PAUL KRETZMANN

Popular Commentary on Joshua, Judges, and Ruth

Just and Sinner

Ithaca, NY 14850

www.JSPublishing.org

First edition

ISBN: 978-1-952295-36-2

This book was professionally typeset on Reedsy. Find out more at reedsy.com

Contents

II   The Book of Judges

I

The Book of Joshua

1

Introduction

The Book of Joshua, so named from its principal character, the successor of Moses, under whose leadership the conquest of Canaan was successfully carried out, covers a period of about twenty-five years (B. C. 1450 to 1425). It takes up the history of Israel after the death of Moses, begins with the commission of the Lord to Joshua, describes in detail the campaigns of the army of Israel, the great successes as well as the occasional reverses, and finally gives an account of the last addresses of Joshua, of his farewell, and of his death. The work entrusted to Joshua was one requiring great intellectual and tactical ability, but above all an unwavering trust in God. Canaan was occupied by great nations and strong, inhabiting strongly fortified cities and able to place armies in the field consisting of skilled warriors. Joshua was fully qualified for the task set before him, since he had not only been associated with Moses during the entire wilderness journey, but was also full of the spirit of wisdom, Deut. 34, 9, possessed of true military ability, and had perfect faith in the word and promise of God, this trust being the source of all his strength and courage.

The chief object of the book is to offer the historical proof of the faithfulness with which God fulfilled the promise made to the patriarchs that He would give the land of Canaan to His chosen people. Accordingly, we are told how the Lord helped Joshua and Israel conquer and occupy Canaan: He led them through the Jordan on dry ground; He fought for them against the heathen inhabitants of Canaan; He drove those wicked, immoral, and foul nations out from before them; He divided the land by lot among the victorious tribes of Israel, and brought them to rest in that "good land flowing with milk and honey."

So far as the author is concerned, the Book of Joshua was probably not written by this great leader himself, although some of the sections, especially the reports of the division of the land, were undoubtedly copied from his notes. Events are related in the book which did not take place until after the death of Joshua, such as Caleb's taking possession of his inheritance at Hebron, chap. 15, 13-19, cp. with Judg. 1, 10-15, the taking of the city of Laish by the Danites, chap. 19, 47, cp. with Judg. 18. Nevertheless, the writer was a contemporary of Joshua, who probably survived him for many years, and it is assumed that one of the elders who entered Canaan with Joshua wrote the book, chap. 5, 1. The very latest date which may be accepted for the composition of the book is that of the time of Samuel, and there are some believing scholars who have regarded this prophet as the author.[1]

---

[1] *Concordia Bible Class*, 1919, 31-34; Fuerbringer, *Einleitung in das Alte Testament*, 20. 27.

2

Joshua 1

Joshua Assumes Command of Israel.

Joshua formally commissioned. — V. 1. **Now, after the death of Moses, the servant of the Lord,** after the completion of the thirty days' mourning for this great prophet whom the Lord so signally distinguished, Num. 12, 7. 8; Deut. 34, 5. 8, **it came to pass that the Lord spake unto Joshua, the son of Nun, Moses' minister,** not his servant, but his assistant, who had been pointed out some 'time before as the successor of Moses, Num. 27, 15-23, had been expressly designated as such by Moses, Deut. 31, 7, and had appeared before the people in that capacity, saying, v. 2. **Moses, My servant, is dead; now, therefore, arise, go over this Jordan, thou and all this people, unto the land which I do give to them, even to the children of Israel,** for Canaan proper was always spoken of as including the territory west of the Jordan only. These words were not spoken to Joshua through the high priest's Urim and Thummim, upon which he had been told to rely in case of difficult questions, Num. 27, 21, but were an immediate revelation of the divine will, in the same

5

way in which the Lord had communicated with Moses. V. 3. **Every place that the sole of your foot shall tread upon, that have I given unto you, as I said unto Moses,** Deut. 11, 24. V. 4. **From the wilderness,** the Desert of Arabia on the south and southeast, **and this Lebanon,** the mountain range in the north, **even unto the great river, the river Euphrates, all the land of the Hittites,** who apparently had been overlords of this entire region at one time and were still occupying the country northwest of the Sea of Chinnereth, afterward that of Galilee, **and unto the great sea toward the going down of the sun,** the Mediterranean Sea, **shall be your coast.** Cp. Deut. 11, 24. 25. V. 5. **There shall not any man,** namely, of the kings and inhabitants of the country, b**e able to stand before thee,** withstand him successfully, **all the days of thy life,** Deut. 31, 8. **As I was with Moses, so I will be with thee; I will not fail thee,** let him sink down in helplessness by withdrawing his hand, **nor forsake thee.** V. 6. **Be strong,** firm, mighty in the trust of Jehovah, **and of a good courage,** altogether undismayed; he must lay hold boldly and with a strong hand, and when he has done so, allow nothing to drive him from his position of firm adherence to Jehovah; **for unto this people shalt thou divide for an inheritance the land which I sware unto their fathers to give them.** Cp. Deut. 31, 7. 23. This condition is still further expanded. V. 7. **Only be thou strong and very courageous,** said with greater emphasis than in v. 6, **that thou mayest observe to do according to all the Law which Moses, My servant, commanded thee,** for the leader of the people must be an example to all his followers. **Turn not from it,** namely, from the roll of the written Law as it was preserved in the Ark of the Covenant, **to the right hand or to the left,** as the slightest deviation was a transgression, **that**

thou mayest prosper, make use of the proper wisdom and thus be successful, whithersoever thou goest. V. 8. **This book of the Law,** as it had been written by Moses and delivered into the hands of the priests, Deut. 31, 26, **shall not depart out of thy mouth,** he should teach it, study it, discuss it; **but thou shalt meditate therein day and night,** trying to penetrate ever more deeply into its scope and meaning, and thus becoming qualified to speak more clearly, pointedly, and powerfully to the people, **that thou mayest observe to do according to all that is written therein,** namely, in the thoughts of the heart and in the deeds of the hands; **for then thou shall make thy way prosperous,** make headway on the path of duty before him, **and then thou shalt have good success,** because of the application of practical wisdom given by the Lord. The Lord now summarizes His charge to Joshua, introducing it by a rhetorical question for the sake of greater effect. V. 9. **Have not I commanded thee? Be strong and of a good courage; be not afraid, neither be thou dismayed; for the Lord, thy God, is with thee whithersoever thou goest.** Thus the assurance gains in strength when to the positive command to be courageous is added the negative to lay aside all fear, as in Deut. 31, 6. 8. We Christians have a similar promise of victory over all our enemies and the eventual enjoyment of the heavenly happiness. But we also have the command of God to read, study, and hear the Word of God to arrange our whole life in accordance with its precepts. Then we also shall have success in the things we undertake under the guidance of God.

The first general order of Joshua. — V. 10. **Then Joshua commanded the officers of the people, saying,** v. 11. **Pass through the host and command the people,** for as keepers of the genealogical records they were also superintendents of the mustering and were primarily concerned with any order pertaining to the mobilizing of the army, **saying, Prepare you victuals,** food for a journey or campaign; **for within three days ye shall pass over this Jordan,** along whose eastern banks their encampment extended, **to go in to possess the land which the Lord, your God, giveth you to possess it.** This order went forth on the seventh of Nisan, chap. 4, 19. V. 12. **And to the Reubenites and to the Gadites and to half the tribe of Manasseh spake Joshua, saying,** v. 13. **Remember the word which Moses, the servant of the Lord,** this being the usual manner in which he is now referred to, **commanded you, saying, The Lord, your God, hath given you rest,** having permitted them to settle in peace, **and hath given you this land,** they had their possession on the east side of Jordan. V. 14. **Your wives, your little ones, and your cattle shall remain in the land which Moses gave you on this side Jordan; but ye shall pass before your brethren armed,** fully equipped and arrayed in battle order, **all the mighty men of valor, and help them,** v. 15. **until the Lord have given your brethren rest, as He hath given you, and they also have possessed the land which the Lord, your God, giveth them. Then ye shall return unto the land of your possession and enjoy it,** make use of all the owners' privileges, **which Moses, the Lord's servant, gave you on this side Jordan toward the sun-rising.** Cp. Num. 32,17-27. V. 16. **And they answered Joshua, saying, All that thou commandest us we will do, and whithersoever thou sendest us we will go,** a fine expression of allegiance and loyalty, of obedience and brotherly love. V. 17. **According as we hearkened unto Moses in all things, so will we hearken unto thee; only the Lord, thy God, be with thee as He was with Moses.** With this assurance and guarantee they were ready to follow Joshua anywhere. V. 18. **Whosoever he be that doth rebel against thy commandment and will not hearken unto thy words in all that thou commandest him, he shall be put to death; only be strong and of a good courage,** a call with which the two and one half tribes intended to give Joshua the assurance which he needed at the beginning of his difficult work that he could depend upon the people whom the Lord had given into his charge. In the New Covenant it is also the will of God that His children help one another in the severe spiritual battles which they must fight, giving one another all possible encouragement at all times. They are assured, even now, of eventual entrance into their rest. "He who follows the Word of God acts wisely and happily, but he who follows his own reason acts unwisely and to no profit." (Luther.)

3

Joshua 2

S**pies Sent to Jericho.**

The spies at Rahab's house. — V. 1. **And Joshua, the son of Hun, sent out of Shittim,** a town in Moabitis, where he had his headquarters, this probably having taken place even before the officers of the host made the proclamation throughout the camp, **two men to spy secretly,** this having reference both to the manner in which the command was given, and the form in which it was carried out, saying, **Go view the land, even Jericho,** both the city and its vicinity. Jericho was located in a beautiful and fertile valley, noted for its palm-trees, some six to eight miles from the Jordan, and the entire neighborhood was thickly settled. **And they went and came into an harlot's house,** where their stay would arouse the least suspicion, **named Rahab, and lodged there,** prepared to stay there overnight. V. 2. **And it was told the king of Jericho,** probably by some of the watch who had marked the coming of the strangers, **saying, Behold, there came men in hither to-night of the children of Israel to search out the country.** This was the natural conclusion which the men of Jericho would reach in finding men of Israel in their city. V. 3. **And the king of Jericho sent unto Rahab, saying, Bring forth the men that are come to thee, which are entered into thine house; for they be come to search out all the country.** The king's messengers did not search her house, but made their demand at the door, relying on her supposed loyalty to produce the spies. V. 4. **And the woman took the two men and hid them,** just as soon as the servant in charge of the door had informed her of the identity of the callers, whereupon she appeared at the door in person, **and said thus, There came men unto me,** literally, "True, there came to me men," **but I wist not whence they were;** v. 5. **and it came to pass about the time of shutting of the gate, when it was dark, that the men went out,** for the gates were closed at sunset, and the short twilight was rapidly succeeded by the falling of darkness; she implied that the spies must have taken advantage of the dusk to make their escape. **Whither the men went I wot** (know) **not; pursue after them quickly; for ye shall overtake them.** V. 6. **But she had brought them up to the roof of the house,** those of the Orient being flat and usually parapeted, a**nd hid them with the stalks of flax,** unbroken lengths spread out there for the purpose of drying, **which she had laid in order upon the roof.** V. 7. **And the men,** the king's messengers, **pursued after them,** the spies, **the way to Jordan unto the fords,** where they were most likely to cross; **and as soon as they which pursued after them were gone out,** they, the keepers, the watchmen, **shut the gate,** to prevent the escape of the spies, if they were still in the city. The obvious terror which had taken hold of the king of Jericho showed that the judgment of the Lord upon the Canaanites had already begun, for it was He who took their courage from them.

The spies saved by Rahab. — V. 8. **And before they were laid down, she came up unto them upon the roof,** where they were preparing to pass the night; v. 9. **and she said unto the men, I know that the Lord,** Jehovah, of whom she had heard and toward whom she felt a reverential awe, **hath given you the land, and that your terror is fallen upon us,** namely, the fear that they would be exterminated by Israel, Deut. 2, 25; 11, 25, **and that all the inhabitants of the land faint because of you,** are terrified and utterly discouraged by the obvious assistance which Jehovah had rendered His people. V. 10. **For we have heard how the Lord dried up the water of the Red Sea for you when ye came out of Egypt,** Ex. 14, 21; **and what ye did unto the two kings of the Amorites that were on the other side Jordan, Sihon and Og, whom ye utterly destroyed,** Num. 21, 21–35. V. 11. **And as soon as we had heard these things,** for Rahab here asserts of all her countrymen what she herself felt, **our hearts did melt,** said of complete discouragement, **neither did there remain any more courage in any man because of you,** they found it impossible to raise a bit of spirit, either to think, plan, or act, so great was their terror; **for the Lord, your God, He is God in heaven above and in earth beneath.** Thus Rahab, in concluding, confessed her faith in Jehovah, the true God. It is strange that the miracles of God's almighty power, which wrought faith in the heart of this great sinner, caused the unbelieving hearts of the other Canaanites to become hardened and thus to be condemned to the judgment of death, of extermination. V. 12. **Now, therefore, I pray you, swear unto me by the Lord, since I have showed you kindness,** in hiding them from the king's messengers, **that ye will also show kindness unto my father's house and give me a true token,** some sign of truth by which they would guarantee immunity to her and her relatives in the general extermination which was sure to come; v. 13. **and that ye will save alive my father, and my mother, and my brethren, and my sisters, and all that they have,** her entire relationship, **and deliver our lives from death.** The sign of truth which she demanded was the solemn oath that they would save the lives of all her kin. V. 14. **And the men answered her,** Our life for yours, literally, "our souls instead of yours to die" (they pledged their very souls for the truth of their promise to spare Rahab and her relatives), **if ye utter not this our business,** that is, if she would not betray them while they were on their way back to the camp of Israel. **And it shall be, when the Lord hath given us the land, that we will deal kindly and truly with thee,** show her this mercy and faithfulness, and save her life. V. 15. **Then she let them down by a cord,** a strong rope, **through the window; for her house was upon the town wall,** built right against it, **and she dwelt upon the wall,** her chamber overhung the wall. V. 16. **And she said unto them** as they stood below after their escape from the city, **Get you to the mountain,** a wild cliff north of Jericho, **lest the pursuers meet you; and hide yourselves there three days, until the pursuers be returned; and afterward may ye go your way.** Being familiar with the distances and all possible roads, she was able to give the spies this shrewd bit of advice. V. 17. **And the men said unto her,** in order to obviate the danger of a false interpretation of their promise and oath, **We will be blameless of this thine oath which thou hast made us swear,** namely, unless she would do as they now directed her to act. V. 18. **Behold, when we come into the land, thou shall bind this line of scarlet thread,** a thin, but strong rope, such as surveyors used, probably the one by which they had made their escape, **in the window which thou didst let us down by; and thou shalt bring thy father, and thy mother, and thy brethren, and all thy father's household,** who apparently were living in their own homes, **home unto thee,** thus having them all together in one house. V. 19. **And it shall be that whosoever shall go out of the doors of thy house into the street,** anywhere outside, **his blood shall be upon his head,** it would be his own fault if some soldier of Israel would strike him down, **and we will be guiltless; and whosoever shall be with thee in the house, his blood shall be on our head if any hand be upon him,** in that case they would assume the blame. That was the second condition. V. 20. **And if thou utter this our business,** in betraying them after their departure, **then we will be quit of thine oath which thou hast made us to swear.** This third condition was really only a repetition of the chief condition made at the time they swore the oath, v. 14. V. 21. **And she said, According unto your words, so be it.** She agreed to all the conditions. **And she sent them away, and they departed; and she bound the scarlet line in the window,** namely, when she found that she needed it for the stipulated purpose. V. 22. **And they went and came unto the mountain, and abode there three days, until the pursuers were returned; and the pursuers sought them throughout all the way,** on every road which they could possibly have taken, **but found them not.** V. 23. **So the two men returned, and descended from the mountain, and passed over,** over the river Jordan, **and came to Joshua, the son of Nun,** by the evening of the third day, **and told him all things that befell them,** gave him a full report of all that had happened to them; v. 24. **and they said unto Joshua, Truly the Lord hath delivered into our hands all the land; for even all the inhabitants of**

the country do faint because of us. Rahab, the harlot, is an example of faith, Heb.11, 31, for the Lord has His elect in the midst of an unbelieving nation. She forsook the sinful business in which she was engaged, and afterward became an ancestress of Jesus, Matt. 1, 5. It was an act of faith on her part to shield those representatives of God's people, Jas. 2, 25; Heb. 11, 31. True faith, love toward God, always shows itself in love toward the fellow-believers, in doing good to the members of God's people and in resisting the enemies of the Lord.

4

Joshua 3

The Passage of Jordan.

The instructions for crossing. - V. 1. **And Joshua rose early in the morning,** on the fourth day after his great proclamation, chap. 1,11. **And they removed from Shittim,** where their headquarters had been situated, **and came to Jordan,** a matter of about two hours' journey, during which they observed the usual order of march, **he and all the children of Israel, and lodged there before they passed over,** they rested for some time, probably during the noon-hour. V. 2. **And it came to pass after three days,** those named in the order of Joshua, chap. 1, 11, **that the officers,** the officials in charge of the mustering, **went through the host,** during this pause in the day's march; v. 3. **and they commanded the people, saying, When ye see the Ark of the Covenant of the Lord, your God,** Ex. 25, 10-22, **and the priests, the Levites,** the priests of the sons of Levi who were charged with this work, **bearing it,** at the head of the army, as it seems to have been done once before, Num. 10, 33, **then ye shall remove from your place, and go after it,** in the orderly array commanded by

16

God. V. 4. **Yet there shall be a space between you and it, about two thousand cubits by measure** (three thousand feet). **Come not near unto it,** they were to observe this respectful distance, lest their vanguard hide the Ark of the Covenant from the great number of the marchers, **that ye may know the way by which ye must go; for ye have not passed this way heretofore.** It was not that the people were in danger of losing their way t3 the river, but that the Lord wanted them to note the miracle by which He opened the way to Canaan before their eyes. V. 5. **And Joshua said unto the people, Sanctify yourselves;** after establishing camp for the night they were to engage in spiritual purification, typified also by the washing of their clothes and of their bodies, thus turning their hearts to God, in faith and trust in His promise, and in willing obedience to His commands, that they might rightly take to heart the miracle of grace which the Lord would perform among them the next day; **for to-morrow the Lord will do wonders among you.** The passage of Jordan took place on the tenth of Nisan, chap. 4, 19. V. 6. **And Joshua spake unto the priests, saying, Take up the Ark of the Covenant and pass over before the people.** This was the special work of the sons of Kohath, Num. 4, 15, and the order referred to the actual time of marching. **And they took up the Ark of the Covenant and went before the people,** this statement either anticipating the actual event, or having reference to the fact that the priests took up their station at the head of the army, ready for the march of the next day. V. 7. **And the Lord said unto Joshua, This day will I begin to magnify thee in the sight of all Israel,** for the miraculous crossing of Jordan was only the first of a series of wonders by which the Lord placed His people in possession of the Land of Promise and confirmed Joshua in his position as leader of the people,

that they may know that, as I was with Moses, so I will be with thee. Cp. chap. 1, 2-9. V. 8. **And thou shalt command the priests that bear the Ark of the Covenant, saying, When ye are come to the brink of the water of Jordan,** the eastern bank or slope of the river, as it descended to the bed of the stream, **ye shall stand still in Jordan,** thus forming, as it were, a dam to hold back the waters rushing down from the north. The Ark of the Covenant here appears as the emblem of God's almighty presence. To this day God has bound His children to the use of certain means of grace, the Word and the Sacraments. Where these are administered, there the true, living God is present, there we find evidences of God's power and mercy, of His protection and blessing.

The miraculous wall of water. – V. 9. **And Joshua said unto the children of Israel, Come hither and hear the words of the Lord, your God,** he addressed them in solemn assembly, as the congregation of Jehovah. V. 10. **And Joshua said, Hereby ye shall know that the living God is among you, and that He will without fail,** most certainly, according to His promise, Deut. 7, 1, **drive out from before you the Canaanites,** occupying chiefly the valley of Jordan and the Plain of Sharon, **and the Hittites,** some tribes of which were living in the northern part of Canaan, northwest of the Sea of Chinnereth, **and the Hivites,** located almost in the center of the country, **and the Perizzites,** just east of them, **and the Girgashites,** west of the Sea of Chinnereth, **and the Amorites,** just west and southwest of the Dead Sea, **and the Jebusites,** in the neighborhood of what was later Jerusalem. V. 11. **Behold, the Ark of the Covenant of the Lord of all the earth passeth over before you into Jordan.** Note that God, where the conquest of the land is in question, is called the Lord of the whole earth, the one to whom the whole earth belongs and who may dispense it at His pleasure, the one in whose almighty power the Israelites should have implicit faith. V. 12. **Now, therefore, take you twelve men out of the tribes of Israel, out of every tribe a man.** The work which these men were to perform is described chap. 4, 3. V. 13. **And it shall come to pass, as soon as the soles of the feet of the priests that bear the ark of the Lord, the Lord of all the earth, shall rest in the waters of Jordan,** the mere touch of their feet being sufficient to bring about the miracle, **that the waters of Jordan,** of the flowing stream before them, **shall be cut off from the waters that come down from above; and they,** the rushing waters above the place of crossing, **shall stand upon an heap,** being held hack by the invisible dam of God's almighty power. V. 14. **And it came to pass, when the people removed from their tents,** struck camp at their departure, **to pass over Jordan, and the priests bearing the Ark of the Covenant before the people,** in the order prescribed by God, v. 15. **and as they that bare the ark were come unto Jordan, and the feet of the priests that bare the ark were dipped in the brim of the water (for Jordan,** barely a hundred feet wide in the dry season, **overfloweth all his banks all the time of harvest,** the melting snows of the northern mountains in the late spring, the season at which the passage took place, at the beginning of the barley harvest, causing the river to overflow its lower banks and to fill even the space which was ordinarily overgrown with reeds and bushes,) v. 16. **that the waters which came down from above stood and rose up upon an heap very far from the city Adam, that is beside Zaretan,** where the lower valley was considerably narrowed by a low range of hills, at some distance from the place of crossing; **and those** (waters) **that came down toward the Sea of the Plain,**

even the Salt Sea, failed, and were cut off, diminished and finally disappeared entirely; **and the people passed over right against Jericho. V. 17. And the priests that bare the Ark of the Covenant of the Lord stood firm on dry ground in the midst of Jordan,** for so completely had the waters disappeared that they had solid ground beneath their feet. **And all the Israelites passed over on dry ground, until all the people were passed clean over Jordan,** and beyond the reach of even the high water which afterward again overflowed the bed of the stream. Thus wonderfully the Lord led His people into the Land of Promise. And He is the same living, almighty God today, opening paths before His children where they are unable to find any, and assisting them in the midst of all dangers, until they reach the promised home above.

5

Joshua 4

The Memorial Stones.

The stones taken from the midst of the river bed. - V. 1. **And it came to pass, when all the people were clean passed over Jordan, that the Lord spake unto Joshua, saying,** v. 2. **Take you twelve men out of the people, out of every tribe a man,** as had been provided for before the crossing began, chap. 3, 12, v. 3. **and command ye them, saying, Take you hence out of the midst of Jordan, out of the place where the priests' feet stood firm,** from the very center of the stream's bed, **twelve stones, and ye shall carry them over with you, and leave them in the lodging-place, where ye shall lodge this night.** It is plain that this entire paragraph, up to and including v. 7, belongs, in point of time, to the morning hours, and is here inserted, together with the actual execution of the order and in explanation of it. V. 4. **Then Joshua called the twelve men, whom he had prepared of the children of Israel,** selected for this particular work, **out of every tribe a man;** v. 5. **and Joshua said unto them, Pass over before the ark of the Lord, your God, into the midst of Jordan,** or, Go

21

over to the place where the ark is now stationed, **and take you up, every man of you, a stone upon his shoulder, according unto the number of the tribes of the children of Israel,** v. 6. **that this may be a sign among you,** serve for a memorial, a monument, in their midst, **that when your children ask their fathers in time to come, saying, "What mean ye by these stones?** v. 7. **then ye shall answer them, That the waters of Jordan were cut off before the Ark of the Covenant of the Lord; when it passed over Jordan, the waters of Jordan were cut off,** as related in the preceding chapter; **and these stones shall be for a memorial unto the children of Israel forever,** to remind every succeeding generation of the great miracle which the Lord performed in keeping His promise and in leading His people safely into the Land of Promise. V. 8. **And the children of Israel did so as Joshua commanded, and took up twelve stones out of the midst of Jordan,** the twelve men acting as the representatives of the entire host or congregation, **as the Lord spake unto Joshua, according to the number of the tribes of the children of Israel, and carried them over with them unto the place where they lodged,** where camp was pitched that evening, **and laid them down there,** in the form of a rough monument. V. 9. **And Joshua set up twelve stones in the midst of Jordan,** where they might become visible when the water was at low stage, **in the place where the feet of the priests which bare the Ark of the Covenant stood; and they are there unto this day,** to the time when this report was put down or this book written. This second monument was erected by Joshua without special divine direction, but nevertheless with a good purpose, for it served to bring home to the people the fact of God's protection and assistance in the conquest of Canaan.

The stones pitched in Gilgal. – V. 10. **For the priests which bare the ark stood in the midst of Jordan until everything was finished that the Lord commanded Joshua to speak unto the people, according to all that Moses commanded Joshua; and the people hasted and passed over,** made as quick a passage as possible. Moses had, according to the command of God, commissioned Joshua to lead the people into the Promised Land, at the same time giving him the assurance that the Lord would be with him. Therefore the execution of the divine command was at the same time an act of obedience to the charge of Moses. During all this time, while the entire host of Israel passed over and while the stones were taken from the bed of the river for the monument, the priests stood in the bed of the stream, their presence with the ark serving as a guarantee for the safe passage of all the people. V. 11. **And it came to pass, when all the people were clean passed over,** when every last one of them had reached the high ground beyond the flood-stage, **that the ark of the Lord passed over,** for it was the emblem of Jehovah, the almighty God, who held back the waves in their mad rush, **and the priests,** who were only the bearers of the sacred chest, **in the presence of the people,** all of them being witnesses of the miraculous happening. V. 12. **And the children of Reuben and the children of Gad and half the tribe of Manasseh passed over armed before the children of Israel, as Moses spake unto them,** that is, their best soldiers, as the representatives of their armies, chap. 1, 14; v. 13. **about forty thousand prepared for war,** fully armed and equipped, **passed over before the Lord,** in whose presence their promise had been given, **unto battle,** for a war of conquest and extermination was before them, **to the plains of Jericho,** the plain or valley extending to that city. These forty thousand warriors represented the flower of the two and one half tribes east of Jordan, the remaining sixty to seventy thousand being left for the protection of the cities and their meadows. V. 14. **On that day the Lord magnified Joshua in the sight of all Israel,** they were filled with the proper reverence for him as the chosen leader of the host; **and they feared him as they feared Moses all the days of his life,** chap. 3, 7. V. 15. **And the Lord spake unto Joshua, saying,** v. 16. **Command the priests that bear the Ark of the Testimony that they come up out of Jordan,** from the midst of the stream where they had been stationed during the passage of the people. V. 17. **Joshua, therefore, commanded the priests, saying, Come ye up out of Jordan.** V. 18. **And it came to pass, when the priests that bare the Ark of the Covenant of the Lord were come up out of the midst of Jordan, and the soles of the priests' feet were lifted up unto the dry land,** literally, "tore themselves loose toward the dry land," said of leaving the bed of the stream and stepping upon the dry bank, **that the waters of Jordan returned unto their place,** flowed down stream in their natural course, **and flowed over all his banks, as they did before.** Thus it must have been plain to all the people that it had been the ark which had served as a dam to hold back the waters of the flooded river. V. 19. **And the people came up out of Jordan on the tenth day of the first month,** on the very day on which, forty years before, their fathers had selected a lamb or a kid for the first celebration of the Passover, Ex, 12, 3, **and encamped in Gilgal, in the east border of Jericho,** of the territory of Jericho. V. 20. **And those twelve stones which they took out of Jordan did Joshua pitch,** set up for a memorial, **in Gilgal.** V.21. **And he spake unto the children of Israel, saying, When your children shall**

ask their fathers in time to come, saying, What mean these stones? v. 22. **then ye shall let your children know,** give them the information as the Lord had commanded in vv. 6 and 7, **saying, Israel came over this Jordan on dry land. V. 23. For the Lord, your God, dried up the waters of Jordan from before you until ye were passed over, as the Lord, your God, did to the Bed Sea, which He dried up from before us, until we were gone over,** the statement being given in poetical form, with epic brevity and force; v. 24. **that all the people of the earth might know the hand of the Lord,** acknowledge His almighty power in affording to His people this miraculous passage, **that it is mighty; that ye might fear the Lord, your God, forever,** Ex. 14, 31; Deut. 6, 2. The remembrance of God's wonderful deed at this time was intended to keep the right fear of the Lord in the hearts of the children of Israel, lest they, in forgetting His blessings, lose the faith and trust of their hearts. We Christians also should be ever mindful of the great and wonderful deeds of God which He performed for the salvation of our soul, in redeeming us from the terrors of the wilderness of His wrath and in leading us into the glorious light of the Gospel, as a surety of our eternal salvation.

6

Joshua 5

Israel at Gilgal.

The circumcision of the people. — V. 1. **And it came to pass, when all the kings of the Amorites, which were on the side of the Jordan westward,** the mighty heathen nations which occupied chiefly the mountainous section of Canaan, for among these the Amorites were the strongest, **and all the kings of the Canaanites which were by the sea,** the heathen nations occupying the lowlands in the neighborhood of the Mediterranean Sea, **heard that the Lord had dried up the waters of Jordan from before the children of Israel, until we were passed over,** for it is an eye-witness who is relating this story, **that their heart melted,** dissolved in apprehension and terror, **neither was there spirit in them any more,** they lost the last vestige of courage, **because of the children of Israel.** It was the terror of the Lord which fallen upon them, causing all life and energy to be taken from them. V. 2. **At that time the Lord said unto Joshua, Make thee sharp knives,** literally, knives of stone, made with a very sharp cutting edge, used extensively at that time, **and circumcise again**

26

the children of Israel the second time. As the people that came out of Egypt had been circumcised, so now there was to be a circumcision of the new generation, by which the solemn rite was solemnly reintroduced. V. 3. **And Joshua made him sharp knives and circumcised the children of Israel at the hill of the foreskins,** for the place was later known as Gibeah-haaraloth, because the foreskins were buried there. V. 4. **And this is the cause why Joshua did circumcise,** why the Lord's order went forth to Joshua, and the latter had the order executed: **All the people that came out of Egypt that were males, even all the men of war, died in the wilderness by the way,** in the course of the desert journey, **after they came out of Egypt,** Num. 14, 29; Deut. 2, 16. V. 5. **Now, all the people that came out were circumcised,** the rite having been observed with all strictness in Egypt; **but all the people that were born in the wilderness by the way as they came forth out of Egypt,** the entire journey in the wilderness being included under this heading, **them they had not circumcised.** V. 6. **For the children of Israel walked forty years in the wilderness, till all the people that were men of war,** mustered as being able to bear arms in battle, **which came out of Egypt, were consumed, because they obeyed not the voice of the Lord; unto whom the Lord sware that He would not show them the land which the Lord sware unto their fathers that He would give us, a land that floweth with milk and honey,** Num. 14, 23. The extraordinary fertility of the country is here once more emphasized, as so often in the Old Testament, Ex. 3, 8. 17; 13, 5; 16, 14; Lev. 20, 24; Num. 13, 27; Deut. 1, 3. The meadow-lands of Canaan, with their rich carpet of grasses and flowers, were well suited for the raising of herds and flocks, while the bees found the abundance of fragrant flowers with their rich nectar eminently satisfactory for the production of honey. V. 7. **And their children, whom He raised up in their stead,** the Lord had them take the place of those who were fallen in the wilderness, **them Joshua circumcised,** their circumcision he ordered; **for they were uncircumcised, because they,** the several fathers of the families, **had not circumcised them by the way.** It was necessary that the present race of young men should receive the sign of the Lord's covenant before they dared undertake the conquest of Canaan. V. 8. **And it came to pass, when they had done circumcising all the people, that they abode in their places in the camp till they were whole,** had recovered from the. effects of the operation. During this time there were at least some three hundred thousand men to take care of the necessary preparations for the celebration of the Passover and to guard against an eventual attack on the part of the heathen armies. V. 9. **And the Lord said unto Joshua, This day have I rolled away the reproach of Egypt from off you,** namely, that resulting from the report that God had led His people out of Egypt merely for the purpose of striking them down in the wilderness, Ex. 32,12; Num. 14, 13-16; Deut. 9, 28. The act of circumcision at Gilgal was God's proclamation of the full restoration of the covenant, as first made with Abraham and at Sinai. **Wherefore the name of the place is called Gilgal** (rolling away) **unto this day.** The sacred covenant rite had now been resumed, and all reproach had been removed. Israel was consecrated for the possession of the Holy Land, for it is an obedient, consecrated people whom the Lord desires for His own.

The Passover celebrated. — V. 10. **And the children of Israel encamped in Gilgal,** having once more been accepted into the full covenant relation with Jehovah, **and kept the Passover** on the fourteenth day of the month at even in the plains of Jericho. V. 11. **And they did eat of the old corn of the land on the morrow after the Passover,** on the fifteenth of Nisan, Lev. 23, 5. 6, **unleavened cakes, and parched corn in the selfsame day,** roasted harvest ears or kernels of grain roasted at the fire, for it was not lawful to eat of the new crop until after the offering of the first sheaves on the sixteenth of Nisan, Lev. 23, 10. 11. V. 12. **And the manna ceased on the morrow after they had eaten of the old corn of the land,** that is, on the sixteenth of Abib, or Nisan, **neither had the children of Israel manna any more; but they did eat of the fruit of the land of Canaan that year.** The people had now arrived in Canaan and no longer needed the bread of the wilderness. It should be noted here once more: "The feeding of the Israelites with manna remains a miracle of God which has, indeed, in nature, a faint analog, but can never be explained on natural principles." (Keil.) V. 13. **And it came to pass, when Joshua was by Jericho,** while the children of Israel were in camp at Gilgal, Joshua, apparently, being engaged in deep meditation and prayer to Jehovah, **that he lifted up his eyes and looked, and, behold, there stood a man over against him with His sword drawn in His hand,** taken from the scabbard and ready for slaughter. That was the Prince of the host of angels, the great Angel of the Lord, the Angel of the Covenant, of one essence with the Lord Himself, who had accompanied Israel from Egypt and from Sinai. **And Joshua went unto Him and said unto Him, Art Thou for us or for our adversaries?** It was a question natural in the circumstances and appropriate for the general of the forces of Israel. V. 14. **And He said, Nay,** He belonged neither to the one nor to the other, **but as Captain of the host of the Lord am I now come,** Prince of the innumerable angelic armies. **And Joshua fell on his face to the earth,** in the attitude of abject submission and entreaty, **and did worship,** recognizing this Prince as a higher being, though not yet sure of His identity, **and said unto Him, What saith my Lord unto His servant?** V. 15. **And the Captain of the Lord's host said unto Joshua, Loose thy shoe from off thy foot,** as Moses did in the presence of the burning bush, Ex. 3, 5; **for the place whereon thou standest is holy.** This undoubtedly reminded Joshua of the experience of Moses, and proved to him that this Prince of the heavenly host was He who had manifested Himself to Moses as the God of Abraham, of Isaac, and of Jacob. **And Joshua did so.** It is then that we may expect manifestations of Christ's divine grace and mercy, when we use the means of grace instituted by Him and are found in the way of our duty. Then it is also that He encamps round about us with the host of His angels and wages war for His Church against the world and the devil.

7

Joshua 6

The Taking of Jericho.

The siege of Jericho. – V. 1. **Now Jericho was straitly shut up,** not only strongly fortified, but also guarded with all strictness, **because of the children of Israel; none went"** out and none came in. This remark is inserted by the historian by way of explanation, before he continues to describe the meeting between Joshua and the Prince of the heavenly host. V. 2. **And the Lord said unto Joshua, See, I have given into thine hand Jericho and the king thereof and the mighty men of valor.** This was the divine plan and intention, assuring the immediate help of God, the overthrow of the city and its staunch and mighty defenders by a miracle. V. 3. **And ye shall compass the city,** surround it completely, **all ye men of war, and go round about the city once,** march completely around it. **Thus shall thou do six days,** on each of six successive days, which probably brought the time around once more to the eve of the Sabbath. V. 4. **And seven priests shall bear before the ark,** which was thus conspicuous in the line of march, **seven trumpets of rams' horns,** very large instruments, with a deep-toned, terrifying sound, especially when the notes were sustained; **and the seventh day ye shall compass the city seven times, and the priests shall blow with the trumpets.** The repetition on the several days of this procession about the city could only be intended to exercise Israel in unconditional faith and patient trust in the power and help of God, and to impress deeply upon the people the fact that it was the almighty power and faithfulness of Jehovah alone which gave into their hands this fortified city, one of the strongest in the land. The last day was surely the strongest test of their faith, for the besieged were probably not sparing in their jeering cries of contempt for a great host that ventured no attack, but continued on its endless procession around the city. V. 5. **And it shall come to pass that, when they make a long blast with the ram's horn,** in a long-sustained, single note, **and when ye hear the sound of the trumpet, all the people shall shout with a great shout,** the cry of an army confident of victory; **and the wall of the city shall fall down flat,** topple over and lie prostrate, **and the people shall ascend up,** the ranks turning to face the city, **every man straight before him,** in perfect order of attack, without turning either to the right or to the left. This was the order of the Prince of the angelic host as it was imparted to Joshua at that wonderful meeting. V. 6. **And Joshua, the son of Nun,** having received this command from the Lord, **called the priests and said unto them, Take up the Ark of the Covenant,** to carry it in the intended procession, **and let seven priests bear seven trumpets of rams' horns before the ark of the Lord. V. 7. And he said unto the people,** the army that was actively engaged in this siege. **Pass on and compass the city, and let him that is armed pass on before the ark of the Lord,** the host of the two and one half tribes probably passing on in review, to be followed afterward by the host of the other tribes. V. 8. **And it came to pass, when Joshua had spoken unto the people, that the seven priests bearing the seven trumpets of rams' horns passed on before the Lord,** before the Ark of the Covenant, which was the visible sign of God's presence among His people, **and blew with the trumpets; and the Ark of the Covenant of the Lord followed them.** V. 9. **And the armed men,** that is, the first division of the army, **went before the priests that blew with the trumpets, and the rearward,** the last division of the army forming the rear-guard, **came after the ark,** probably in the same manner as on the march through the desert, **the priests going on and blowing with the trumpets,** sounding without intermission. V. 10. **And Joshua had commanded the people, saying, Ye shall not shout, nor make any noise with your voice, neither shall any word proceed out of your mouth, until the day I bid you shout; then shall ye shout.** The grim and silent procession, moving forward without a sound but the tramping of marching feet and the blasts from the priests' horns, must have made the impression of unwavering determination. V. 11. **So the ark of the Lord,** the most conspicuous feature in the procession, **compassed the city, going about it once; and they came into the camp and lodged in the camp,** they spent the night there. V. 12. **And Joshua rose early in the morning,** on the second day, **and the priests took up the ark of the Lord.** V. 13. **And seven priests, bearing seven trumpets of rams' horns before the ark of the Lord, went on continually and blew with the trumpets,** without intermission; **and the armed men went before them; but the rearward came after the ark of the Lord, the priests going on and blowing with the trumpets.** V. 14. **And the second day they compassed the**

city once and returned into the camp; so they did six days, observing the same procedure every day. It was a strange siege and one which tested the faith of the children of Israel strongly. For it was against all human reason and prudence for the army to lay aside all weapons and, instead, to march around the city with the sound of trumpets. But they followed the command of the Lord strictly and literally. It is a mark of true faith for a person to set reason aside, simply believe the Word, and trust the Lord in everything.

Rahab saved at the overthrow of Jericho. – V. 15. **And it came to pass on the seventh day that they rose early about the dawning of the day,** when the first indications of the new day were visible in the east, **and compassed the city after the same manner seven times; only on that day they compassed the city seven times,** the greater part of the day, probably till near sundown, being occupied with this marching. V. 16. **And it came to pass at the seventh time, when the priests blew with the trumpets,** or, the priests had sounded the blast on the trumpets, for the description in the Hebrew is more vivid than in the translation, **Joshua said unto the people, Shout; for the Lord hath given you the city.** V. 17. **And the city shall be accursed,** devoted to the Lord as under His curse and condemnation, **even it and all that are therein, to the Lord; only Rahab, the harlot, shall live, she and all that are with her in the house, because she hid the messengers that we sent,** chap. 2, 4. V. 18. **And ye, in any wise,** by all means, **keep yourselves from the accursed thing, lest ye make yourselves accursed,** become polluted with the curse which God had pronounced upon the city and all it contained, **when ye take of the accursed thing, and make the camp of Israel a curse, and trouble it,** since the transgression of a single person would be charged to the entire people. "A devoted thing, Num. 21, 2. 3; Deut. 7, 2; 20, 17, was that which had been doomed to the Lord, which no man might employ for his own use, but which was either put away and destroyed utterly to the honor of God, as the men and beasts in this passage, a propitiation, as it were, to the divine justice, that this might be glorified; or it was consecrated to the special service of God, as here all precious and useful metals." (Starke.) V. 19. **But all the silver and gold and vessels of brass and iron are consecrated unto the Lord,** literally, "holiness are they to the Lord," and therefore not to be taken and used for profane purposes; **they shall come into the treasury of the Lord. V. 20. So the people shouted when the priests blew with the trumpets,** at the long blast after the seventh trip around the city on this last day. **And it came to pass, when the people heard the sound of the trumpet, and the people shouted with a great shout,** as commanded by the Lord, v. 5, **that the wall fell down flat,** toppled over and crumbled to pieces, **so that the people,** the attacking soldiers, **went up into the city, every man straight before him, and they took the city,** by an obvious, almighty interposition of the Lord. V. 21. **And they utterly destroyed all that was in the city, both man and woman, young and old, and ox, and sheep, and ass, with the edge of the sword,** for it was the Lord's war of extermination. V. 22. **But Joshua had said unto the two men that had spied out the country, Go into the harlot's house, and bring out thence the woman, and all that she hath, as ye sware unto her,** chap. 2, 14. V. 23. **Arid the young men that were spies,** who had performed the work of spies in the instance referred to, **went in and brought out Rahab,** her house having evidently not fallen, although it was built against the city wall, **and her father, and her mother,**

and her brethren, and all that she had; and they brought out all her kindred, chap. 2, 13, **and left them without the camp of Israel,** until they should have performed all the rites which were necessary to admit them into the congregation of the Lord. V. 24. **And they,** the soldiers of Israel, **burned the city with fire, and all that was therein; only the silver and the gold and the vessels of brass and of iron they put into the treasury of the house of the Lord.** Thus was Jericho offered up as a first-fruits of the conquered land, because "this was the first city of Canaan which Jehovah had given into the hands of His people. This city, therefore, Israel should offer to the Lord, and even consecrate to Him as devoted, for a sign or token that they received the whole land from His hand, as a loan of what had fallen to Him, and not what they could obtain for themselves." V. 25. **And Joshua saved Rahab, the harlot, alive, and her fathers household, and all that she had; and she dwelleth in Israel even unto this day,** being alive and considered a member of the people of the Lord at the time when this account was written, cp. Matt. 1, 5; **because she hid the messengers which Joshua sent to spy out Jericho.** It was a reward of her act of faith. V. 26. **And Joshua adjured them,** the soldiers of Israel, **at that time, saying, Cursed be the man before the Lord that riseth up and buildeth this city Jericho; he shall lay the foundation thereof in his first-born,** lose his oldest son at that time, **and in his youngest son shall he set up the gates of it,** he being taken by death at the completion of the building of the city. This threat was literally fulfilled, as the history of Israel shows, 1 Kings 16, 34. V. 27. **So the Lord was with Joshua; and his fame was noised throughout all the country,** his military ability as well as his success under the guidance of Jehovah. The overthrow of Jericho showed plainly that Jehovah was battling for His people, for the walls of the city fell by faith, Heb. II, 30. This faith is the victory which overcomes the world. But in the fall of Jericho we also see a type of the final overthrow of all the powers of the world, death, and hell. At the end of the world the Lord will come with the voice of the archangel, and with the trumpet of God, 1 Thess. 4,16, and the whole world will fall down in ruins as He proceeds to carry out His judgment upon His enemies.

8

Joshua 7

The Transgression and Punishment of Achan. Israel's defeat at Ai. — V. 1. **But the children of Israel committed a trespass in the accursed thing,** the sin of one man being regarded as compromising all and making the entire host of Israel guilty in the sight of God; **for Achan, the son of Carmi, the son of Zabdi** (or Zimri, 1 Chron. 2, 6), **the son of Zerah, of the tribe of Judah, took of the accursed thing,** appropriated some of the booty of the city, all of which had been declared devoted to the Lord, for his own use; **and the anger of the Lord was kindled against the children of Israel,** it was fanned to a blaze, like a flame which shoots up with destructive force. Achan's sin had robbed the entire people of that purity and holiness which it was supposed to have in the sight of God, just as the impurity of a single member in the body infects all the members. V. 2. **And Joshua sent men from Jericho to Ai, which is beside Bethaven, on the east side of Bethel,** northeast of Jericho and almost due north of Jerusalem, **and spake unto them, saying, Go up and view the country.** They were spies, entrusted with the task

38

of obtaining the information necessary to send a successful expedition against the city. **And the men went up and viewed Ai.** V. 3. **And they returned to Joshua and said unto him, Let not all the people,** the entire army, **go up, but let about two or three thousand men,** literally, "two thousand men or some three thousand men," **go up and smite Ai; and make not all the people to labor thither; for they are but few.** The city having but 12,000 inhabitants, chap. 8, 25, the number of able-bodied defenders probably did not exceed between two and three thousand, according to the estimate of the scouts. V. 4. **So there went up thither of the people about three thousand men; and they fled before the men of Ai.** They not only were unable to accomplish their purpose, but they were even put to shameful flight. V. 5. **And the men of Ai smote of them about thirty and six men; for they chased them from before the gate,** where the attack had been delivered, **even unto Shebarim,** stone quarries at some distance toward the south, **and smote them in the going down,** as they fled toward the valley of the Jordan; **wherefore the hearts of the people melted** and became as water, in utter discouragement and despondency. V. 6. **And Joshua rent his clothes,** as a sign of the deepest distress and mourning, a**nd fell to the earth upon his face before the ark of the Lord until the eventide,** in a silent and yet eloquent appeal to the Lord, **he and the elders of Israel, and put dust upon their heads,** another custom betokening the deepest mourning, 1 Sam. 4, 12; 2 Sam. 1, 2; 13, 19. V. 7. **And Joshua said,** in a mournful complaint, **Alas, O Lord God, wherefore hast Thou at all brought this people over Jordan to deliver us into the hand of the Amorites,** the heathen nation in this part of Canaan, **to destroy us?** For the defeat of the small army was a sign that the Lord had withdrawn His assistance. **Would to God we had been content and dwelt on the other side Jordan!** literally, "Had we but made up our minds to remain on the east aide of Jordan!" It was the bold language of a faith battling with the Lord, unable to understand the ways of the Lord and including the most urgent appeal to the Lord to continue as the Ally of Israel. To this complaint is added an anxious question. V. 8. **O Lord, what shall I say when Israel turneth their backs before their enemies** in shameful flight? V. 9. **For the Canaanites and all the inhabitants of the land shall hear of it, and shall environ us round,** completely surrounding them, **and cut off our name from the earth,** destroy them so completely that even their memory would be forgotten; **and what wilt Thou do unto Thy great name?** Joshua implies that the Lord had not had the due consideration of His honor in mind in permitting this misfortune to strike Israel, that it would now be a difficult matter to secure His honor against misunderstanding and blasphemy. Note: If any Christian congregation suffers a transgressor to remain in its midst, then all the members are guilty before the Lord.

Achan found guilty and punished. — V. 10. **And the Lord said unto Joshua, Get thee up; wherefore liest thou thus upon thy face?** This direct answer of Jehovah implied that Joshua had no reason to doubt the faithfulness of the Lord, but that the fault lay with the people. V. 11. **Israel hath sinned, and they have also transgressed My covenant which I commanded them.** It was Israel that had broken faith by setting aside the obligations of the covenant of Jehovah; **for they have even taken of the accursed thing,** thus far have they forgotten themselves, **and have also stolen, and dissembled also,** acting a lie before Jehovah, **and they have put it even**

among their own stuff. Since the stolen goods were devoted to Jehovah by His express command, their being taken for private use was the height of blasphemous violence. The language of the Lord is very dramatic, laden with the most intense emotion. V. 12. **Therefore the children of Israel could not stand before their enemies, but turned their backs before their enemies, because they were accursed,** lying under the ban of Jehovah, destined for destruction unless the cause were removed; **neither will I be with you any more except ye destroy the accursed from among you,** the person actually guilty, who had involved the entire people in his guilt. V. 13. **Up, sanctify the people and say, Sanctify yourselves against to-morrow,** as in chap. 3, 5; **for thus saith the Lord God of Israel, There is an accursed thing,** something under Jehovah's ban, **in the midst of thee, O Israel; thou canst not stand before thine enemies until ye take away the accursed thing from among you.** V. 14. **In the morning, therefore, ye shall be brought,** into the presence of Jehovah, before the Tabernacle, **according to your tribes; and it shall be that the tribe which the Lord taketh shall come according to the families thereof; and the family which the Lord shall take shall come by households; and the household which the Lord shall take shall come man by man.** So lots were to be cast, first upon the tribes, then upon the clans into which the guilty tribe was divided, then upon the houses of the fathers, the groups of families under one patriarchal ancestor, and finally upon the heads of the households included in the guilty house of the fathers. V. 15. **And it shall be that he that is taken with the accursed thing shall be burned with fire,** after having been stoned to death. Lev. 20, 14, **he and all that he hath, because he hath transgressed the covenant of**

the Lord and because he hath wrought folly in Israel, moral foolishness and iniquity, resulting in trouble for the entire people. V. 16. **So Joshua rose up early in the morning and brought Israel by their tribes; and the tribe of Judah was taken,** declared to be the guilty one by the falling of the lots, under the direction of Jehovah. V. 17. **And he brought the family of Judah,** the various clans into which the tribe of Judah was divided; **and he took the family of the Zarhites; and he brought the family,** or clan, **of the Zarhites man by man,** the heads of the various houses of the fathers; **and Zabdi was taken; v. 18. and he brought his household man by man,** all the heads of the individual families; **and Achan, the son of Carmi, the son of Zabdi, the son of Zerah, of the tribe of Judah, was taken,** declared to be the guilty man by the testimony of the lots, whose falling or drawing was directed by Jehovah. V. 19. **And Joshua said unto Achan, My son, give, I pray thee, glory to the Lord God of Israel,** a very solemn formula of adjuration, **and make confession unto Him;** by admitting the truth Achan was to give praise to God, declaring His judgments to be righteous, also in the matter of his own punishment; **and tell me now what thou hast done; hide it not from me.** Achan should confess his sin in order to clear the rest of the people and to receive forgiveness for himself, although he had outwardly fallen under the irrevocable sentence of God. V. 20. **And Achan answered Joshua and said, Indeed I have sinned. against the Lord God of Israel, and thus and thus have I done: v. 21. when I saw among the spoils a goodly Babylonish garment,** a very precious, skillfully woven mantle, such as were made in Babylon and sold far and wide in the neighboring countries, **and two hundred shekels of silver** (about $128), **and a wedge**

of gold, a piece of jewelry in the form of a tongue, **of fifty shekels' weight** (worth about $480); **then. I coveted them and took them; and, behold, they are hid in the earth in the midst of my tent, and the silver under it.** That is the progress of sin: seeing, coveting, taking, hiding, dissembling. V. 22. **So Joshua sent messengers, and they ran into the tent; and, behold, it,** the stolen mantle, **was hid in his tent, and the silver under it.** V. 23. **And they took them out of the midst of the tent and brought them unto Joshua and unto all the children of Israel,** as they were assembled before the Lord, **and laid them out before the Lord,** probably in the court of the Tabernacle. V. 24. **And Joshua, and all Israel with him, took Achan, the son of Zerah, and the silver, and the garment, and the wedge of gold,** the detailed enumeration serving to emphasize his guilt, a**nd his sons, and his daughters,** since they shared in their father's guilt by concealing his theft, and his oxen, **and his asses, and his sheep, and his tent, and all that he had,** all his possessions coming under the curse; **and they brought them unto the Valley of Achor.** V. 25. **And Joshua said, Why hast thou troubled us,** brought misfortune upon us? **The Lord shall trouble thee this day.** Achan, as the chief transgressor, is addressed. **And all Israel stoned him with stones,** this form of punishment signifying that Achan had by his robbery violated the honor of God, in the same way as blasphemers did, **and burned them,** his sons and daughters with him, **with fire, after they had stoned them with stones.** V. 26. **And they raised over him a great heap of stones unto this day,** commemorating his disgrace and serving as a warning for many years, until this account was embodied in the book. **So the Lord,** after the punishment of the guilty, **turned from the fierceness of His anger,** which includes the certainty that His assistance was assured for the future. **Wherefore the name of that place was called The Valley of Achor** (trouble) **unto this day.** The story of Achan contains an earnest lesson; for, although he was truly repentant, yet he had to suffer the penalty of his transgression. Thus a repentant sinner may be assured of the forgiveness of God and yet be obliged to suffer the punishment which was set upon his transgression. It is in this connection that a false sentimentalism is working more harm than good and making hypocrites out of many criminals who learn to play upon men's feelings.

9

Joshua 8

Ai Taken. The Law Proclaimed.

Preparations for the taking of Ai. — V. 1. **And the Lord,** having restored His favor to Israel by the expiation of Achan's death, **said unto Joshua, Fear not, neither be thou dismayed,** cast down and filled with apprehension. **Take all the people of war with thee,** the entire army, **and arise, go up to Ai; see, I have given into thy hand the king of Ai, and his people, and his city, and his land,** the territory of which Ai was capital; v. 2. **and thou shalt do to Ai and her king as thou didst unto Jericho and her king,** exterminate all human beings; **only the spoil thereof,** in money and goods, **and the cattle thereof shall ye take for a prey unto yourselves,** for only Jericho, as first-fruits, had been devoted to the Lord. **Lay thee an ambush for the city behind it. V. 3. So Joshua arose and all the people of war,** the entire army, as ordered by God, **to go up against Ai,** he gave the command that all should be mustered. **And Joshua chose out thirty thousand mighty men of valor and sent them away by night,** since the distance was such as to be made easily in

45

one night's march. V. 4. **And he commanded them, saying, Behold, ye shall lie in wait against the city,** ready for an attack, **even behind the city. Go not very far from the city, but be ye all ready;** v. 5. **and I and all the people that are with me,** the main division of the army, **will approach unto the city,** along the road which led to it from the southeast; **and it shall come to pass, when they come out against us, as at the first, that we will flee before them,** employ this ruse to draw them out of the city, v. 6. **(for they will come out after us) till we have drawn them from the city. For they will say, They flee before us as at the first; therefore we will flee before them,** thus strengthening the enemy in their false supposition and causing them to abandon caution. V. 7. **Then ye shall rise up from the ambush and seize upon the city,** capture it without difficulty; **for the Lord, your God, will deliver it into your hand. V. 8. And it shall be, when ye have taken the city, that ye shall set the city on fire; according to the commandment of the Lord shall ye do. See, I have commanded you. V. 9. Joshua therefore sent them forth; and they went to lie in ambush, and abode between Bethel and Ai, on the west side of Ai,** there being some rocky ridges to the southwest, where concealment could easily be made. **But Joshua lodged that night among the people,** in camp with the larger division of his army, which marched less swiftly. V. 10. **And Joshua rose up early in the morning and numbered the people,** mustered them, **and went up, he and the elders of Israel,** for it behooved them to take the lead in the attack, **before the people of Ai,** so that the watchmen of the city could see them. V. 11. **And all the people, even the people of war that were with him, went up, and drew nigh, and came before the city, and pitched on the north side of Ai. Now, there was a valley between them**

and Ai. Thus their camp was plainly visible from Ai, but could not easily be attacked. V. 12. **And he took about five thousand men, and set them to lie in ambush between Bethel and Ai, on the west side of the city,** for there was a second ridge toward the northwest. V. 13. **And when they had set the people,** assigned to every company and every individual the place which he was to occupy in the attack, **even all the host that was on the north of the city, and their liers-in-wait on the west of the city, Joshua went that night into the midst of the valley,** moved forward, as though for an attack, under cover of darkness. Thus the main part of the army was on the north side of the city, the ambush of thirty thousand was on the southwest, directly behind the city, and the smaller ambush of five thousand men was ready to attack the flank of the enemy. It was not merely Joshua's military genius which appears in this story, for the plan was made by the Lord, whose purpose was to reassure the army of Israel.

Ai taken and destroyed. — V. 14. **And it came to pass, when the king of Ai saw it, that they hasted and rose up early,** believing they had only the army to the north of the city to deal with; **and the men of the city went out against Israel to battle, he** (the king) **and all his people, at a time appointed, before the plain,** in the only place where a battle in open formation was possible, near the steppes of Beth-aven, east of Bethel; **but he wist not that there were liers-in-ambush against him behind the city.** V. 15. **And Joshua and all Israel made as if they were beaten before them,** they feigned fear and weakness, **and fled by the way of the wilderness.** V. 16. **And all the people that were in Ai,** all the able-bodied men, **were called together to pursue after them; and they pursued after Joshua, and were drawn away from the city,** leaving the latter altogether unprotected. V. 17. **And there was not a man left in Ai or Bethel,** the inhabitants of the latter city having joined the forces of Ai, **that went not out after Israel; and they left the city open, and pursued after Israel,** thinking that the army of Israel was fleeing in utter and hopeless rout. V. 18. **And the Lord said unto Joshua, Stretch out the spear that is in thy hand toward Ai; for I will give it into thine hand.** Joshua was probably occupying some higher point from which he was easily visible, or he may have been mounted and his figure easily distinguishable even at a distance. **And Joshua stretched out the spear that he had in his hand toward the city.** V. 19. **And the ambush,** to whom the outposts had immediately signaled to that effect, **arose quickly out of their place, and they ran as soon as he had stretched out his hand; and they entered into the city,** whose defenders were all engaged in the pursuit of the Israelites, **and took it, and hasted and set the city on fire.** V. 20. **And when the men of Ai looked behind them,** their attention being drawn in that direction by the behavior of the Israelites, who turned to watch for the signal of the smoke's rising, **they saw, and, behold, the smoke of the city ascended up to heaven, and they had no power to nee this way or that way,** they were paralyzed with sudden terror; **and the people that fled to the wilderness turned back upon the pursuers.** The whole situation of the men of Ai, who now saw before them the enemy, behind them the burning town, is admirably pictured in a few strokes. V. 21. **And when Joshua and all Israel saw that the ambush had taken the city, and that the smoke of the city ascended,** for this was the sign for which they had been waiting, **then they turned again, and slew the men of Ai.** V. 22. **And the other,** the Israelites who had lain in ambush, issued out of the city against them; so they were in the midst of Israel, some on this side and some on that side, caught in a trap from which there was no escape. And they, the Israelites, smote them, so that they let none of them remain or escape, the entire army of Ai, together with its allies, being destroyed. V. 23. And the king of Ai they took alive, and brought him to Joshua, who was to rule regarding his disposal. V. 24. And it came to pass, when Israel had made an end of slaying all the inhabitants of Ai in the field, in the wilderness, wherein they chased them, and when they were all fallen on the edge of the sword, until they were consumed, that all the Israelites returned unto Ai, and smote it with the edge of the sword, put all its inhabitants to death. V. 25, And so it was that all that fell that day, both of men and women, were twelve thousand, even all the men of Ai, the adult inhabitants. V. 26. For Joshua drew not his hand back wherewith he stretched out the spear until he had utterly destroyed all the inhabitants of Ai. This he did according to the universal rule of the ancients, which required the general to hold the signal of battle aloft until he desired the battle to be ended. V. 27. Only the cattle and the spoil of that city Israel took for a prey unto themselves, according unto the word of the Lord which He commanded Joshua, v. 2. V. 28. And Joshua burned Ai, and made it an heap forever, a heap of ashes and broken stones, even a desolation unto this day; its ruins were still visible at the time when the author wrote this account. V. 29. And the king of Ai he hanged on a tree until eventide, Num. 25, 4; and as soon as the sun was down, Joshua commanded that they should take his carcass down from the tree, Deut. 21, 23, and cast it at the entering of the gate of the city, and raise thereon a great heap of stones, that remaineth unto this day. The entire story teaches that we should indeed use all our physical and mental powers in the work given us by the Lord, but that everything depends upon His almighty power and blessing. It is He who must give us the victory in every battle.

Blessing and curse proclaimed. — V. 30. **Then Joshua built an altar unto the Lord God of Israel in Mount Ebal,** as the Lord had commanded, Deut. 27, 4. 5, v. 31. **as Moses, the servant of the Lord, commanded the children of Israel, as it is written in the book of the Law of Moses, an altar of whole stones, over which no man hath lift up any iron,** Ex. 20, 25. **And they offered thereon burnt offerings unto the Lord, and sacrificed peace-offerings.** V. 32. **And he** (Joshua) **wrote there upon the stones a copy of the Law of Moses, which he wrote in the presence of the children of Israel,** Deut. 27, 2. 8. V. 33. **And all Israel and their elders and officers and their judges stood on this side the ark and on that side, before the priests, the Levites,** the ark thus occupying the center between the two divisions of the tribes, **which bare the Ark of the Covenant of the Lord, as well the stranger as he that was born among them, half of them. over against Mount Gerizim and half of them over against Mount Ebal,** Deut. 11, 29; 27, 11-26, **as Moses, the servant of the Lord, had commanded before, that they should bless the people of Israel.** V. 34. **And afterward he read all the words of the Law, the blessings and cursings,** fulfilling the Law being in itself a blessing and transgressing it being in itself a curse, Deut. 11, 26, **according to all that is written in the book of the Law.** V. 35. **There was not a word of all that Moses commanded which Joshua read not before all the congregation of Israel, with the women and the little ones and the strangers that were conversant among** (living with) **them,** who had chosen to cast their lot with that of Israel. We believers of the New Covenant will ever be mindful of the revelation of the New Testament, of the Gospel, never leaving it out of our eyes. For upon a man's attitude toward the Gospel of Jesus Christ depends, in the last analysis, his eternal weal or woe.

10

Joshua 9

The Craft of the Gibeonites.

The Gibeonites deceive Joshua and the princes. – V. 1. **And it came to pass, when all the kings which were on this side Jordan,** on the west side, in the hills, in the entire mountain country of Canaan, **and in the valleys,** the lowland toward the south and west, **and in all the coasts of the great sea,** the Mediterranean Sea, **over against Lebanon,** in the entire strip of open coast, from the neighborhood of Joppa well into Phenicia, **the Hittite, and the Amorite, the Canaanite, the Perizzite, the Hivite, and the Jebusite,** chap. 3, 10, **heard thereof,** namely, of all the deeds which Israel had undertaken till now, v. 2. **that they gathered themselves together,** they formed a league, **to fight with Joshua and with Israel, with one accord,** there being only one opinion expressed among them, namely, that they must maintain an alliance in order to overcome the invaders. V. 3. **And when the inhabitants of Gibeon,** the capital of a small independent state in the mountains northwest of Jerusalem, the principality containing a number of smaller cities as well, v. 17. **heard** what Joshua had done unto Jericho and Ai, v. 4. **they did work wilily,** they made use of a stratagem, **and went and made as if they had been ambassadors,** or, they provided themselves with victuals, **and took old sacks upon their asses and wine-bottles,** specially prepared skins, as they were used for transporting liquids, **old, and rent, and bound up,** v. 5. **and old shoes and clouted upon their feet,** sandals worn and patched, **and old garments upon them; and all the bread of their provision was dry and moldy,** the mold having eaten spots into the bread. V. 6. **And they went to Joshua, unto the camp at Gilgal,** either that near Jericho, or, more probably, that in Mount Ephraim, about midway between Jerusalem and Shechem, **and said unto him and to the men of Israel, We be come from. a far country; now, therefore, make ye a league with us.** V. 7. **And the men of Israel said unto the Hivites,** for that is what the Gibeonites were, as the Israelites later found out, **Peradventure ye dwell among us; and how shall we make a league with you?** This question was prompted by the suspicious aspect of the entire matter, which made it seem probable that the ambassadors were members of some Canaanitish nation. V. 8. **And they said unto Joshua, We are thy servants,** which was really a meaningless form of courtesy and not at all satisfactory. **And Joshua,** not satisfied with this evasive attitude, said unto them, **Who are ye, and from whence come ye?** It was a direct and definite inquiry. V. 9. **And they said unto him, From a very far country thy servants are come because of the name of the Lord, thy God; for,** as they add in explanation, **we have heard the fame of Him, and all that He did in Egypt,** v. 10. **and all that He did to the two kings of the Amorites that were beyond Jordan, to Sihon, king of Heshbon, and to Og, king of Bashan, which was at**

Ashtaroth. They wisely make no mention of the miraculous passage of Jordan and of the taking of Jericho, in order not to contradict their statement of having been on the way a long time. V. 11. **Wherefore our elders,** the officials of their republic, **and all the inhabitants of our country spake to us, saying, Take victuals with you for the journey, and go to meet them,** the Israelites, a**nd say unto them, We are your servants; therefore, now, make ye a league with us.** V. 12. **This our bread we took hot,** straight from the oven, **for our provision out of our houses on the day we came forth to go unto you, but now, behold, it is dry, and it is moldy;** v. 13. **and these bottles, skins, of wine, which we filled, were new, and, behold, they be rent; and these our garments and our shoes are become old by reason of the very long journey.** It was a bold stroke by which the messengers pointed to their provisions and to their clothing in corroboration of their story. V. 14. **And the men,** the princes of Israel, **took of their victuals,** either to convince themselves of the truth of the statements presented to them, or in an act implying readiness to make a league with the Gibeonites, **and asked not counsel at the mouth of the Lord,** thus transgressing an explicit command of the Lord, Num. 27, 21; for that was one of the functions of the high priest, to ask advice of the Lord in all difficult questions by means of Urim and Thummim. V. 15. **And Joshua made peace with them, and made a league with them,** to their advantage, **to let them live; and the princes of the congregation sware unto them.** In the entire transaction Joshua and the heads of Israel acted very foolishly, and the result was a transgression of God's command, who had made the strict rule that no covenants were to be made with the nations of Canaan, Ex.-23, 32; 34, 12. The neglect to consult the Word of God in important questions has plunged many a Christian into severe sins.

The deception discovered and punished. V. 16. **And it came to pass at the end of three days, after they had made a league with them, that they,** the Israelites, **heard that they,** the Gibeonites, **were their neighbors, and that they dwelt among them,** almost in the center of Canaan. V. 17. **And the children of Israel journeyed, and came unto their cities on the third day. Now, their cities were Gibeon, and Chephirah, and Beeroth, and Kirjath-jearim,** the location of all of which is pretty definitely known, west and northwest of Jerusalem. V. 18. **And the children of Israel smote them not, because the princes of the congregation had sworn unto them by the Lord God of Israel,** namely, to spare their lives, and they felt themselves bound in conscience, by their reverence of the oath in itself, Lev. 19, 12, although, strictly speaking, the condition of the ambassadors' having come from a distant country was attached to the oath and rendered it invalid. **And all the congregation murmured against the princes.** V. 19. **But all the princes said unto all the congregation, We have sworn unto them by the Lord God of Israel; now, therefore, we may not touch them.** V. 20. **This we will do to them: we will even let them live, lest wrath be upon us, because of the oath which we sware unto them.** The punishment of God did strike Israel later, at the time of David, because Saul, not paying any attention to this oath and the subsequent provision, had tried to exterminate the Gibeonites, 2 Sam. 21. V. 21. **And the princes said unto them, Let them live, but let them be hewers of wood and drawers of water unto all the congregation; as the princes had promised them.** So their lives were spared, but they were given the most menial position in Israel; they were made slaves of the Sanctuary, being obliged to perform the lowest tasks there, as servants of the entire congregation. In this way the danger of their attempting to lead Israel into idolatry was also removed. Thus the matter was decided upon and adjusted. V. 22. **And Joshua called for them, and he spake unto them, saying, "Wherefore have ye beguiled us, saying, We are very far from you, when ye dwell among us?** It was a just rebuke of the lying craftiness of the Gibeonites. V. 23. **Now, therefore, ye are cursed, and there shall none of you be freed from being bondmen,** they were never to cease being slaves, that was to be their social status in Israel forever, **and hewers of wood and drawers of water for the house of my God,** reckoned among the lowest class of the people, Deut. 29, 10. 11. Together with captives taken in war and devoted for like purposes to the Sanctuary, they bore, at a later period, the name *Nethinim*, 1 Chron. 9, 2; Neh. 7, 43. 46. V. 24. **And they answered Joshua,** in attempting to justify their action, and said, **Because it was certainly told thy servants how that the Lord, thy God, commanded His servant Moses to give you all the land, and to destroy all the inhabitants of the land from before you, therefore we were sore afraid of our lives because of you, and have done this thing.** V. 25. **And now, behold, we are in thine hand; as it seemeth good and right unto thee to do unto us,** do. It was an unconditional submission, by which they left their fate entirely in the hands of Joshua. V. 26. **And so he did unto them,** as had been decided upon, **and delivered them out of the hand of the children of Israel, that they slew them not,** which they, in their warlike zeal, would have been only too willing to do. V. 27. **And Joshua made them that day hewers of wood and drawers of water for the congregation and for the altar of the Lord even unto this day,** at the Tabernacle, **in the**

place which He should choose, this note proving that the book was written before the building of Solomon's Temple. Yet the Gibeonites, condemned to everlasting servitude as they were, were received into the fellowship of the blessings of Jehovah. There are always some souls, even among the outcasts of the world, who hear of the mercy of the Lord and are moved to accept His invitation in the Gospel. Mark: An oath in uncertain things may be the cause of much trouble and unpleasantness, if it does not lead to severe transgressions of the will of God.

11

Joshua 10

The Destruction of the Five Kings.
The defeat of the five kings on a day of miraculous length. — V. 1. **Now, it came to pass, when Adoni-zedec, king of Jerusalem, had heard how Joshua had taken Ai and had utterly destroyed it, (as he had done to Jericho and her king, so he had done to Ai and her king,** a judgment of extermination having been carried out upon them,) **and how the inhabitants of Gibeon had made peace with Israel and were among them,** in alliance with them, the entire Central Canaan thus being in the hands of the invaders, v. 2. **that they feared greatly, because Gibeon was a great city, as one of the royal cities,** the capitals occupied by the sheiks, or kings, of the various tribes and nations, **and because it was greater than Ai and all the men thereof were mighty. V. 3. Wherefore Adoni-zedec, king of Jerusalem, sent unto Hoham, king of Hebron,** the ancient city in Southern Canaan, **and unto Piram, king of Jarmuth, and unto Japhia, king of Lachish, and unto Debir, king of Eglon,** these cities being in the lowlands toward the southwest, bordering on Philistia, **saying,** v. 4. **Come**

up unto me and help me that we may smite Gibeon; for it hath made peace with Joshua and with the children of Israel. The campaign was not directed against Israel, but against Gibeon, for the action of the Gibeonites was construed as a betrayal of the Canaanites' cause, as a going over to the enemy. V. 5. **Therefore the five kings of the Amorites, the king of Jerusalem, the king of Hebron, the king of Jarmuth, the king of Lachish, the king of Eglon, gathered themselves together,** formed an alliance, **and went up, they and all their hosts, and encamped before Gibeon, and made war against it.** Thus these kings hardened their hearts against the obvious proofs of God's power and plunged headlong into their destruction. V. 6. **And the men of Gibeon sent unto Joshua, to the camp, to Gilgal,** for they were now in alliance with Israel, **saying, Slack not thy hand from thy servants,** do not withdraw it in this emergency; **come up to us quickly, and save us, and help us,** the appeal being in the form of a climax; **for all the kings of the Amorites that dwell in the mountains are gathered together against us.** Since the Amorites of the mountains, the Jebusites, were the strongest among the allies, the entire army of the enemy is described accordingly. V. 7. **So Joshua ascended from Gilgal,** in a forced night march, **he and all the people of war with him and all the mighty men of valor,** a picked portion of the army. V. 8. **And the Lord said unto Joshua, Fear them not, for I have delivered them into thine hand; there shall not a man of them stand before thee.** Cp. chap. 2, 24; 6, 2; 8, 1. 18. V. 9. **Joshua, therefore, came unto them suddenly,** in a surprise attack, the rapid march being a proof of his great military genius, **and went up from Gilgal all night.** V. 10. **And the Lord discomfited them,** the Amorites, **before Israel,** made them confused and helpless at this sudden attack, **and slew them with a great slaughter at Gibeon, and chased them along the way that goeth up to Beth-horon,** the pass in the mountains which led to the plains beyond, **and smote them to Azekah and unto Makkedah,** far down in the lowlands of Philistia, the battle thus rapidly changing to flight and pursuit over a distance of some thirty miles. V. 11. **And it came to pass, as they fled from before Israel, and were in the going down to Beth-horon,** where the foothills converge into the plains of Philistia, **that the Lord cast down great stones from heaven upon them unto Azekah,** in a terrible hailstorm, **and they died; they were more which died with hailstones than they whom the children of Israel slew with the sword.** The Israelites were to see and understand that it was not their own strength, but the divine assistance of Jehovah, which gave them the victory. V. 12. **Then spake Joshua to the Lord in the day when the Lord delivered up the Amorites before the children of Israel, and he said in the sight of Israel,** in a mighty prayer of faith, **Sun, stand thou still upon Gibeon,** wait, delay some time; **and thou, Moon, in the Valley of Ajalon.** This must, therefore, have happened while the moon was in its first quarter. The command was a heroic prayer to the Lord and Creator of the world to interfere in the order of nature and not to permit the setting of the main lights controlling the division of time until Israel would have completed her vengeance upon her enemies. V. 13. **And the sun stood still, and the moon stayed,** they were held back, they did not continue their course, **until the people had avenged themselves upon their enemies,** completely destroyed them. **Is not this written in the Book of Jasher** (of the righteous), a book of poems praising the great deeds of Jehovah? **So the sun stood still in the midst of heaven, and hasted not to go**

down, made no progress toward the west, **about a whole day. V. 14. And there was no day like that before it or after it, that the Lord hearkened unto the voice of a man; for the Lord fought for Israel.** Thus the living, almighty God wrought a great miracle, for the religious destiny of all the world was here at stake. All the efforts of Bible-scholars and critics to explain away this fact avail them nothing; the text is too clear and too powerful.

The five kings put to death. — V. 15. **And Joshua returned, and all Israel with him, unto the camp, to Gilgal,** this central location being convenient for all campaigns. V. 16. **But these five king's fled, and hid themselves in a cave at Makkedah,** for the lime- and chalk-rocks of this neighborhood contain many suitable caves. V. 17. **And it was told Joshua, saying", The five king's are found hid in a cave at Makkedah.** V. 18. **And Joshua said, Roll great stones upon the mouth of the cave, and set men by it for to keep them,** to guard the entrance, **lest they escape; v. 19. and stay ye not, but pursue after your enemies, and smite the hindmost of them,** the rear-guard, so far as there was still a semblance of order in their ranks; **suffer them. not to enter into their cities,** to escape into fortified places; **for the Lord, your God, hath delivered them into your hand. V. 20. And it came to pass, when Joshua and the children of Israel had made an end of slaying them with a very great slaughter, till they were consumed, that the rest which remained of them,** a small remnant, entered into fenced cities, where they were safe for the time being. V. 21. **And all the people returned to the camp, to Joshua, at Makkedah,** where he had pitched for the purpose of continuing the campaign, **in peace; none moved his tongue against any of the children of Israel,** Ex. 11, 7. The enemies were so thoroughly subdued and frightened that no one ventured to do any harm to any of the children of Israel, although they must have been scattered far and wide in their pursuit of the Amorite army. V. 22. **Then said Joshua, Open the mouth of the cave, and bring out those five kings unto me out of the cave.** V. 23. **And they did so, and brought forth those five kings unto him out of the cave, the king of Jerusalem, the king of Hebron, the king of Jarmuth, the king of Lachish, and the king of Eglon.** V. 24. **And it came to pass, when they brought out those kings unto Joshua, that Joshua called for all the men of Israel, and said unto the captains of the men of war which went with him, Come near and put your feet upon the necks of these kings,** in token of their complete subjection and of the conquest of all enemies of the Lord. **And they came near and put their feet upon the necks of them.** V. 25. **And Joshua said unto them,** to the officers of his army, **Fear not, nor be dismayed,** filled with terror, **be strong and of good courage; for thus shall the Lord do to all your enemies against whom ye fight.** V. 26. **And afterward,** after this symbolical act, **Joshua smote them,** the five kings, **and slew them, and hanged them on five trees; and they were hanging upon the trees until the evening.** Cp. chap. 8, 29. V. 27. **And it came to pass at the time of the going down of the sun that Joshua commanded, and they took them down off the trees,** Deut. 21,23, **and cast them into the cave wherein they had been hid, and laid great stones in the cave's mouth, which remain until this very day,** or, which the Israelites had kept in the mouth of the cave to the day when the kings were executed. It was an act of God's punishment, and shows the manner in which He is able to deal with all His enemies and those who interfere with His plans in His Church.

The conquest of southern Canaan. — V. 28. **And that day,** while the five kings were suspended from trees, **Joshua took Makkedah, and smote it with the edge of the sword, and the king thereof he utterly destroyed, them and all the souls that were therein,** in the same manner of extermination employed in the case of Jericho and Ai; **he let none remain; and he did to the king of Makkedah as he did unto the king of Jericho,** chap. 6, 21. V. 29. **Then Joshua passed from Makkedah, and all Israel with him, unto Libnah,** a few miles to the south, **and fought against Libnah;** v. 30. **and the Lord delivered it also and the king thereof into the hand of Israel; and he smote it with the edge of the sword and all the souls that were therein; he let none remain in it, but did unto the king thereof as he did unto the king of Jericho.** V. 31. **And Joshua passed from Libnah, and all Israel with him, unto Lachish,** following up every advantage immediately, **and encamped against it, and fought against it.** V. 32. **And the Lord delivered Lachish,** which was almost in the center of the country of the Philistines, southwest of Libnah, **into the hand of Israel, which took it on the second day, and smote it with the edge of the sword, and all the souls that were therein, according to all that he had done to Libnah.** V. 33. **Then Horam, king of Gezer,** in Northern Philistia, **came up,** from the lowlands, **to help Lachish; and Joshua smote him and his people until he had left him none remaining.** V. 34. **And from Lachish Joshua passed unto Eglon,** a few miles to the east, **and all Israel with him; and they encamped against it, and fought against it;** v. 35. **and they took it on that day, and smote it with the edge of the sword, and all the souls that were therein he utterly destroyed that day, according to all that he had done to Lachish.** V. 36. **And Joshua went up from Eglon, and all**

Israel with him, unto Hebron, in the mountains, some thirty miles east; **and they fought against it;** v. 37. **and they took it, and smote it with the edge of the sword, and the king thereof,** the successor to him who had been executed at Makkedah, **and all the cities thereof,** the tributary suburbs, **and all the souls that were therein; he left none remaining, according' to all that he had done to Eglon; but destroyed it utterly and all the souls that were therein.** V. 38. **And Joshua returned,** turned back, toward the southwest, **and all Israel with him, to Debir,** some ten miles from Hebron, **and fought against it.** V. 39. **And he took it and the king thereof and all the cities thereof,** those under its jurisdiction; **and they smote them with the edge of the sword, and utterly destroyed all the souls that were therein; he left none remaining; as he had done to Hebron, so he did to Debir and to the king thereof; as he had done also to Libnah and to her king.** This territory, the extreme southern part of Canaan, was afterward again occupied by the Anakim and the Amorites, which made a second conquest of Hebron and the vicinity necessary. V. 40. **So Joshua smote all the country of the hills,** the mountainous section of Central and Southern Canaan, **and of the south,** the plain forming the southern portion of Judea, **and of the vale,** the lowlands of the southwest, **and of the springs,** the foothills section, or piedmont region, from Joppa to Gaza, **and all their kings; he left none remaining, but utterly destroyed all that breathed, as the Lord God of Israel commanded,** Deut. 20, 16. 17. V. 41. **And Joshua smote them from Kadesh-barnea even unto Gaza,** all the land between the Jordan valley and the Mediterranean in one direction, **and all the country of Goshen,** a section of the southern mountains, **even unto Gibeon,** from the heights of Gibeon to the wilderness. V.

42. **And all these kings and their land did Joshua take at one time,** in one campaign, **because the Lord God of Israel fought for Israel.** V. 43. **And Joshua returned, and all Israel with him, unto the camp, to Gilgal,** where he still had his headquarters, and where his soldiers could rest after their strenuous exploits. God is great and wonderful and past understanding in His judgments, but also at all times holy and righteous.

12

Joshua 11

The Conquest of Northern Canaan.

The second alliance of heathen kings and their defeat. – V.1. **And it came to pass, when Jabin, king of Hazor,** a city in the extreme northern part of Canaan, southeast of Tyre, **had heard those things,** the conquest of the entire southern part of Canaan, **that he sent to Jobab, king of Madon,** a city near the brook Kishon, **and to the king of Shimron, and to the king of Achshaph,** v. 2. **and to the kings that were on the north of the mountains,** what was later the mountainous region of Naphtali, a**nd of the plains south of Chinneroth,** the wide part of the valley of Jordan, south of the Sea of Galilee, **and in the valley,** the strip bordering the Mediterranean Sea between Akko and Sidon, **and in the borders of Dor on the west,** a Phenician city south of Tyre, overlooking the sea, later occupied by Manassites, v. 3. **and to the Canaanite on the east and on the west,** for their tribes occupied the lowlands, **and to the Amorite,** mainly in the mountain districts, **and the Hittite,** northwest of the Sea of Galileo, **and the Perizzite,** in the foothill country farther south,

and the Jebusite in the mountains, the highlands of Judah, **and to the Hivite under Hermon in the land of Mizpeh,** in the far north, in the spurs of the Lebanon range. So the alliance included all the tribes from Mount Hermon to Mount Carmel, some of the mightiest being those of the Plain of Eadraelon. V. 4. **And they went out, they and all their hosts with them, much people,** a mighty army, **even as the sand that is upon the seashore in multitude, with horses and chariots very many.** V. 5. **And when all these kings were met together,** had joined their forces by definite appointment, **they came and pitched together at the Waters of Merom,** a small lake about three miles in diameter, north of the Sea of Galileo, hardly more than a swamp in the dry season, **to fight against Israel.** It was a strategically strong position, for the army shielded the important cities to the north and west, while it was ready to meet the army of Joshua with every prospect of victory. V. 6. **And the Lord said unto Joshua, Be not afraid because of them; for to-morrow about this time will I deliver them up all slain before Israel; thou shall hough,** hamstring, **their horses, and burn their chariots with fire.** Evidently Joshua was already on his way to Northern Canaan when his scouts brought him the news of the enemy's strength, and the words of the Lord were intended to reassure him. V. 7. **So Joshua came,** after one of his characteristic rapid marches, **and all the people of war with him, against them,** the heathen armies, **by the Waters of Merom suddenly,** in a surprise attack; **and they fell upon them.** V. 8. **And the Lord delivered them into the hand of Israel, who smote them, and chased them unto great Zidon,** the ancient capital of Phenicia, **and unto Misrephoth-maim,** a place of springs at the foot of a steep precipice, over which a part of the enemy's army was forced, and, having dispersed the main body of their opponents, **unto the Valley of Mizpeh eastward,** into the foothills of the Lebanon toward the northeast; **and they smote them until they left them none remaining. V. 9. And Joshua did unto them as the Lord bade him: he houghed their horses,** by severing the tendons of their hind legs, **and burned their chariots with fire,** whose bodies therefore were certainly of wood. V. 10. **And Joshua at that time turned back and took Hazor,** whose king was the leader in the alliance, a**nd smote the king thereof with the sword; for Hazor beforetime was the head of all these kingdoms,** the chief city of the northern confederacy. V. 11. **And they,** the Israelites, **smote all the souls that were therein with the edge of the sword, utterly destroying them,** as being under the ban of Jehovah; **there was not any left to breathe. And he burned Hazor with fire,** purposely dealing more harshly with this city than with the rest. V. 12. **And all the cities of those kings,** who had been in the confederacy, **and all the kings of them did Joshua take, and smote them with the edge of the sword; and he utterly destroyed them, as Moses, the servant of the Lord, commanded,** Num. 33, 52; Deut. 7, 2. V. 13. **But as for the cities that stood still in their strength,** every one on its height or hill, as the inland cities were usually built, **Israel burned none of them,** although it overthrew or destroyed them, **save Hazor only; that did Joshua burn.** These cities remained in their old locations, many of them rising out of their ruins to new splendor. V. 14. **And all the spoil of these cities and the cattle the children of Israel took for a prey unto themselves; but every man,** all the human inhabitants, both young and old, **they smote with the edge of the sword until they had destroyed them, neither left they any to breathe,** Deut. 20, 16. V. 15. **As the Lord**

commanded Moses, His servant, so did Moses command Joshua, and so did Joshua; he left nothing undone of all that the Lord commanded Moses. If the children of God trust in Him with full obedience, the Lord gives them the victory over all their enemies.

The conquest of western Palestine. — V. 16. **So Joshua took all that land, the hills,** the mountainous sections of Canaan proper, **and all the south country,** the great steppes of Judah, **and all the land of Goshen,** the foothills country toward the west, **and the valley,** the plains in the central and northwestern section, **and the plain,** probably that of Sharon, **and the mountain of Israel,** Ephraim, in the center of the land, **and the valley of the same,** its lowland on the west; v. 17. **even from the Mount Halak that goeth up to Seir,** the smooth or bald mountain in the Azazimeh range in the south, whose chalk cliffs probably gave it the name, **even unto Baal-gad, in the Valley of Lebanon, under Mount Hermon,** in the extreme north; **and all their kings he took, and smote them and slew them.** Thus the entire campaign, lasting some seven years, is summarized. V. 18. **Joshua made war a long time with all these kings.** V. 19. **There was not a city that made peace with the children of Israel save the Hivites, the inhabitants of Gibeon,** chap. 9, 3. 7; **all other they,** the children of Israel, **took in battle.** V. 20. **For it was of the Lord,** it was His dispensation, **to harden their hearts that they should come against Israel in battle, that He might destroy them utterly, and that they might have no favor,** no compassionate sympathy from Him, **but that He might destroy them, as the Lord commanded Moses,** Deut. 20, 16. 17. Theirs was an obduration, a hardening of heart, like that of Pharaoh, Ex. 4, 21. V. 21. **And at that time,** in the course of the conquest of the entire country, **came Joshua and cut off the Anakim,** the race of giants, Num. 13, 28 ff., **from the mountains, from Hebron, from Debir,** chap. 10, 36. 38, **from Anab,** another city south of Hebron, **and from all the mountains of Judah, and from all the mountains of Israel; Joshua destroyed them utterly with their cities.** This account supplements that of the preceding chapter and shows that the giant race was by no means unconquerable, as the spies had reported on their return to the camp of Israel in Kadesh-barnea. V. 22. **There was none of the Anakim left in the land of the children of Israel; only in Gaza, in Gath,** the city of Goliath, **and in Ashdod,** the city of the idol Dagon, these three being cities of Philistia, **there remained.** V. 23. **So Joshua took the whole land, according to all that the Lord said unto Moses; and Joshua gave it for an inheritance unto Israel according to their divisions by their tribes,** as related in the subsequent account. **And the land rested from war,** not because all the Canaanites had been exterminated or even all their cities taken, but because their power was broken, their dominion a thing of the past, and Israel master of the entire land. The remnants of the heathen nations might easily have been conquered and annihilated, if Israel had but remained faithful to Jehovah, for with His help, in His power, everything is possible.

13

Joshua 12

AList of Canaanitish Kings and Their Conquered Kingdoms.

On the east side of Jordan. — V. 1. **Now, these are the kings of the land which the children of Israel smote, and possessed their land on the other side Jordan toward the rising of the sun, from the river Arnon,** the northern boundary of Moab, **unto Mount Hermon,** in the Anti-Lebanon range, **and all the plain on the east,** the valley of Jordan with its eastern tributaries: v. 2. **Sihon, king of the Amorites, who dwelt in Heshbon, and ruled from Aroer, which is upon the bank of the river Arnon, and from the middle of the river,** that is, from the middle of the valley, from the city of Ar, or Areopolis, **and from half Gilead,** the hilly section on the south side of Jabbok, **even unto the river Jabbok, which is the border of the children of Ammon,** that is, in its upper reaches; v. 3. **and from the plain,** the Arabian Desert, **to the sea of Chinneroth on the east, and unto the sea of the plain, even the Salt Sea, on the east, the way to Bethjeshimoth,** which was located near the mouth of the Jordan; **and from the**

south, under Ashdothpisgah, under the foothills of the range flanking the Dead Sea on the east, all this country, as thus bounded, being included in the kingdom of Sihon, who was defeated by the army of Israel, Num.21; Deut.2; v. 4. **and the coast of Og, king of Bashan, which was of the remnant of the giants,** a descendant of the ancient giant races, **that dwelt at Ashtaroth and at Edrei,** Deut. 1, 4; 3, 11; Num. 21, 33, v. 5. **and reigned in Mount Hermon and in Salcah,** Deut. 3, 10, on the southern border of the Hauran, **and in all Bashan,** the Hauran proper, the entire upper valley of the Hieromax River, **unto the border of the Geshurites and the Maachathites,** the former located on the southeastern, the latter on the southwestern slopes of Mount Hermon, **and half Gilead,** the part north of the Jabbok, **the border of Sihon, king of Heshbon.** V. 6. **Them did Moses, the servant of the Lord, and the children of Israel smite; and Moses, the servant of the Lord, gave it for a possession unto the Reubenites and the Gadites and the half tribe of Manasseh,** Num. 32, 33. These kings of the Amorites had been powerful monarchs, but they had been helpless before the army of the Lord.

The conquered kings west of Jordan. — V. 7. **And these are the kings of the country which Joshua and the children of Israel smote on this side Jordan on the west, from Baal-gad, in the Valley of Lebanon,** in the north, **even unto the Mount Halak, that goeth up to Seir,** chap. 11,17; **which Joshua gave unto the tribes of Israel for a possession according to their divisions;** v. 8. **in the mountains, and in the valleys, and in the plains, and in the springs, and in the wilderness, and in the south country; the Hittites, the Amorites, and the Canaanites, the Perizzites, the Hivites, and the Jebusites,** cp. chap. 10, 40-42; 11,16: v. 9. **the king of Jericho, one; the**

king of Ai, which is beside Bethel, one; v. 10. **the king of Jerusalem, one; the king of Hebron, one;** v. 11. **the king of Jarmuth, one; the king of Lachish, one;** v. 12. **the king of Eglon, one,** the last five being those defeated at Gibeon, and executed at Makkedah, chap. 10; **the king of Gezer, one,** chap. 10,33; v. 13. **the king of Debir, one; the king of Geder,** in the lowlands of Judah, **one;** v. 14. **the king of Hormah,** on the extreme southern boundary, **one; the king of Arad,** south of Hebron, **one;** v. 15. **the king of Libnah, one; the king of Adullam, one;** v. 16. **the king of Makkedah, one; the king of Bethel, one,** all those named till now being in the central and southern part of Canaan; v. 17. **the king of Tappuah,** in the Plain of Jezreel, near the river Kishon, **one; the king of Hepher,** in the same region, **one;** v. 18. **the king of Aphek, one; the king of Lasharon, one;** v. 19. **the king of Madon, one; the king of Hazor, one,** he being the leader in the northern confederacy, chap. 11, 10; v. 20. **the king of Shimronmeron, one; the king of Achshaph, one;** v. 21. **the king of Taanach, one; the king of Megiddo,** one, both these cities being situated in the Valley of Jezreel; v. 22. **the king of Kedesh,** on the mountains of Naphtali, **one; the king of Jokneam of Carmel, one;** v. 23. **the king of Dor in the coast of Dor,** chap. 11, 2, **one; the king of the nations of Gilgal,** not far from Naphothdor, **one;** v. 24. **the king of Tirzah,** north of Shechem, in Samaria, **one: all the kings thirty and one.** The enumeration of these conquered kings served as a reminder to the children of Israel never to forget the powerful and miraculous help of Jehovah, by which He gave them possession of the country promised to their fathers and them. It is only by always keeping the great deeds of God for our salvation before our eyes that we appreciate them with any degree of proper gratitude.

14

Joshua 13

oncerning the Distribution of Canaan. The command to distribute the land. — V. 1. **Now, Joshua was old and stricken in years,** literally, "well advanced in days," said of one whose age is showing plainly; **and the Lord said unto him, Thou art old and stricken in years, and there remaineth yet very much land to be possessed.** These sections are now, by way of parenthesis, enumerated. V. 2. **This is the land that yet remaineth: all the borders of the Philistines,** literally, all the circles of the Philistines, the five city-states of the country being referred to, the capitals with their suburbs and vicinity being joined in a confederacy, **and all Geshuri,** a small principality south of the Philistines, on the border of Egypt, 1 Sam. 27, 8, v. 3. **from Sihor, which is before Egypt,** the so-called brook of Egypt, 1 Chron. 13, 5, for this actually flows northeastwardly from or before Egypt, **even unto the borders of Ekron northward,** for thus far the territory of the Philistines extended, **which is counted to the Canaanite: five lords of the Philistines: the Gazathites, and the Ashdothites,**

the Eshkalonites, the Gittites, and the Ekronites, that is, the inhabitants of Gaza, mentioned frequently in the Old and also in the New Testament, of Ashdod, of Ashkelon, of Gath, and of Ekron, all of which have been identified with the exception of Gath, which seems to have been totally destroyed; **also the Avites,** or Avim, a small tribe living southwest of Gaza; **from the south,** that is, in the south; v. 4. **all the land of the Canaanites,** of the Phenicians living along the coast to the northwest, **and Mearah that is beside the Sidonians,** a well-known cave on Lebanon, east of Sidon, **unto Aphek,** a small city northeast of what is now Beirut, **to the borders of the Amorites,** the country of Bashan; for the entire Leontes Valley and the region in the neighborhood of Damascus was really included in the territory as the Lord intended it for Israel ; v. 5. **and the land of the Giblites,** of the race of Gebal, on the Mediterranean Sea, north of what is now Beirut, **and all Lebanon,** the entire region included within this range with its foothills, **toward the sun-rising, from Baal-gad, under Mount Hermon,** chap. 12, 7, **unto the entering into Hamath,** a small territory in the Orontes Valley, Num. 34, 8. V. 6. **All the inhabitants of the hill country from Lebanon unto Misrephothmaim,** chap. 11, 8, the present promontory of Ra-sen-Nakura, **and all the Sidonians,** an ancient name for all the Phenicians, **them will I drive out from before the children of Israel; only,** although it is not yet conquered, **divide thou it by lot unto the Israelites for an inheritance, as I have commanded thee.** The distribution of the country was to go on with a view toward the eventual possession of the entire country, as here described by the Lord. Israel afterward neglected to drive out the nations occupying all this territory, thereby not only reducing its own heritage, but also keeping these tribes as a continual temptation to idolatry. V. 7. **Now, therefore, divide this land for an inheritance unto the nine tribes and the half tribe of Manasseh,** those that had not yet been assigned a part of Canaan, v. 8. **with whom the Reubenites and the Gadites have received their inheritance,** they had already entered upon the possession of the territory assigned to them, **which Moses gave them beyond Jordan eastward, even as Moses, the servant of the Lord, gave them,** there was no change made either in the extent or in the boundaries of their possessions: v. 9. **from Aroer, that is upon the bank of the river Arnon, and the city that is in the midst of the river,** of the valley of the Arnon, chap. 12, 2, **and all the plain of Medeba unto Dibon,** the plateau east of Mount Pisgah, so named after its principal city; v. 10. **and all the cities of Sihon, king of the Amorites, which reigned in Heshbon, unto the border of the children of Ammon;** v. 11. **and Gilead, and the border of the Geshurites and Maachathites,** chap. 12, 5, **and all Mount Hermon, and all Bashan unto Salcah;** v. 12. **all the kingdom of Og in Bashan, which reigned in Ashtaroth and in Edrei, who remained of the remnant of the giants; for these did Moses smite, and cast them out,** Num. 21, 24-35. V. 13. **Nevertheless, the children of Israel expelled not the Geshurites nor the Maachathites,** chap. 15, 63; 16, 10; 17, 12. 13; **but the Geshurites and the Maachathites dwell among the Israelites until this day.** V. 14. **Only unto the tribe of Levi he gave none inheritance,** no separate territory; **the sacrifices of the Lord God of Israel made by fire are their inheritance, as he said. unto them,** Num. 18, 20-24. They possessed no earthly inheritance; with all the greater zeal they should therefore devote themselves to Jehovah and His worship. In a similar manner Christians know that they have here no continuing city, but they seek one to come, Heb. 13,14.

The territory of the two and one half tribes. — V. 15. **And Moses gave unto the tribe of the children of Reuben inheritance according to their families,** Num. 32. V. 16. **And their coast,** their boundary, **was from Aroer, that is on the bank of the river Arnon, and the city that is in the midst of the river,** Ar in the valley of the Arnon, **and all the plain by Medeba,** east of the Dead Sea; v. 17. **Heshbon,** the former capital of Sihon, **and all her cities that are in the plain; Dibon,** about four miles north of Arnon, **and Bamothbaal,** Num. 24, 20, **and Bethbaalmeon,** a short distance southeast of Heshbon, Num. 32, 38, v. 18. **and Jahaza,** where Sihon was defeated, almost at the eastern edge of the plateau, **and Kedemoth,** later a city of the Levites, 1 Chron. 6, 79, **and Mephaath,** another Levite city, v. 19. **and Kirjathaim,** where Chedorlaomer defeated the Enim, Gen. 14, 5, **and Sibmah,** a suburb of Heshbon, **and Zarethshahar in the mount of the valley,** nearer to the Dead Sea than Heshbon, v. 20. **and Bethpeor,** opposite Jericho, on the slopes of Mount Peor, **and Ashdothpisgah,** on the northeastern shore of the Dead Sea, **and Bethjeshimoth,** near the mouth of the Jordan, v. 21. **and all the cities of the plain, and all the kingdom, of Sihon, king of the Amorites,** so far as it was contained in this plateau, **which reigned in Heshbon, whom Moses smote with the princes of Midian,** Num. 21, 24, **Evi, and Rekem, and Zur, and Hur, and Reba, which were dukes of Sihon,** vassals or tributaries, **dwelling in the country,** Num. 31, 8. V. 22. **Balaam, also, the son of Beor, the soothsayer,** the diviner by the casting of lots, a name which brands him a false prophet, **did the children of Israel slay with the sword among them that were slain by them,** Num. 22, 5; 31, 8. V.

23. **And the border,** the boundary, **of the children of Reuben was Jordan and the border thereof,** to the territory of the Jordan in the west, for its main part was east of the Dead Sea. **This was the inheritance of the children of Reuben after their families, the cities and the villages thereof,** the latter being open towns, without walls or fortifications. V. 24. **And Moses gave inheritance unto the tribe of Gad, even unto the children of Gad, according to their families.** V. 25. **And their coast,** their boundary, as it included their territory, **was Jazer,** a city taken from the Amorites, Num. 21, 32, **and all the cities of Gilead,** that is, its southern part, below the Jabbok, the part of Ammonitis between the Arnon and the Jabbok, which the Amorites under Sihon had taken from the Ammonites (both the Aroer and the Rabbah here mentioned are not to be confounded with those of Moabitis); v. 26. **and from Heshbon,** which was practically on the northern boundary of Reuben, **unto Ramathmizpeh,** that is, Ramoth in Gilead, **and Betonim,** these being the most important cities in the north; **and from Mahanaim,** Gen. 32, 2, a Levite city north of Jabbok, **unto the border of Debir,** or Lidhbir, probably on the heights which border the Jordan; v. 27. **and in the valley, Betharam,** later Libias, Num. 32,36, **and Bethnimrah, and Succoth,** where Jacob lived for some time. Gen. 33, 17, **and Zaphon, the rest of the kingdom of Sihon, king of Heshbon, Jordan and his border,** the river valley proper, **even unto the edge of the Sea of Chinnereth,** the southern end of the Sea of Galilee, **on the other side Jordan eastward.** While the Jabbok was, generally speaking, the northern boundary of the territory of Gad, the latter extended northward at least to include the plateau of Mahanaim and the Jordan valley to the Sea of Galileo. V. 28. **This is the inheritance of the children of Gad after their**

families, the cities, and their villages. V. 29. **And Moses gave inheritance unto the half tribe of Manasseh; and this was the possession of the half tribe of the children of Manasseh by their families.** V. 30. **And their coast was from Mahanaim,** from the boundaries of this city, **all Bashan, all the kingdom of Og, king of Bashan, and all the towns of Jair which are in Bashan, threescore cities,** Num. 32, 41; v. 31. **and half Gilead,** the northern half, **and Ashtaroth, and Edrei, cities of the kingdom of Og in Bashan, were pertaining unto the children of Machir, the son of Manasseh, even to the one half of the children of Machir by their families.** V. 32. **These are the countries which Moses did distribute for inheritance in the Plains of Moab,** while the children of Israel were encamped there, **on the other side Jordan, by Jericho, eastward. V. 33. But unto the tribe of Levi Moses gave not any inheritance; the Lord God of Israel was their inheritance, as he said unto them,** Num. 18, 20; Deut. 10, 9. Note: The end of Balaam is an example of warning. Like him all those who come to the knowledge of the truth, but reject it, preferring the froth of this world to the substance of eternity, will be subject to a severe condemnation.

15

Joshua 14

The Possession of Caleb.

The beginning of the distribution. — V. 1. **And these are the countries which the children of Israel inherited,** received for their possession, **in the land of Canaan, which Eleazar, the priest, and Joshua, the son of Nun, and the heads of the fathers of the tribes of the children of Israel, distributed for inheritance to them,** to remain in their possession, and to be transferred from one generation to the next. V. 2. **By lot was their inheritance, as the Lord commanded by the hand of Moses, for the nine tribes and for the half tribe,** Num. 26, 52-56. The location of the territory of the various tribes was determined by lot, but the size of each tribal state was fixed according to the numerical strength of the individual tribe. V. 3. **For Moses had given the inheritance of two tribes and an half tribe on the other side Jordan,** as described in detail in the preceding chapter; **but unto the Levites he gave none inheritance among them.** V. 4. **For the children of Joseph were two tribes, Manasseh and Ephraim; therefore they gave no part unto the Levites**

in the land, save cities to dwell in, with their suburbs for their cattle and for their substance, forty-eight cities with their meadows or pasture-lands, Num. 35. V. 5. As the Lord commanded Moses, so the children of Israel did, and they divided the land, they made preparations for its distribution by lot, under the direction of the leaders appointed by God, although some time elapsed before the division of the land was actually completed.

Caleb granted Hebron for an inheritance. — V. 6. **Then the children of Judah came unto Joshua in Gilgal,** this being the first interruption in the work of distributing the land; and **Caleb, the son of Jephunneh, the Kenezite, said unto him, Thou knowest the thing that the Lord said unto Moses, the man of God, concerning me and thee in Kadesh-barnea,** namely, in promising them a possession in the land of Canaan, Num. 14,24, for the stand which they took over against the other spies after their return from their scouting expedition. The men presenting this petition were not representatives of the tribe of Judah in general, but only of the house of fathers out of that tribe which bore the name of Kenaz, a descendant of Hezron. V. 7. **Forty years old was I when Moses, the servant of the Lord, sent me from Kadesh-barnea,** where Israel was then encamped, **to espy out the land; and I brought him word again as it was in mine heart,** with a bold and confident spirit, which was not easily discouraged like that of the rest of the spies. V. 8. **Nevertheless my brethren that went up with me made the heart of the people melt,** the other spies discouraged the children of Israel by their unfavorable attitude; **but I wholly followed the Lord, my God,** rendered Him unconditional, cheerful obedience. V. 9. **And Moses sware on that day, saying, Surely the land whereon thy feet**

have trodden shall be thine inheritance and thy children's forever, because thou hast wholly followed the Lord, my God. This account supplements that given Num. 14, for it can be understood only of a direct promise made to Caleb, with special reference to Hebron and its vicinity, where the giants lived who had so terrified the other spies. V. 10. **And now, behold, the Lord hath kept me alive, as He said, these forty and five years, even since the Lord spake this word unto Moses, while the children of Israel wandered in the wilderness; and now, lo, I am this day fourscore and five years old,** having thus been fully thirty-eight at the time of the departure from Egypt. In order to establish his claim, Caleb now mentions another factor. V. 11. **As yet I am as strong this day as I was in the day that Moses sent me; as my strength was then, even so is my strength now for war, both to go out and to come in.** He was as yet unaffected by the weakness of old age and was able to hold his own in battle even with the young men of the army. V. 12. **Now, therefore, give me this mountain whereof the Lord spake in that day,** the mountainous region of Hebron; **for thou heardest in that day how the Anakim were there,** the giants who had filled the hearts of the scouts with fear, **and that the cities were great and fenced,** strongly fortified; **if so be the Lord will be with me,** that is his sincere wish and prayer, **then I shall be able to drive them out, as the Lord said.** Since Joshua had not garrisoned these cities after his conquest of them, the Anakim had returned and built them again. V. 13. **And Joshua blessed him, and gave unto Caleb, the son of Jephunneh, Hebron for an inheritance,** this city being named as the capital to which the entire neighborhood down to Debir belonged. V. 14. **Hebron, therefore, became the inheritance of Caleb, the**

son of Jephunneh, the Kenezite, unto this day, because that he wholly followed the Lord God of Israel, having trusted faithfully in the almighty power of Jehovah. V. 15. **And the name of Hebron before,** when it was first founded, **was Kirjatharba; which Arba was a great man among the Anakim,** the most renowned of their tribe. **And the land had rest from war,** affairs were now in such a condition that the division and the occupation of the country by Israel could continue. Those who are firm in tribulation and loyal to the Lord grow in His power, ever renewing and increasing their strength and receiving His blessings in rich measure.

Joshua 15

Territory of the Tribe of Judah.

The boundaries of Judah. — V. 1. **This, then, was the lot of the tribe of the children of Judah by their families,** as it was drawn from the urn or as it fell upon casting; **even to the border of Edom,** the land be longing to the Edomites, south of the Dead Sea, **the Wilderness of Zin southward was the uttermost part of the south coast.** The territory of Judah thus extended to the very edge of the great desert in which the people had spent so many weary years. V. 2. **And their south border was from the shore of the Salt Sea,** the Dead Sea, **from the bay that looketh southward,** the swampy tongue or branch of the Dead Sea toward the southwest; v. 3. **and it went out to the south side to Maaleh-acrabbim,** where the country rises to the foothills of the mountains which form the boundary of the wilderness, **and passed along to Zin,** either a city or a mountain in the Wilderness of Zin, **and ascended up on the south side unto Kadesh-barnea,** Num. 34, 3, **and passed along to Hezron,** turning to the west after passing Kadesh, **and went up to Adar,** and fetched a compass to Karkaa; v. 4. **from thence it passed toward Azmon, and went out unto the river of Egypt,** Num. 34, 4. 5; **and the goings out of that coast were at the sea,** the boundary followed this brook or river to the Mediterranean Sea; **this shall be your south coast. V. 5. And the east border was the Salt Sea, even unto the end,** the mouth, **of Jordan. And their border in the north quarter,** on the north side, **was from the bay of the sea at the uttermost part of Jordan,** just where it entered the Dead Sea; v. 6. **and the border went up to Bethhogia,** between Jericho and the Jordan, **and passed along by the north,** that is, northwardly, **of Betharabah,** not far from the northwest end of the Dead Sea; **and the border went up to the stone of Bohan, the son of Reuben,** toward the west or southwest; v. 7. **and the border went up toward Debir,** in the neighborhood of Gilgal, **from the Valley of Achor,** where Achan was executed, chap. 7, 26, **and so northward, looking toward Gilgal, that is before the going up to Adummim, which is on the south side of the river,** of a small watercourse coming down from the neighborhood of Jerusalem; **and the border passed toward the waters of Enshemesh,** the sun-spring, some two or three miles northeast of Jerusalem, **and the goings out thereof were at Enrogel,** the fullers' spring on the south side of Jerusalem, at the junction of the Kidron and the Hinnom valleys; v. 8. **and the border went up,** almost due west, **by the valley of the son of Hinnom unto the south side of the Jebusite,** just below the city of Jerusalem; **the same is Jerusalem; and the border went up to the top of the mountain that lieth before the Valley of Hinnom westward, which is at the tend of the Valley of the Giants northward,** a rocky ridge overlooking the fertile valleys; v. 9. **and the border was drawn,** brought around, bent, **from the top of the**

hill unto the fountain of the water of Nephtoah, one hour northwest of Jerusalem, a**nd went out to the cities of Mount Ephron,** a prominent ridge, **and the border was drawn to Baalah, which is Kirjath-jearim,** three hours northwest of Jerusalem; v. 10. **and the border compassed from Baalah westward unto Mount Seir,** a small range of hills, **and passed along unto the side of Mount Jearim, which is Chesalon,** on the north side, toward the north, a wooded hill, now called Kesia, **and went down,** on the other side of the mountain, **to Bethshemesh, and passed on to Timnah,** later the home of Samson, Judg. 14, 1-4; v. 11. **and the border went out unto the side of Ekron,** the Philistine city, a small line of hills running parallel with the coast, **and went out unto Jabneel,** the small Philistine town of Jabneh; **and the goings out of the border were at the sea.** V. 12. **And the west border was to the Great Sea,** the Mediterranean Sea, **and the coast thereof,** from Jabneh to the river of Egypt. **This is the coast of the children of Judah round about according to their families.** It was a large and rich territory, well suited for the governing tribe in Israel.

Caleb's possession. — V. 13. **And unto Caleb, the son of Jehunneh, he,** Joshua, **gave a part among the children of Judah, according to the commandment of the Lord to Joshua, even the city of Arba, the father of Anak,** the ancestor of the Anakim, **which city is Hebron.** V. 14. **And Caleb drove thence,** as he had promised, chap. 14, 12, **the three sons of Anak, Sheshai, and Ahiman, and Talmai, the children of Anak.** V. 15. **And he went up thence to the inhabitants of Debir; and the name of Debir before was Kirjathsepher,** which, meanwhile, seems to have been fortified very strongly. V. 16. **And Caleb said, He that smiteth Kirjathsepher and**

taketh it, to him will I give Achsah, my daughter, to wife, this being the reward or prize held out before the young men to spur them on to their best efforts. V. 17. **And Othniel, the son of Kenaz, the brother of Caleb, took it; and he,** Caleb, **gave him Achsah, his daughter, to wife.** V. 18. **And it came to pass, as she came unto him,** on her way over from Hebron in the company of her father, to celebrate the nuptials, **that she moved him,** her husband-to-be, **to ask of her father a field,** a piece of land fit for cultivation as her dowry; **and she lighted,** quickly sprang down, **off her ass,** thus humbling herself before her father; **and Caleb said unto her, What wouldest thou?** V. 19. **Who answered, Give me a blessing; for thou hast given me a south land,** by marrying her to Othniel, he had caused her to inhabit a dry land, at and near Debir; **give me also springs of water,** a piece of land containing springs. **And he gave her the upper springs and the nether springs,** a strip of land well watered in every respect. V. 20. **This is the inheritance of the tribe of the children of Judah according to their families.** This is the subscription or conclusion of the first division of this chapter, with which the description of the bounds of the inheritance of Judah closes.

Catalog of the cities of Judah. — V. 21. **And the uttermost of the tribe of the children of Judah toward the coast of Edom southward were Kabzeel, and Eder, and Jagur,** v. 22. **and Kinah, and Dimonah, and Adadah,** v. 23. **and Kedesh, and Hazor, and Ithnan,** v. 24. **Ziph, and Telem, and Bealoth,** v. 25. **and Hazor, Hadattah, and Kerioth, and Hezron,** or Kerioth-hezron, **which is Hazor,** v. 26. **Amam, and Shema, and Moladah,** v. 27. **and Hazargaddah, and Hesh-mon, and Beth-palet,** v. 28. **and Hazar-shual, and Beer-sheba, and Bizjothjah,** v. 29. **Baalah, and Iina, and Azem,** v. 30.

and Eitolad, and Chesil, and Hormah, v. 31. **and Ziklag, and Madmannah, and Sansannah,** v. 32. **and Lebaoth, and Shilhim, and Ain, and Bimmon. All the cities are twenty and nine, with their villages,** in addition to which seven cities are named which were afterwards occupied by the tribe of Simeon, chap. 19, 1. These were cities of the south country, in the extreme southern part. V. 33. **And in the valley,** in the lowland and foothills, **Eshtaol, and Zoreah, and Ashnah,** v. 34. **and Zanoah, and En-gannim, Tappuah, and Enam,** v. 35. **Jarmuth, and Adullam, Socoh, and Azekah,** v. 36. **and Sharaim, and Adithaim, and Gederah, and Gederothaim: fourteen cities with their villages,** for the last two are probably the same city, and the names should be connected with "or." V. 37. **Zenan, and Hadashah, and Migdalgad,** v. 38. **and Dilean, and Mizpeh, and Joktheel,** v. 39. **Lachish, and Bozkath, and Eglon,** v. 40. **and Cabbon, and Lahmam, and Kithlish,** v. 41. **and Gederoth, Bethdagon, and Waamah, and Makkedah: sixteen cities with their villages.** V. 42. **Libnah, and Ether, and Ashan,** v. 43. **and Jiphtah, and Ashnah, and Nezib,** v. 44. **and Keilah, and Achzib, and Mareshah: nine cities with their villages;** v. 45. **Ekron, with her towns and her villages;** v. 46. **from Ekron even unto the sea, all that lay near Ashdod, with their villages:** v. 47. **Ashdod, with her towns and her villages, Gaza, with her towns and her villages, unto the river of Egypt and the Great Sea and the border thereof. V. 48. And in the mountains, Shamir, and Jattir, and Socoh,** v. 49. **and Dannah, and Kirjath-sannah, which is Debir,** v. 50. **and Anab, and Eshtemoh, and Anim,** v. 51. **and Goshen, and Holon, and Giloh: eleven cities with their villages;** v. 52. **Arab, and Dumah, and Eshean,** v. 53. **and Janum, and Beth-tappuah, and Aphekah,** v. 54. **and**

Humtah, and Kirjatharba, which is Hebron, and Zior: nine cities with their villages; v. 55. Maon, Carmel, and Ziph, and Juttah, v. 56. and Jezreel, and Jokdeam, and Zanoah, v. 57. Cain, Gibeah, and Timnah: ten cities with their villages; v. 58. Halhul, Bethzur, and Gedor, v. 59. and Maarath, and Bethanoth, and Eitekon; six cities with their villages; v. 60. Kirjathbaal, which is Kirjathjearim, and Babbah: two cities with their villages. V. 61. In the wilderness, near the Dead Sea, Betharabah, Middin, and Secacah, v. 62. and Nibshan, and the City of Salt, and Engedi: six cities with their villages. Some of these cities, as those in the Philistine country, were not occupied by the tribe of Judah, and others were in the hands of the children of Israel for only a short time. The site of a large number of these cities has been fixed with a fair degree of certainty, while others are mentioned in the various narratives and will be located as the history calls for a more exact geographical description. V. 63. **As for the Jebusites, the inhabitants of Jerusalem, the children of Judah could not drive them out; but the Jebusites dwell with the children of Judah at Jerusalem unto this day.** It was not till the time of David that this city was finally taken by the army of the Lord's people, 2 Sam. 5, 5-9. It is a dangerous thing for the soldiers of the Lord to grow weary in battle, for then their enemies are likely to gain strength beyond their ability to overcome them.

17

Joshua 16

The Borders of Ephraim.

The general boundaries of the sons of Joseph. — V. 1. **And the lot of the children of Joseph fell,** came out from the urn or was drawn to give the boundaries, **from Jordan by Jericho,** that part of the Jordan Valley which touches upon the territory of Jericho, **unto the water of Jericho on the east,** the Fountain of Elisha, between Jericho and the Jordan, **to the wilderness that goeth up from Jericho throughout Mount Bethel,** toward the northwest. V. 2. **And** (the boundary) **goeth out from Bethel,** from this mountain, **to Luz,** for the ancient name of the city is still used at times, **and passeth along unto the borders of Archi to Ataroth,** southwestward and then south, v. 3. **and goeth down westward to the coast of Japhleti,** or, of the Japhletite, **unto the coast of Beth-horon the nether,** located on a slight elevation below Upper Beth-horon, **and to Gezer,** still farther to the west; **and the goings out thereof are at the sea,** the place not being so exactly located as in the case of Judah. V. 4. **So the children of Joseph, Manasseh and Ephraim, took their inheritance,** their territory being located north of this line, and that of Benjamin between their possession and that of Judah.

The special borders of Ephraim. — V. 5. **And the border of the children of Ephraim according to their families was thus: even the border of their inheritance on the east side,** from the east, beginning where the detailed description of v. 3. ended, **was Atarothaddar, unto Beth-horon the upper,** and thence onward to the west as in v. 3. V. 6. **And the** (northern) **border,** reckoning from some central point or watershed, **went out toward the sea,** the Mediterranean Sea, **to Michmethah on the north side,** not far from Shechem; **and the border,** from that same central point, **went about eastward unto Taanath-shiloh,** southeast of Shechem, **and passed by it on the east to Janohah,** still farther to the southeast; v. 7. **and it went down from Janohah to Ataroth,** probably on the edge of the Jordan Valley, **and to Naarath,** two hours northwest of Jericho, **and came to Jericho,** the territory of this city, **and went out at Jordan,** just about east of Jericho. V. 8. **The border,** the western half of the northern boundary, **went out from Tappuah,** north or northwest of Shechem, **westward unto the river Kanah** (reed-brook); **and the goings out thereof were at the sea. This is the inheritance of the tribe of the children of Ephraim by their families.** V. 9. **And the separate cities for the children of Ephraim,** certain cities set apart for Ephraimites within the province of the Manassitea, **were among the inheritance of the children of Manasseh, all the cities with their villages.** To these cities Tappuah belonged, chap. 17, 8. V. 10. **And they drave not out the Canaanites that dwelt in Gezer,** in the Plain of Sharon; **but the Canaanites dwell among the Ephraimites unto this day,** to the time that this book was written, **and serve under tribute,** being subject to tributary service. This foolish indulgence later proved disastrous to the Israelites, for the heathen seduced the people of God to idolatry. Christians who love the world and enter into friendships with unbelievers are in danger of accepting the wrong views of the enemies of God, to the detriment of their souls.

Joshua 17

The Portion of Manasseh.

The boundaries and cities. — V. 1. **There was also a lot for the tribe of Manasseh,** namely, that east of Jordan, which has already been described several times; **for he was the first-born of Joseph; to wit, for Machir, the first-born of Manasseh, the father of Gilead; because he was a man of war, therefore he had Gilead and Bashan.** Deut. 3,15. Since Manasseh was the first-born of Joseph, therefore his descendants, in whom the rights of Joseph were vested, received not only a portion in the conquered territory of Og, but also a lot in Canaan proper. V. 2. **There was also a lot for the rest of the children of Manasseh by their families,** not only for the descendants of Machir: **for the children. of Abiezer, and for the children of Heiek, and for the children of Asriel, and for the children of Shechem, and for the children of Hepher, and for the children of Shemida,** Num. 26, 30-32; **these were the male children of Manasseh, the son of Joseph, by their families,** the distinction being expressly made in this instance on account of the next statement. V. 3. **But**

Zeiophehad, the son of Hepher, the son of Gilead, the son of Machir, the son of Manasseh, had no sons, but daughters, Num. 26, 33; 27, 1; 36, 2; and these are the names of his daughters, Mahlah, and Noah, Hoglah, Milcah, and Tirzah. According to the precept which was formulated at the request of the daughters of Zeiophehad at that time, women in a similar position were known as heir-daughters. V. 4. And they came near before Eleazar, the priest, and before Joshua, the son of Nun, and before the princes, the official representatives of the people, saying, The Lord commanded Moses to give us an inheritance among our brethren, Num. 27, 2-11. Since the land was now being divided, they claimed their right. Therefore, according to the commandment of the Lord, he, Joshua, gave them an inheritance among the brethren of their father. V. 5. And there fell ten portions to Manasseh, in the country west of Jordan, beside the land of Gilead and Bashan, which were on the other side Jordan, v. 6. because the daughters of Manasseh had an inheritance among his sons; and the rest of Manasseh's sons, those of the line of Machir, had the land of Gilead. The statement concerning the ten portions allotted to the Manassites is to be understood as follows: "According to this the inheritance coming to the Manassites had to be divided into ten parts, since the male posterity fell into five families, and so received five parts, while the sixth family, that of Hepher, was divided again into five families, through his granddaughters, the five daughters of Zelophehad, who married men of the other families of their paternal tribe and received each her special share of the land." (Keil.) V. 7. And the coast of Manasseh was from Asher, a city some sixteen miles northeast of Shechem, to Michmethah, that lieth before Shechem, chap. 16,5; and

the border went along on the right hand, probably on the south side, **unto the inhabitants,** that is, the territory, **of En-tappuah,** the whole region being mentioned in this case on account of the following statement. V. 8. **Now, Manasseh had the land of Tappuah,** the entire country which had formerly been a Canaanitish city-state; **but Tappuah, on the border of Manasseh, belonged to the children of Ephraim,** for it is the south boundary of Manasseh which is here described; v. 9. **and the coast descended unto the river Kanah** (reed-brook), **southward of the river,** the brook being the boundary, chap. 16, 8. **These cities of Ephraim. are among the cities of Manasseh,** that is, the territory on the south side of the brook really belonged to Manasseh, but the cities on the south side of the brook were Ephraim's. **The coast of Manasseh also was on the north side of the river, and the outgoings of it were at the sea.** V. 10. **Southward it was Ephraim's, and northward it was Manasseh's, and the sea,** the Mediterranean Sea, **is his** (western) **border; and they met together in Asher on the north and in Issachar on the east.** Their territory bounded that of the tribe of Asher north of them, and that of the tribe of Issachar east of them, or to the northeast. The description makes it doubtful whether the portions of Ephraim and Manasseh were intended to be effectually separated. Cp. chap. 16, 1-4. V. 11. **And Manasseh,** in addition to the territory as now described, **had in Issachar and in Asher,** in the territories of these two tribes, **Bethshean and her towns,** on the edge of the Jordan Valley, east of Mount Gilboa, **and Ibleam and her towns, and the inhabitants of Dor and her towns, and the inhabitants of Endor and her towns,** 1 Sam. 28, 9; Ps. 83, 11, **and the inhabitants of Taanach and her towns, and the inhabitants of Megiddo and her towns, even**

three countries, three heights; for three of the cities, Endor, Taanach, and Megiddo, were situated on hills, and the last-named cities were in the territory of Asher, on the southwest border of the Plain of Esdraelon. V. 12. **Yet the children of Manasseh could not drive out the inhabitants of those cities,** they made no real effort to exterminate the heathen; **but the Canaanites would dwell in that land,** in the cities allotted to Manasseh. V. 13. **Yet it came to pass, when the children of Israel were waxen strong, that they put the Canaanites to tribute; but did not utterly drive them out.** They were content with making the heathen tributary servants, lacking the spirit which was needed to exterminate them according to the word of the Lord. To become indifferent in the Lord's battle is often equivalent to a surrender to the enemy's forces.

Joshua's advice to the children of Joseph. — V. 14. **And the children of Joseph,** the tribes of Ephraim and Manasseh, **spake unto Joshua, saying, Why hast thou given me but one lot and one portion to inherit,** for the two tribes had been treated as one in the division of the land west of Jordan, **seeing I am a great people, forasmuch as the Lord hath blessed me hitherto?** So great had been Jehovah's blessing, that is their contention, up to this time, that they had become a numerous people and needed more room. But their objection was not well taken, for not only were the two tribes together less numerous than either Judah or Dan, but the territory assigned to them was also immensely fertile, the plateaus and valleys of this section of Canaan being unsurpassed in this respect. V. 15. **And Joshua answered them,** in a well-deserved reproof, **If thou be a great people, then get thee up to the wood country,** the wooded range of hills, either to the northeast toward Mount Gilboa, or to the northwest toward Mount Carmel, **and cut**

down for thyself there, clear the forest, **in the land of the Perizzites and of the giants,** of the Rephaim, who were still in possession of that country, **if Mount Ephraim be too narrow for thee.** If they would but drive out the heathen who still occupied parts of the territory allotted to them, especially the Plain of Jezreel, or Esdraelon, in the north, they would have room enough. V. 16. **And the children of Joseph said, The hill,** Mount Ephraim with its tributary ranges, **is not enough for us; and all the Canaanites that dwell in the land of the valley have chariots of iron,** built of wood, but covered with iron, and with heavy iron tires, **both they who are of Beth-shean and her towns, and they who are of the Valley of Jezreel.** Here the real reason for the request appears, namely, the unwillingness to undertake the conflict, although Jehovah had promised His assistance. V. 17. **And Joshua spake unto the house of Joseph,** denying their request, **even to Ephraim and to Manasseh, saying, Thou art a great people and hast great power; thou shall not have one lot only;** v. 18. **but the mountain shall be thine,** by clearing the forested highlands throughout the territory allotted to them they would, as it were, obtain a second lot or portion; **for it is a wood, and thou shall cut it down; and the outgoings of it shall be thine,** the fields and plains adjoining the forests; **for thou shall drive out the Canaanites, though they have iron chariots, and though they be strong.** He wanted to direct their thoughts to the promise of God's assistance and encourage them in the task assigned to them. He who desired the blessings of the Promised Land did not dare to give up the battle. He who refuses to fight on the Lord's side virtually surrenders to the enemy and loses the eternal blessings.

19

Joshua 18

Further Steps toward Permanent Settlement. The tabernacle set up. — V.1. **And the whole congregation of the children of Israel assembled together at Shiloh,** a little more than one half the distance between Jerusalem and Shechem, **and set up the Tabernacle of the Congregation there.** Shiloh, approximately in the center of the country, was the city of the Sanctuary for several centuries, until the time of Eli. So the Ark of the Covenant had now found a place of rest and thus served as a sign encouraging the people to strive for the true rest which is reserved for the children of God, Heb. 4. **And the land was subdued before them,** and there was nothing hindering the division of the land. V. 2. **And there remained among the children of Israel seven tribes which had not yet received their inheritance,** Reuben, Gad, Judah, Ephraim, and Manasseh having been provided for. V. 3. **And Joshua said unto the children of Israel, How long are ye slack to go to possess the land which the Lord God of your fathers hath given you?** The chief strongholds of the heathen inhabitants had fallen before the vigorous onslaughts of Joshua and the army of Israel, and it now remained merely to take possession of the land and to complete the extermination of the heathen. Apparently the tribes of Israel were not at all eager to exchange the nomadic form of life with that of settled abodes, and the thought of taking possession of their land with their weapons in their hand did not appeal to them. V. 4. **Give out from among you, select and set forth, three men for each tribe; and I will send them, and they shall rise, and go through the land, and describe it according to the inheritance of them,** with reference to its being taken possession of by the seven remaining tribes. Their chief work consisted in their making a list of the cities and their vicinity, the physical aspect of the land, and the condition of the soil. **And they shall come again to me,** their report serving as the basis of the subsequent division of the land. V. 5. **And they shall divide it,** the land still remaining, **into seven parts; Judah shall abide in their coast on the south, and the house of Joseph shall abide in their coasts on the north,** no changes being made in the possessions of these tribes. V. 6. **Ye shall therefore describe the land into seven parts, and bring the description,** the list as thus made out, **hither to me,** to Shiloh, **that I may cast lots for you here before the Lord, our God,** probably in the court of the Tabernacle, chap. 19, 51. V. 7. **But the Levites have no part among you,** chap. 13, 33; Num. 18, 20; **for the priesthood of the Lord is their inheritance,** and as ministers of the Sanctuary they were granted certain privileges which compensated, in a way, for the fact that they had not received a definite section of the Promised Land as their home; **and Gad and Reuben and half the tribe of Manasseh have received their inheritance beyond Jordan on the east, which Moses, the servant of the Lord, gave them,** Num. 32. The weakness of the children of God in waging the war which is their lot in life may easily result in disaster of the worst kind for them.

The lot of Benjamin. — V. 8. **And the men,** the twenty-one chosen from the tribes, **arose and went away; and Joshua charged them that went to describe the land, saying, Go and walk through the land, and describe it, and come again to me, that I may here cast lots for you before the Lord in Shiloh.** V. 9. **And the men went and passed through the land, and described it by cities,** with special reference to the cities found throughout the unclaimed sections, **into seven parts in a book, and came again to Joshua, to the host at Shiloh.** V. 10. **And Joshua cast lots for them in Shiloh before the Lord; and there Joshua divided the land unto the children of Israel according to their divisions.** V. 11. **And the lot of the tribe of the children of Benjamin came up,** namely, when it was drawn from the urn, **according to their families; and the coast of their lot,** the territory allotted to them, **came forth between the children of Judah and the children of Joseph,** north of Judah and south of Ephraim. V. 12. **And their border on the north side was from Jordan,** beginning at the river; **and the border went up to the side of Jericho on the north side,** the site of this city thus being included in the territory of Benjamin, **and went up through the mountains westward,** west and northwest of this city, chap. 16, 1; **and the goings out thereof,** the continuation of the boundary line, **were at the wilderness of Bethaven,** the bare and rocky heights east of Bethel. V. 13. **And the border went over from thence toward Luz, to the side of Luz, which is Bethel, southward,** the city itself thus being included in this territory; **and the border descended to Atarothadar, near the hill that lieth**

on the south side of the nether Bethhoron, chap. 16, 2. V. 14. **And the border was drawn thence, and compassed the corner of the sea southward,** it turned southward on the western boundary of Benjamin, **from the hill that lieth before Bethhoron southward; and the goings out thereof were at Kirjathbaal, which is Kirjathjearim, a city of the children of Judah,** chap. 15, 9; **this was the west quarter. V. 15. And the south quarter was from the end of Kirjathjearim,** from the boundaries of this city, **and the border went out on the west,** westward, **and went out to the well of the waters of Nephtoah,** chap. 15, 9; v. 16. **and the border came down to the end of the mountain that lieth before the valley of the son of Hinnom, and which is in the Valley of the Giants on the north, and descended to the Valley of Hinnom, to the side of Jebusi,** Jerusalem, **on the south, and descended to Enrogel,** v. 17. **and was drawn from the north,** northward, **and went forth to Enshemesh, and went forth to Geliloth,** toward the west, **which is over against the going up of Adummim, and descended to the stone of Bohan, the son of Reuben,** v. 18. and passed along. **toward the side over against Arabah,** the eastern plain, **northward, and went down unto Arabah,** the plain in which Jericho is situated; v. 19. **and the border passed along to the side of Bethhoglah northward; and the outgoings of the border were at the north bay of the Salt Sea at the south end,** the mouth, **of Jordan; this was the south coast.** This description coincides with that of the north border of Judah, chap. 15, 5–9, only the southeast corner being determined a little more exactly. V. 20. **And Jordan was the border of it,** Benjamin's territory, **on the east side. This was the inheritance of the children of Benjamin, by their coasts thereof round about, according to their families.** V.

21. Now the cities of the tribe of the children of Benjamin according to their families were Jericho, and Bethhoglah, and the valley of Keziz, Emekkeziz, between Jerusalem and Jericho, v. 22. **and Betharabah, and Zemaraim, and Bethel,** v. 23. **and Avim,** probably the same as Ai, **and Parah, and Ophrah,** v. 24. **and Chepharhaamonai, and Ophni, and Gaba,** some ten miles north of Jerusalem: **twelve cities with their villages,** those of the eastern half of the territory of Benjamin. V. 25. **Gibeon,** chap. 10, 1-15, **and Ramah, and Beeroth,** v. 26. **and Mizpeh,** 1 Sam. 7, 5-15, **and Chephirah,** near Gibeon, **and Mozah,** v. 27. **and Rekem, and Irpeel, and Taralah,** v. 28. **and Zeiah, Eleph, and Jebusi, which is Jerusalem, Gibeath,** later known as Gibeah of Saul, 1 Sam. 10, 26; 11, 4; 15, 34, **and Kirjath: fourteen cities with their villages,** all of them in the western part of Benjamin's territory. **This is the inheritance of the children of Benjamin according to their families.**

20

Joshua 19

The Territory of the Six Remaining Tribes. The possession of Simeon, Zebulun, Issachar, Asher, Naphtali, and Dan. — V. 1. **And the second lot came forth to Simeon,** was drawn forth from the urn, **even for the tribe of the children of Simeon according to their families; and their inheritance was within the inheritance of the children of Judah.** Since the territory assigned to the latter tribe was too large for them, Simeon was given certain cities within their boundaries, the curse of Jacob concerning the distribution of Simeon in Jacob, Gen. 49, 7, thus being fulfilled. The tribe of Simeon afterwards practically lost its identity, although the genealogical records were carefully preserved. V. 2. **And they had in their inheritance Beersheba,** a city known from the time of the patriarchs, in the center of the southern steppes, **and Sheba, and Moladah,** v. 3. **and Hazar-shual, and Balah, and Azem,** v. 4. **and Eitolad, and Bethul, and Hormah,** on the extreme southern boundary, v. 5. **and Zik-lag,** in the Philistine country, **and Beth-marcaboth, and Hazar-susah,** v. 6. **and Beth-lebaoth, and Sharuhen: thirteen cities and**

their villages: v. 7. **Ain, Remmon, and Ether, and Ashan: four cities and their villages;** v. 8. **and all the villages that were round about these cities to Baalath-beer, Ramath of the south.** All these cities have already, chap. 15, 26-32. 42, been enumerated in the list of the cities of Judah, and are again listed 1 Chron. 4, 28-32. That the prophecy of the scattering was literally fulfilled appears even at this point, for the cities inhabited by Simeon were not even grouped according to any definite plan. **This is the inheritance of the tribe of the children of Simeon according to their families.** V. 9. **Out of the portion of the children of Judah was the inheritance of the children of Simeon; for the part of the children of Judah was too much for them; therefore the children of Simeon had their inheritance within the inheritance of them,** literally, "in the midst of their inheritance," and not in a specially defined part of Canaan. V. 10. **And the third lot came up for the children of Zebulun according to their families; and the border of their inheritance was unto Sarid,** this city, from the whole description, being the center of the southern boundary; v. 11. **and their border went up,** from Sarid, **toward the sea,** westward toward the Mediterranean, **and Mara-lah, and reached to,** or struck, **Dabbasheth, and reached to,** or struck, **the river that is before Jokneam,** this watercourse very probably being the Kishon, which flows at the foot of the Carmel range; v. 12. **and turned from Sarid,** as the starting-point, **eastward toward the sun-rising unto the border of Chisloth-tabor,** on the slopes of Mount Tabor, **and then goeth out to Daberath,** also in the foothills of Tabor, a city of the Levites, **and goeth up to Japhia,** a little farther to the east, v. 13. **and from thence passeth on along on the east,** still toward the east, **to Gittah-hepher, to Ittah-kazin,**

and goeth out to Bemmon [-methoar], **which is drawn to Neah,** thus extending to a place which was somewhat north of Nazareth; v. 14. **and the border compasseth it,** the territory of Zebulun, on the **north side to Hannathon,** this being the eastern boundary, going north; **and the outgoings thereof are in the Valley of Jiphthahel,** a wide valley extending down toward the Kishon; v. 15. **and Kattath, and Nahallal, and Shimron, and Idalah, and Bethlehem,** these cities indicating the western or northwestern boundary of Zebulun: **twelve cities with their villages.** V. 16. **This is the inheritance of the children of Zebulun according to their families, these cities with their villages.** It was a fertile country with an outlet to the sea, which assured the inhabitants a participation in its blessings also, as Jacob had foretold. V. 17. **And the fourth lot came out to Issachar, for the children of Issachar according to their families.** V. 18. **And their border was toward Jezreel,** their territory included the fertile and beautiful Plain of Jezreel, or Esdraelon, **and Chesulloth, and Shunem,** on the western slopes of the Little Hermon, appearing several times in later history, v. 19. **and Haphraim,** or Chepharaim, **and Shihon, and Anaharath,** v. 20. **and Babbith, and Kishion,** or Kedesh, a city of the Levites, **and Abez,** v. 21. **and Bemeth, and En-gan-nim,** another Levitical city, with a rich supply of fine water from large springs above the town, **and En-haddah, and Beth-pazzez;** v. 22. **and the coast reacheth to Tabor,** a city on the boundary of Zebulun, **and Sha-hazimah, and Beth-shemesh,** in the Jordan Valley, near Mount Tabor; **and the outgoings of their border were at Jordan: sixteen cities with their villages.** V. 23. **This is the inheritance of the tribe of the children of Issachar according to their families, the cities and their villages.** So Issachar was richly blessed with material prosperity and gave himself up to the enjoyment of the pleasures of life. V. 24. **And the fifth lot came out for the tribe of the children of Asher according to their families.** V. 25. **And their border was Helkath,** a Levitical city northeast of Acco, a**nd Hali, and Beten, and Achshaph,** v. 26. **and Alammelech,** not far from the Kishon, **and Amad,** on or near the site of the modern Haifa, **and Misheal,** a Levitical city on the sea, near Mount Carmel; **and reacheth to Carmel westward, and to Shihor-libnath,** a small stream on the southern slopes of Carmel; v. 27. **and turneth toward the sunrising to Beth-dagon, and reacheth to Zebulun, and to the valley of Jiphthahel toward the north side of Beth-emek and Neiel,** places on the boundary of Zebulun, **and goeth out to Cabul on the left hand,** on the north side of it, four hours southeast of Acco, v. 28. **and Hebron,** or Abdon, **and Rehob, and Hammon, and Kanah, even unto great Zidon,** the ancient capital of Phenicia. V. 29. **And then the coast turneth to Ramah, and to the strong city Tyre,** fortified strongly even at that time, and later the rich and proud capital of Phenicia; **and the coast turneth to Hosah; and the outgoings thereof are at the sea from the coast to Achzib,** three hours north of Acco; v.30. **Umnah also, and Aphek, and Rehob,** in the foothills of the Lebanon range: **twenty and two cities with their villages.** Thus the territory of Asher extended from the southern slopes of Mount Carmel to Acco along the Mediterranean Sea, and from there to the northern boundary of Canaan, just skirting the narrow coast country of the Pheriicians, with the cities Tyre and Sidon. V. 31. **This is the inheritance of the tribe of the children of Asher according to their families, these cities with their villages.** Asher was also richly blessed, both the agricultural and the commercial possibilities of the country being exceptionally good. V. 32. **The sixth lot came out to the children of Naphtali, even for the children of Naphtali according to their families.** V. 33. **And their coast was from Heleph, from Allon to Zaanannim,** northwest of the Sea of Merom, **and Adami,** on the road that leads through the pass toward Baalbek, **Nekeb, and Jabneel, unto Lakum; and the outgoings thereof were at Jordan,** the upper Jordan, also above the Waters of Merom; v. 34. **and then the coast turneth westward to Aznoth-tabor, and goeth out from thence to Hukkok, and reacheth to Zebulun on the south side, and reacheth to Asher on the west side, and to Judah,** here apparently a city on the boundary of Asher; **upon Jordan toward the sun-rising,** for the upper Jordan was Naphtali's eastern boundary. V. 35. **And the fenced cities,** the fortified towns, **are Ziddim, Zer, and Ham-math, Rakkath, and Chinnereth,** v. 36. **and Adamah, and Ramah, and Hazor,** v. 37. **and Kedesh, and Edrei,** not that in Bashan, **and En-hazor,** v. 38. **and Iron, and Mig-dal-el, Horem, and Beth-anath, and Beth-shemesh,** not to be confounded with the cities of the same name in Judah and Issachar: **nineteen cities with their villages.** So Naphtali's territory was largely in the forested foothills of the Lebanon and Anti-Lebanon ranges. The tribe was a liberty-loving mountain people, for which reason they had been compared by Jacob with a hind let loose. V. 39. **This is the inheritance of the tribe of the children of Naphtali according to their families, the cities and their villages.** V. 40. **And the seventh lot came out for the tribe of the children of Dan according to their families.** V. 41. **And the coast of their inheritance,** west of Benjamin, north of Judah, south of Ephraim, **was Zorah, and Eshtaol, and Irshemesh,** three cities of Judah which were yielded to the Danites, the last named being assigned to the Levites, v. 42. **and Shaalabbin, and. Ajalon, and Jethlah,** v. 43. **and Elon, Thimnathah, and Ekron,** chap. 15, 10. 11, v. 44. **and Elte-keh, and Gibbethon, and Baalath,** v. 45. **and Jehud, and Beneberak, and Gath-rimmon,** v. 4G. **and Me-jarkon, and Bak-kon, with the border before Japho,** over against Joppa, or Jaffa, that is, extending to the gardens or suburbs of this nourishing seaport. V. 47. **And the coast of the children of Dan went out too little for them,** there was hardly room enough for their rapidly growing tribe; **therefore the children of Dan went up to fight against Leshem,** or Laish, in the extreme northern part of Canaan, north of the territory of Naphtali, **and took it, and smote it with the edge of the sword, and possessed it, and dwelt therein, and called Leshem Dan, after the name of Dan, their father.** The story of this campaign is related in detail Judg. 18. V. 48. **This is the inheritance of the tribe of the children of Dan according to their families, these cities with their villages.** The Danites did not occupy the territory allotted to them altogether, being hindered in their attempts by the heathen inhabitants of the plains, Judg. 1, 34, and apparently unable to muster men and courage for a successful venture.

The inheritance of Joshua. — V. 49. **When they had made an end of dividing the land for inheritance by their coasts,** according to the allotment of the various parts of the Promised Land, **the children of Israel gave an inheritance to Joshua, the son of Nun, among them,** a special tract of land belonging to him exclusively; v. 50. **according to the word of the Lord,** probably a divine promise which was given to Joshua at the same time when Caleb was assured a distinct inheritance in Canaan, **they gave him the city which he asked, even Timnath-serah in Mount Ephraim,** now the ruins of Tibneh, seven hours north of Jerusalem; **and he built the city and dwelt therein.** V. 51. **These are the inheritances which Eleazar, the priest, and Joshua, the son of Nun, and the heads of the fathers of the tribes of the children of Israel,** as the representatives of the people, **divided for an inheritance by lot in Shiloh before the Lord,** chap. 18, 1. 10, **at the door of the Tabernacle of the Congregation,** before the face, in the presence, of the Lord. **So they made an end of dividing the country.** It was the Lord Himself who decided the division of the country, and in such a manner as to fulfill the prophecies of Jacob and Moses. It is God who distributes to all His children what they need in this life, but the most blessed portion is reserved for them in heaven.

21

Joshua 20

The Cities of Refuge.

Since the Lord had commanded, Num. 35, that cities of refuge should be chosen in various parts of the country, this matter was next attended to. V. 1. **The Lord also spake unto Joshua, saying,** v. 2. **Speak to the children of Israel, saying, Appoint out for you cities of refuge, whereof I spake unto you by the hand of Moses,** Ex. 21, 13; Num. 35. 6. 11. 14; Deut. 19, 2, 9, v. 3. **that the slayer that killeth any person unawares and unwittingly,** without malice, without evil intention, **may flee thither; and they shall be your refuge from the avenger of blood,** as had been provided for in detail by the precepts governing such cases. V. 4. **And when he that doth flee unto one of those cities shall stand at the entering of the gate of the city,** when begging for admission to the safety of its sacred precincts, **and shall declare his cause in the ears of the elders of that city, they shall take him into the city unto them,** the preliminary hearing at the gate being made to safeguard their interests, **and give him a place that he may dwell among them.** V. 5. **And if the avenger**

of blood, the relative upon whom the duty of requiring an atonement devolved, **pursue after him, then they shall not deliver the slayer up into his hand, because he smote his neighbor unwittingly, and hated him not beforetime,** the slaying thus evidently being an accident. V. 6. **And he shall dwell in that city until he stand before the congregation for judgment, and until the death of the high priest that shall be in those days; then shall the slayer return and come unto his own city and unto his own house, unto the city from whence he fled.** "He might not be delivered to the avenger of blood, but ... to the congregation of his own city, which should hold judgment upon him, and either, if they found him guilty, give him up to the avenger of blood or, if they esteemed him innocent, send him back to the city of refuge, where he must remain until the death of the anointed high priest, Num. 35,25, that is, of the ruling high priest. After the death of the latter there follows, somewhat as upon the death of an anointed prince, an amnesty, and the manslayer is at liberty to return to his home. If, however, he presumptuously leaves his asylum sooner, he is exposed to the anger of the avenger, Num. 35, 26. 28." 2) V. 7. **And they,** in accordance with this express order of the Lord, **appointed Kedesh in Galilee in Mount Naphtali,** in the extreme northern part of Canaan, **and Shechem in Mount Ephraim,** in the approximate center, **and Kirjath-arba, which is Hebron, in the mountain of Judah,** in the southern part of the land. V. 8. **And on the other side Jordan, by Jericho eastward,** in the territory of the two and one half tribes, **they assigned Bezer in the wilderness upon the plain out of the tribe of Reuben,** in the south, and **Ramoth in Gilead, out of the tribe of Gad,** in the center, **and Golan in Bashan out of the tribe of Manasseh,** in the north, as Moses had directed, Deut. 4, 43. V. 9. **These were the cities appointed for all the children of Israel,** literally, "the cities of appointment," **and for the stranger that sojourneth among them, that whosoever killeth any person at unawares might flee thither, and not die by the hand of the avenger of blood, until he stood before the congregation** and thus had the opportunity of proving the absence of any evil intention in the slaying which had happened. The entire chapter testifies to the grace and mercy of the Lord. We Christians learn here that even sins that are done unintentionally, unwittingly, are nevertheless transgressions of God's holy Law, just as is the inherited tendency to all sins which we bear in our hearts. But God has placed before us the true city of refuge, in the Gospel of Jesus Christ. Every one who flees to the Redeemer and His mercy, relying upon His atonement alone, will in no wise be cast out.

22

Joshua 21

The Cities of the Levites.

The allotment in general. — V. 1. **Then came near the heads of the fathers of the Levites unto Eleazar, the priest, and unto Joshua, the son of Nun, and unto the heads of the fathers of the tribes of the children of Israel;** v. 2. **and they spake unto them at Shiloh, in the land of Canaan,** where the division of the land had taken place, this city being the capital of the tribes, **saying, The Lord commanded by the hand of Moses to give us cities to dwell in, with the suburbs,** meadow-lands, **thereof for our cattle,** Num. 35, 2-6. The Levites had not deemed it opportune to urge their claims before, mainly because they knew that they would receive these cities for their habitation only after the other tribes had been given their inheritance. V. 3. **And the children of Israel gave unto the Levites out of their inheritance, at the commandment of the Lord, these cities and their suburbs,** as listed in this catalog, in the present chapter. V. 4. **And the lot came out for the families of the Kohathites,** descendants of the second son of Levi, the families of whose three sons,

Izhar, Hebron, and Uzziel, together with the descendants of Moses, formed the division of the Kohathite Levites, while the descendants of Aaron were vested with the priesthood. Note that the cities were selected by the Israelites themselves, but that the Lord decided, by directing the drawing of the lots, which of these cities each particular family should have. **And the children of Aaron, the priest, which were of the Levites,** descendants of Levi, **had by lot out of the tribe of Judah and out of the tribe of Simeon and out of the tribe of Benjamin,** all in Southern Canaan, **thirteen cities.** So it was even at this time that the Lord arranged to settle the priests in the cities near the place where He intended to have the permanent Sanctuary. There is never an element of chance in His government of the world and of His Church. V. 5. **And the rest of the children of Kohath,** who were Levites only, **had by lot out of the families of the tribe of Ephraim and out of the tribe of Dan and out of the half tribe of Manasseh,** all in Central Canaan, **ten cities.** V. 6. **And the children of Gershon had by lot out of the families of the tribe of Issachar and out of the tribe of Asher and out of the tribe of Naphtali,** in Northern Canaan, **and out of the half tribe of Manasseh in Bashan,** in the northern section of the territory east of Jordan, **thirteen cities.** V. 7. **The children of Merari by their families had out of the tribe of Reuben and out of the tribe of Gad,** in the southern section east of Jordan, **and out of the tribe of Zebulun,** this one portion of Northern Canaan, **twelve cities.** V. 8. **And the children of Israel gave by lot unto the Levites these cities with their suburbs,** their pasture- or meadowlands, **as the Lord commanded by the hand of Moses.** While provision was here made also for the future, it should be noted that the priests and Levites did not occupy these cities alone, but other people lived there as well. It was merely that they were sure of a place to live, and that they, by living in the very midst of the people, should serve as an example to the entire nation.

The cities of the priests. — V. 9. **And they gave out of the tribe of the children of Judah and out of the tribe of the children of Simeon,** out of the possessions allotted to these tribes, **these cities which are here mentioned by name,** v. 10. **which the children of Aaron, being of the families of the Kohathites, who were of the children of Levi, had; for theirs was the first lot.** V. 11. **And they gave them the city of Arba, the father of Anak,** chap. 15, 13. 14, **which city is Hebron, in the hill country of Judah, with the suburbs thereof found about it,** the grazing-land for cattle immediately adjoining the city. V. 12. **But the fields of the city,** the farm-land, **and the villages thereof,** the towns tributary to it, **gave they to Caleb, the son of Jephunneh, for his possession,** chap. 14, 12-14. V. 13. **Thus they gave to the children of Aaron, the priest, Hebron with her suburbs, to be a city of refuge for the slayer,** for this it was at the same time, chap. 20, 7; **and Libnah with her suburbs,** v. 14. **and Jattir with her suburbs, and Eshtemoa with her suburbs,** v. 15. **and Holon with her suburbs, and Debir with her suburbs,** v. 16. **and Ain with her suburbs, and Juttah with her suburbs, and Beth-shemesh with her suburbs: nine cities out of those two tribes,** all of them being mentioned in the catalog of the cities of Judah and of Simeon, chap. 15, 21-62; 19, 7. V. 17. **And out of the tribe of Benjamin, Gibeon with her suburbs,** a fact which tended to curb any idolatrous notions of its heathen inhabitants, chap. 9, **Geba with her suburbs,** v. 18. **Anathoth with her suburbs, and Almon with her suburbs,** chap. 18, 24. 25; 1 Chron. 6,

60: **four cities. V. 19. All the cities of the children of Aaron, the priests, were thirteen cities with their suburbs.** Thus the men in charge of the worship in the Jewish Church were provided for with all that they needed to support their body and life, even as it is the will of the Lord to-day that they who preach the Gospel should live of the Gospel.

The cities of the Kohathites, the Gershonites, and the Merabites. — V. 20. **And the families of the children of Kohath,** the descendants of Izhar, Hebron, and Uzziel, and of Moses, **the Levites which remained of the children of Kohath,** namely, after the priests, the children of Aaron, had received their allotment, **even they had the cities of their lot out of the tribe of Ephraim.** V. 21. **For they gave them,** the Levites, **Shechem with her suburbs in Mount Ephraim, to be a city of refuge for the slayer,** chap. 20, 7; **and Gezer with her suburbs, v. 22. and Kibzaim with her suburbs, and Beth-horon with her suburbs: four cities. V. 23. And out of the tribe of Dan, El-tekeh with her suburbs, Gibbe-thon with her suburbs, v. 24. Aijalon with her suburbs, Gath-rimmon with her suburbs,** chap. 19, 42-15; **four cities. V. 25. And out of the half tribe of Manasseh,** west of Jordan, **Tanach with her suburbs, and Gath-rimmon,** or, Bileam (Ibleam), **with her suburbs,** chap. 17,11: **two cities. V.26. All the cities were ten with their suburbs,** their meadow-lands, **for the families of the children of Kohath that remained. V. 27. And unto the children of Gershon, of the families of the Levites, out of the other half tribe of Manasseh,** east of Jordan, **they gave Golan in Bashan with her suburbs, to be a city of refuge for the slayer,** chap. 20, 8; **and Beesh-terah with her suburbs: two cities. V. 28. And out of the tribe of Issachar, Kishon with her suburbs, Dabareh with her suburbs, v. 29. Jarmuth with** her suburbs, **En-gan-nim with her suburbs,** chap. 19, 12-21: **four cities. V. 30. And out of the tribe of Asher, Mishal with her suburbs, Abdon with her suburbs,** v.31. **Helkath with her suburbs, and Rehob with her suburbs,** chap. 19, 25-28: **four cities. V. 32. And out of the tribe of Naphtali, Kedesh in Galilee with her suburbs, to be a city of refuge for the slayer,** chap. 20, 7; **and Hammoth-dor with her suburbs, and Kartan with her suburbs,** chap. 19, 35-37: **three cities. V. 33. All the cities of the Gershonites according to their families were thirteen cities with their suburbs. V. 34. And unto the families of the children of Merari, the rest of the Levites,** the last family to be supplied, **out of the tribe of Zebulun, Jokneam with her suburbs and Kartah with her suburbs,** v. 35. **Dimnah,** or Rimmono, **with her suburbs, Nahalal,** or Tabor, **with her suburbs,** chap. 19,11-15: **four cities. V. 36. And out of the tribe of Reuben, Bezer, with her suburbs, and Jahazah with her suburbs,** v. 37. **Kedemoth with her suburbs, and Mephaath with her suburbs,** chap. 20, 8; 13, 18; Deut. 4, 43: **four cities. V. 38. And out of the tribe of Gad,** in Southern Gilead, **Ramoth in Gilead with her suburbs, to be a city of refuge for the slayer; and Mahanaim with her suburbs,** v. 39. **Heshbon with her suburbs, Jazer with her suburbs,** chap. 20, 8; 13,17-26: **four cities in all. V. 40. So all the cities for the children of Merari by their families, which were remaining of the families of the Levites, were by their lot twelve cities. V. 41. All the cities of the Levites within the possession of the children of Israel were forty and eight cities with their suburbs,** including the six cities set apart as cities of refuge. **V. 42. These cities were every one with their suburbs round about them,** the meadow-land was distinctly included for the perpetual use of the Levites; **thus were all these cities. V. 43.**

And the Lord, by this distribution of the country, **gave unto Israel all the land which He sware to give unto their fathers,** Gen. 12, 7; 15, 18; Num. 11,12; Deut.21, 12; **and they possessed it and dwelt therein.** V. 44. **And the Lord gave them rest round about,** all the heathen nations being subdued for the time being, **according to all that He sware unto their fathers; and there stood not a man of all their enemies before them,** not one was able to offer a successful resistance; **the Lord delivered all their enemies into their hand.** Although not entirely subjugated, the enemies were in a condition where they dared no enterprise against the Israelites while Joshua lived. V. 45. **There failed not aught of any good thing which the Lord had spoken unto the house of Israel; all came to pass.** God is always faithful in His promises, but we, through unbelief and indifference, stand in His way. Perfection, true happiness, lasting joy, will be ours in the rest of yonder life, Heb. 4.

23

Joshua 22

The Return of the Two and One Half Tribes.

The dismissal . — V. 1. **Then,** namely, at some time after the conquest of Canaan, probably after the division of the land was completed, **Joshua called the Reubenites and the Gadites and the half tribe of Manasseh,** the soldiers out of these tribes, who had served in the army of Israel during these years of conquest, chap. 1, 12-15, v. 2. **and said unto them, Ye have kept all that Moses, the servant of the Lord, commanded you,** Num. 32, 20; Deut. 3, 18, **and have obeyed my voice in all that I commanded you,** to which they had agreed before the people passed over Jordan. V. 3. **Ye have not left your brethren these many days unto this day,** having been thoroughly loyal to the obligations of relationship, **but have kept the charge of the commandment of the Lord, your God.** All this the praise of Joshua duly acknowledges, as an encouragement to further efforts in unselfish assistance. V. 4. **And now the Lord, your God, hath given rest unto your brethren, as He promised them; therefore, now, return ye, and get you unto your tents,** a standing expression for returning home, **and unto the land of your possession, which Moses, the servant of the Lord, gave you on the other side Jordan,** Num. 32, 33; Deut. 29, 8. V. 5. **But take diligent heed,** watch with the greatest carefulness, **to do the commandment and the Law,** both that of the general Moral Law and that of the special precepts given to Israel, **which Moses, the servant of the Lord, charged you, to love the Lord, your God, and to walk in all His ways, and to keep His commandments, and to cleave unto Him, and to serve Him with all your heart and with all your soul.** This parting admonition of Joshua shows his understanding of the human heart with its changeableness, deceitfulness, and wickedness. Cp. Deut. 4, 2. 29; 6, 5; 8, 6. V. 6. **So Joshua blessed them, and sent them away,** dismissed them honorably; **and they went unto their tents,** they started for their homes on the east side of Jordan. V. 7. **Now to the one half of the tribe of Manasseh,** to the children of Machir, **Moses had given possession in Bashan; but unto the other half thereof gave Joshua among their brethren on this side Jordan westward.** This is here repeated in order to make the situation perfectly clear, according to the ancient style of Hebrew narrative. **And when Joshua sent them away also unto their tents, then he blessed them,** v. 8. **and he spake unto them, saying, Return with much riches,** their share of the booty of the wars, **unto your tents, and with very much cattle, with silver, and with gold, and with brass, and with iron, and with very much raiment,** for the cities of the Canaanites which they had captured, beginning with Ai, had contained great treasures, all of which fell into the hands of the invaders. **Divide the spoil of your enemies with your brethren,** namely, the sixty to seventy thousand who had remained to garrison the cities east of Jordan and to protect the homes and the herds of the two and one half tribes while the conquest of Canaan proper was going on. V. 9. **And the children of Reuben and the children of Gad and the half tribe of Manasseh returned, and departed from the children of Israel out of Shiloh, which is in the land of Canaan, to go unto the country of Gilead, to the land of their possession, whereof they were possessed, according to the word of the Lord by the hand of Moses,** Num. 32, 20-22. That is the important thing, not only to come to the Lord, but to continue in His Word, to love Him with all one's heart, and with all one's soul, and with all one's mind, and to show this love in one's entire life.

The building of the altar and the investigation following. — V. 10. **And when they came unto the borders of Jordan that are in the land of Canaan,** the regions of Jordan, the valley proper of Jordan, in this case probably the eastern side, as the context seems to indicate, **the children of Reuben and the children of Gad and the half tribe of Manasseh built there an altar by Jordan,** on the very boundary line of their possession, **a great altar to see to,** great-looking, great in appearance, great as compared with other altars. V. 11. **And the children of Israel,** the ten western tribes, **heard say, Behold, the children of Reuben and the children of Gad and the half tribe of Manasseh have built an altar over against the land of Canaan, in the borders,** circles, regions, **of Jordan, at the passage of the children of Israel,** in the land opposite the sons of Israel. V. 12. **And when the children of Israel heard of it, the whole congregation of the children of Israel,** all the able-bodied men, **gathered themselves together at Shiloh to go up to war against them,** for they took the erection of this altar as an evidence of apostasy, as a transgression of God's precept concerning the unity of the altar of burnt offering, Lev. 17, 8. 9; Deut. 12, 4-14, and therefore prepared to carry out His command of extermination upon the apostate tribes, Deut. 13. V. 13. **And the children of Israel sent unto the children of Reuben and to the children of Gad and to the half tribe of Manasseh,** as the ordinance of Jehovah provided, Deut. 13, 14, **into the land of Gilead,** the general designation of the land east of Jordan, **Phinehas, the son of Eleazar, the priest,** who had once before distinguished himself by his zeal for the Lord, v. 14. **and with him ten princes,** heads of father-houses, **of each chief house a prince throughout all the tribes of Israel,** that rank at least the men selected had to hold; **and each one was an head of the house of their fathers among the thousands of Israel.** V. 15. **And they came unto the children of Reuben and to the children of Gad and to the half tribe of Manasseh, unto the land of Gilead, and they spake with them, saying,** Phinehas probably acting as the spokesman: v. 16. **Thus saith the whole congregation of the Lord, What trespass is this that ye have committed against the God of Israel,** in open rebellion against Jehovah, **to turn away this day from following the Lord,** by an act of faithlessness and disloyalty, **in that ye have builded you an altar, that ye might rebel this day against the Lord?** Even though the language may be considered strong, the zeal which prompted it was, at any rate, praiseworthy, since the altar, although not built for a place of sacrifice, yet might easily be perverted to that use, and lead the whole people into the sin of idolatry. At all events, the two and one half tribes ought not to have undertaken the building of this altar without first consulting with Joshua or with the high priest. V. 17. **Is the iniquity of Peor,** when the Midianite women seduced the men of Israel to adultery and idolatry, **too little for us, from which we are not cleansed until this day,** for it seems that many Israelites in their hearts were still idolaters, lacking only the courage to show their preference openly, **although there was a plague in the congregation of the Lord,** consuming a total of 24,000 people, v. 18. **but that ye must turn away this day from following the Lord?** And it will be, seeing ye rebel today against the Lord, **that tomorrow He will be wroth with the whole congregation of Israel,** for Jehovah would hold all the tribes responsible for the defection of those east of Jordan. V. 19. **Notwithstanding, and indeed, if the land of your possession be unclean,** making it necessary for them to have an altar for the expiation of sins in their immediate neighborhood, **then pass ye over unto the land of the possession of the Lord,** Canaan proper, west of Jordan, **wherein the Lord's Tabernacle dwelleth, and take possession among us; but rebel not against the Lord, nor rebel against us, in building you an altar beside the altar of the Lord, our God,** who had commanded that the altar of the Tabernacle should be the only one erected for His worship and would seriously punish the erection of any altar to another god. V. 20. **Did not Achan, the son of Zerah, commit a trespass in the accursed thing,** in taking of spoil devoted to Jehovah, chap. 7, 1. 5, **and wrath fell on all the congregation of Israel? And that man perished not alone in his iniquity,** since not only his children were involved, but also, through the unfortunate attack on Ai, the entire congregation. Thus did the ten tribes voice their zeal for Jehovah through their delegates.

The explanation made and accepted. — V. 21. **Then the children of Reuben and the children of Gad and the half tribe of Manasseh answered,** in defending themselves against the reproach and charge made against them, **and said unto the heads of the thousands of Israel,** v. 22. **The Lord God of gods, the Lord God of gods,** or, God, God Jehovah, repeated for the sake of impressiveness, in the form of a solemn oath, **He knoweth, and Israel, he shall know; if it be in rebellion, or if in transgression against the Lord,** or, Surely not in rebellion and surely not in disloyalty toward Jehovah was this done. And in order to remove every doubt concerning the truth of their assertion, they include an imprecation upon themselves in case their words should be found false: **(Save us not this day,)** namely, if it was done in apostasy. The oath is now continued, v. 23. **That we have built us an altar to turn from following the Lord,** with idolatrous intention, **or if to offer thereon burnt offering or meat-offering, or if to offer peace-offerings thereon,** in flagrant disobedience against the Lord's command, **let the Lord Himself require it,** by visiting the transgressors with His punishment; v. 24. **and if we have not rather done it for fear of this thing, saying, In time to come your children,** those of the Israelites west of Jordan, **might speak unto our children, saying, What have ye to do with the Lord God of Israel?** V. 25. **For the Lord hath made Jordan a border between us and you, ye children of Reuben and children of Gad; ye have no part in the Lord; so shall your children make our children cease from fearing the Lord.** So it was their anxiety for their children and for the latter's possible exclusion from the worship of Jehovah, the true God, which had prompted the two and one half tribes to erect the great altar on the bank of the Jordan. V. 26. **Therefore we said, Let us now prepare to build us an altar, not for burnt offering, nor for sacrifice,** v. 27. **but that it may be a witness between us and you and our generations after us,**

that we might do the service of the Lord before Him, have the right to appear at the Tabernacle and worship Jehovah, **with our burnt offerings and with our sacrifices and with our peace-offerings; that your children may not say to our children in time to come, Ye have no part in the Lord.** V. 28. **Therefore said we that it shall be, when they should so say to us or to our generations in time to come, that we may say again, Behold the pattern, copy, likeness, of the altar of the Lord which our fathers made, not for burnt offerings nor for sacrifices; but it is a witness between us and you.** V. 29. **God forbid that we should rebel against the Lord, and turn this day from following the Lord, to build an altar for burnt offerings, for meat-offerings, or for sacrifices, beside the altar of the Lord, our God, that is before His Tabernacle.** So this copy of Jehovah's altar was simply to serve as a witness of the fact that the tribes on both sides of Jordan worshiped the same God. V. 30. **And when Phinehas, the priest, and the princes of the congregation and heads of the thousands of Israel which were with him heard the words that the children of Reuben and the children of Gad and the children of Manasseh spake, it pleased them,** the explanation satisfied them in every way. V. 31. **And Phinehas, the son of Eleazar, the priest, said unto the children of Reuben and to the children of Gad and to the children of Manasseh, This day we perceive that the Lord is among us, the entire nation, because ye have not committed this trespass against the Lord,** the disloyalty of which the western tribes suspected them; **now ye have delivered the children of Israel out of the hand of the Lord,** for He would surely have visited the iniquity of the offending tribes upon the whole people if they had been guilty. V. 32. **And Phinehas, the**

son of Eleazar, the priest, and the princes returned from the children of Reuben and from the children of Gad out of the land of Gilead,** east of Jordan, **unto the Land of Canaan,** the Land of Promise in the narrower sense, **to the children of Israel,** the ten western tribes, **and brought them word again. V. 33. And the thing pleased the children of Israel; and the children of Israel blessed God,** thanking Him for adjusting the matter in such a satisfactory way, **and did not intend,** had no further thought, **to go up against them in battle, to destroy,** devastate, **the land wherein the children of Reuben and Gad dwelt. V. 34. And the children of Reuben and the children of Gad called the altar Ed; for it shall be a witness between us that the Lord is God.** The entire sentence served as the name of the altar, for it should be regarded as a continual witness, for all times, that the tribes east of Jordan also accepted Jehovah as the one true God. It is well-pleasing to God if Christians are zealous for His honor, but He also expects us to discuss matters which may lead to quarrels in a proper, brotherly manner, lest we harm some one by an unjust suspicion.

24

Joshua 23

Admonition to Be Faithful to the Covenant.

The urgent exhortation to be faithful to the Lord. — V. 1. **And it came to pass a long time after that the Lord had given rest unto Israel from all their enemies round about,** when the heathen nations had been brought to a state of fear which kept them from undertaking any attack against Israel, **that Joshua waxed old and stricken in age,** advanced in days, with the infirmities of old age in evidence. V. 2. **And Joshua called for all Israel,** in its representatives, **and for their elders, and for their heads, and for their judges, and for their officers,** the first designation being the general one, and the heads being divided into judges and officers, both the judicial and the executive branches of the government thus being represented, **and said unto them,** the meeting taking place either at his home, at Timnath-serah, or, more probably, at Shiloh, **I am old and stricken in age;** v. 3. **and ye have seen all that the Lord, your God, hath done unto all these nations because of you; for the Lord, your God, is He that hath fought for you,** for it had been evident throughout that the Lord was battling for Israel. V. 4. **Behold, I have divided unto you by lot these nations that remain,** those that had not yet been exterminated, **to be an inheritance for your tribes, from Jordan, with all the nations that I have cut off, even unto the Great Sea westward,** toward the going down of the sun; for tribes of the heathen nations were still living in the Valley of Jordan and in parts of the plain along the coast of the Mediterranean. But these sections had been included in the allotment of land, and so the duty of driving them out was before the people. V. 5. **And the Lord, your God, He shall expel them. from before you,** thrust them out altogether, **and drive them from out of your sight; and ye shall possess their land as the Lord, your God, hath promised unto you,** Ex. 23, 23; Num. 33, 53. V. 6. **Be ye therefore very courageous to keep and to do all that is written in the Book of the Law of Moses,** for that was the condition of the covenant upon which the Lord insisted, **that ye turn not aside therefrom to the right hand or to the left;** v. 7. **that ye come not among these nations, these that remain among you,** to enter into any fellowship with them; **neither make mention of the name of their gods,** namely, for the purpose of calling upon them or of proclaiming them, to swear by them, to serve them by offerings, and to bow down to them in prayer, Ex. 23, 13; Deut. 6, 13; 10, 20, as Joshua adds; **nor cause to swear by them, neither serve them, nor bow yourselves unto them;** v. 8. **but cleave unto the Lord, your God, as ye have done unto this day,** for the congregation as such had adhered firmly to the worship of Jehovah while Joshua was leader. V. 9. **For the Lord hath driven out from before you great nations and strong,** Deut. 4, 38; **but** (or "and") **as for you, no man hath been able to stand before you unto this day,** the assistance of Jehovah making them invincible and giving them the power to conquer everything before them, Deut. 7, 24. V. 10. **One man of you shall chase a thousand,** as Moses had promised, Lev. 26, 8; Deut. 32, 30; **for the Lord, your God, He it is that fighteth for you, as He hath promised you,** Ex. 14, 14; 23, 27; Deut. 3, 22. V. 11. **Take heed, therefore, unto yourselves,** they were to watch very carefully over their own souls, in keeping them in the Law of the Lord, **that ye love the Lord, your God;** for this love is the fulfillment of the Law. V. 12. **Else if ye do in any wise go back, and cleave unto the remnant of these nations,** be joined to them in friendship and affection, **even these that remain among you, and shall make marriages with them,** thus entering into the most intimate relationship with them and setting aside the loyalty toward Jehovah, **and go in unto them and they to you,** in a social fellowship and intercourse which the Lord had forbidden them, Ex. 34,12-16; Deut. 7, 3, v. 13. **know for a certainty that the Lord, your God, will no more drive out any of these nations from before you,** an achievement which was possible only with His assistance, **but they shall be snares and traps unto you,** Num. 33, 55; Is. 8, 14. 15, **and scourges in your sides,** to punish them, **and thorns in your eyes,** infinitely more painful than motes, **until ye perish from off this good land which the Lord, your God, hath given you.** Joshua heaps the figures picturing the affliction and the misery which would follow their act of disloyalty in entering into friendships and other intimate relationships with the heathen nations; for the Lord knew that no warning could be made too impressive in this connection. The blessings of God's goodness should be the strongest inducement to all Christians to cling to Him alone with all their heart and to shun all intimacy with the children of this world.

An earnest warning. — V. 14. **And, behold, this day I am going the way of all the earth,** for Joshua was on his way to the land of darkness and the shadow of death; and ye know in all your hearts and in all your souls that not one thing hath failed of all the good things which the Lord, your God, spake concerning you, not a single word, a single promise of the Lord fell to the ground, became void, remained unfulfilled, as they well knew; **all are come to pass unto you, and not one thing hath failed thereof.** But the very greatness of the Lord's goodness and mercy laid additional obligations upon the whole people. V. 15. **Therefore it shall come to pass that, as all good things are come upon you which the Lord, your God, promised you, so shall the Lord bring upon you all evil things,** as He had threatened, Lev. 26, 14–33; Deut. 28, 15–68, **until He have destroyed you from off this good land which the Lord, your God, hath given you.** V. 16. **When ye have transgressed the covenant of the Lord, your God, which He commanded you, and have gone and served other gods,** for faithfulness to Jehovah was the essence of the covenant, **and bowed yourselves to them, then shall the anger of the Lord be kindled against you, and ye shall perish quickly from off the good land which He hath given unto you,** Deut. 11, 17. To abstain from intimacy with the world is a form of protecting our souls. Carelessness in this respect may result in the loss of our inheritance and in bringing God's wrath and curse upon us.

25

Joshua 24

Joshua's Farewell Address and Death.

A review of God's mercies. — V. 1. **And Joshua gathered all the tribes of Israel to Shechem,** a gigantic assembly of people in the place which was hallowed by so many memories, ever since the time of Abraham, **and called for the elders of Israel, and for their heads, and for their judges, and for their officers,** chap. 23, 2; **and they presented themselves before God,** for this last appeal was made in the name of Jehovah. V. 2. **And Joshua said unto all the people, Thus saith the Lord God of Israel,** as whose representative Joshua was here addressing the people, **Your fathers,** progenitors, **dwelt on the other side of the flood,** of the great stream Euphrates, **in old time, even Terah, the father of Abraham, and the father of Nachor,** who lived first in Ur of the Chaldees and then in Haran, Gen. 11, 28. 31; **and they,** Terah with his family, **served other gods,** namely, teraphim. Gen. 31, 19. V. 3. **And I took your father Abraham from the other side of the flood,** the great river Euphrates, out of these dangerous surroundings, **and led him throughout all the land of Canaan,**

and multiplied his seed, and gave him Isaac, in making true the promise concerning his great progeny. V. 4. **And I gave unto Isaac Jacob and Esau,** Gen. 25, 24; **and I gave unto Esau Mount Seir to possess it,** Gen. 36, 8; Deut. 2, 5; **but Jacob and his children went down into Egypt,** Gen. 46, 1.6. Thus everything was prepared for the second great proof of God's mercy, the miraculous deliverance of Israel from the bondage of Egypt. V. 5. **I sent Moses also and Aaron, and I plagued Egypt, according to that which I did among them,** in the matter of the great plagues, Ex. 7-10; **and afterward I brought you out,** Ex. 12. V. 6. **And I brought your fathers out of Egypt,** Ex. 12, 51; **and ye came unto the sea,** the Red Sea, Ex. 14, 2; **and the Egyptians pursued after your fathers with chariots and horsemen unto the Red Sea,** Ex. 14, 9. V. 7. **And when they cried unto the Lord, He put darkness between you and the Egyptians,** Ex. 14,10. 20, a**nd brought the sea upon them, and covered them,** Ex. 14, 27; **and your eyes have seen what I have done in Egypt,** in punishing both the land and the people; **and ye dwelt in the wilderness a long season,** forty years, chap. 5, 6. The entire description is a noble, impressive account. The Lord now recalls the third proof of His favor and merciful kindness. V. 8. **And I brought you into the land of the Amorites,** this one name standing for all the heathen nations, but here designating the two branches of this nation dwelling east of Jordan, **which dwelt on the other side Jordan; and they fought with you,** the armies of Sihon and of Og, Num. 21, 21. 33; **and I gave them into your hand that ye might possess their land; and I destroyed them from before you. V. 9. Then Balak, the son of Zippor, king of Moab, arose and warred against Israel,** he made ready for a campaign against Israel, in case he could get Balaam to curse the invaders, **and sent**

and called Balaam, the son of Beor, to curse you, Num. 22, 5, since he lacked the courage to attack Israel outright; v. 10. **but I would not hearken unto Balaam,** Jehovah frustrated the evil intentions of the soothsayer; **therefore he blessed you still,** in spite of himself; **so I delivered you out of his hand.** Thus were the plans of Balak overthrown and everything made ready for the fourth proof of God's favor, the conquest of Canaan proper. V. 11. **And ye went over Jordan,** by a miraculous passage, chap. 3, 14, **and came unto Jericho; and the men of Jericho fought against you,** chap. 6, 1, and not only they, but also **the Amorites, and the Perizzites, and the Canaanites, and the Hittites, and the Girgashites, the Hivites, and the Jebusites,** chap. 3, 10; **and I delivered them into your hand.** V. 12. **And I sent the hornet before you,** in terrifying the nations of the land, Ex. 23, 28; Deut. 7, 20, **which drave them out from before you, even the two kings of the Amorites,** Sihon and Og, as representatives of the entire heathen host; **but not with thy sword nor with thy bow,** for it was not Israel's prowess which had subdued the land. V. 13. **And I have given you a land for which ye did not labor, and cities which ye built not, and ye dwell in them; of the vineyards and olive-yards which ye planted not do ye eat.** Thus Israel, without any merit on its part, through God's goodness and merciful kindness alone, had received a glorious land, a rich and fertile country, in whose cultivation they were not obliged to labor in the sweat of their brow, but which was given to them in the finest condition, ready to enjoy. We Christians are also obliged to confess, with regard to both the temporal and the spiritual blessings of the Lord, that we are not worthy of the least of all His benefits.

The exaction of the promise to be faithful. — V. 14. **Now, therefore,** with all these blessings and merciful kindnesses in mind, **fear the Lord, and serve <u>Him</u> in sincerity and in truth,** without all pretense and feigned devotion, for all hypocrisy and false piety is an abomination in the sight of the Lord; **and put away the gods which your fathers served on the other side of the flood,** in Mesopotamia, **and in Egypt,** for heathenish, idolatrous superstition was still found among the people, although not in its gross form, Lev. 17, 7; **and serve ye the Lord.** V. 15. **And if it seem evil unto you to serve the Lord,** for true service requires the conviction of the heart, **choose you this day whom ye will serve, whether the gods which your fathers served that were on the other side of the flood,** beyond Euphrates, **or the gods of the Amorites,** the Canaanitish nations, **in whose land ye dwell,** this form of challenge being the very strongest admonition to loyalty. **But as for me and my house, we will serve the Lord.** This declaration of Joshua, with all its simplicity, contained a mighty appeal, just as all similar confessions do, arousing the sluggish and strengthening the weak to rally around the Lord. V. 16. **And the people,** evidently deeply affected by Joshua's fervent sincerity, **answered and said, God forbid that we should forsake the Lord to serve other gods,** the very idea of such apostasy was far from their minds; v. 17. **for the Lord, our God, He it is that brought us up and our fathers out of the land of Egypt, from the house of bondage, and which did those great signs in our sight, and preserved us in all the way wherein we went,** as the Lord had reminded them in the address of Joshua, a**nd among all the people through whom. we passed;** v. 18. **and the Lord drave out from before us all the people, even the Amorites which dwelt in the land,** as they here gratefully acknowledge; **therefore will we also serve the Lord, for He is our God.** They turn from the service of other gods with every indication of extreme loathing, of deep aversion. V. 19. **And Joshua said unto the people,** in testing the sincerity of their position, **Ye cannot serve the Lord,** that is, not without His assistance, for He it is who must work both to will and to do; **for He is an holy God; He is a jealous God,** Ex. 19, 6; 20, 5; **He will not forgive your transgressions nor your sins.** So they should not promise faithfulness lightly, but in the full consciousness of the import of their words. V. 20. **If ye forsake the Lord and serve strange gods,** Gen. 35, 4, **then He will turn,** assume an entirely different attitude toward them, **and do you hurt and consume you after that He hath done you good.** Jehovah demands unwavering loyalty, steadfast allegiance. V. 21. **And the people said unto Joshua, Nay; but we will serve the Lord.** They persist in their determination and uphold their resolution. V. 22. **And Joshua said unto the people, Ye are witnesses against yourselves,** their declaration would serve as a testimony against them, **that ye have chosen you the Lord to serve Him. And they said, We are witnesses.** They fully agreed to all that Joshua had said. V. 23. **Now, therefore, put away, said he, the strange gods which are among you,** even the last remnant of idolatrous superstition, **and incline your heart unto the Lord God of Israel,** who demands all the heart, all the soul, and all the mind in His service. V. 24. **And the people said unto Joshua, The Lord, our God, will we serve, and His voice will we obey.** It was the third solemn assurance of loyalty and obedience. V. 25. **So Joshua made a covenant with the people that day,** in exacting this promise from them, **and set them a statute and an ordinance in Shechem.** It was a second renewal of the covenant made with Israel on Mount Sinai, Ex. 19, 20; Deut. 28, 69. It is a great and serious thing to serve the Lord, a matter which no man can perform in his own reason and strength, but only in the strength of the grace of God.

Joshua's death and burial. — V. 26. **And Joshua wrote these words,** the entire account of the renewal of the covenant, **in the Book of the Law of God,** as an addition to the law-book of Moses, **and took a great stone, and set it up there under an oak that was by the Sanctuary of the Lord,** in the space consecrated by the altars of Abraham and Jacob, Gen. 12, 7; 33, 20, and by the solemn service which had been held there shortly after the coming of Israel into the Land of Promise, chap. 7, 30. V. 27. **And Joshua said unto all the people, Behold, this stone shall be a witness,** a monument and memorial, **unto us; for it hath heard all the words of the Lord which He spake unto us,** during the meeting which had gone before; **it shall be therefore a witness unto you, lest ye deny your God,** it would always serve to remind them of their solemn promise, lest they deny Jehovah by thought, word, or deed. V. 28. **So Joshua let the people depart; every man unto his inheritance,** to his possession in the section of the country allotted to his tribe. V. 29. **And it came to pass after these things that Joshua, the son of Nun, the servant of the Lord,** as he is now also called in recognition of his loyalty to Jehovah, **died, being an hundred and ten years old,** as his progenitor, the patriarch Joseph, before him. V. 30. **And they buried him in the border of his inheritance in Timnath-serah, which is in Mount Ephraim, on the north side of the hill of Gaash,** evidently a well-known hill at that time, Judg. 2, 9; 2 Sam. 23, 30. V. 31. **And Israel served the Lord all the days of Joshua, and all the days of the elders that overlived Joshua,** literally, "whose days extended beyond those of Joshua,"

and which had known all the works of the Lord that He had done for Israel. The experiences which these men had gone through in their youth and early manhood served to keep them loyal to the covenant God, and their example influenced the people accordingly. V. 32. **And the bones of Joseph which the children of Israel brought up out of Egypt buried they in Shechem,** Gen. 50, 25. **in a parcel of ground which Jacob bought of the sons of Hamor, the father of Shechem, for an hundred pieces of silver,** Gen. 33, 19; **.and it became the inheritance of the children of Joseph.** This was in their territory, on the boundary between Manasseh and Ephraim, and thus belonged to them in a twofold sense of the word, by inheritance and by allotment. V. 33. **And Eleazar, the son of Aaron, died,** the second high priest whom Israel had had; **and they burled him in a hill that pertained to Phinehas, his son,** that is, at Gibeah-Phinehas, a city in central Canaan, **which was given him in Mount Ephraim.** Thus the righteous, enter into their reward and rest in the security of their tombs to the great day of resurrection.

II

The Book of Judges

26

Introduction

The Book of Judges covers a period of some three hundred and fifty years, from approximately 1440 to 1090 B. C. It is named from the heroes who were appointed by God as leaders of Israel in the period succeeding Joshua and ending with the rise of Samuel. The exploits of these champions of Israel, whom the Lord endowed with miraculous power in conquering their heathen enemies, form the central and principal part of the book, They are called Judges because they held the highest civil authority in the nation, and they are called Saviors because they repeatedly delivered Israel from its enemies.

The author, after characterizing the political condition and the religious life of Israel during the time of the Judges, gives a brief account of the Judges themselves. The following Judges are named in the book: Othniel, Ehud, Shamgar, the woman Deborah and Barak, Gideon, Abimelech, Tola, Jair, Jephthah, Ibzan, Elon, Abdon, and Samson, The deeds of Deborah and Barak, of Gideon, Jephthah, and Samson against the Canaanites, Midianites, Ammonites, and Philistines are treated in greater detail than the others.

Of the general character of the period the following may be said. In his farewell address Joshua had earnestly warned the people against idolatry and solemnly exhorted them to remain faithful to Jehovah, the God of their fathers. They gave their solemn promise, which was kept for that one generation. But their children and descendants turned from the Lord to idolatry and provoked Him to anger. When the Lord thereupon punished them by giving them into the hands of their enemies to spoil them, they repented and walked in the ways of Jehovah until they had been delivered. But the lesson was invariably soon forgotten; the people relapsed into idolatry, and thus sin, punishment, repentance, and deliverance followed in succession through those centuries. The purpose of the book is to offer a history of Israel from the death of Joshua to the days of Samuel in an account of the chief events and thus to demonstrate the working of the divine justice and mercy as a lesson for all future generations.

Regarding the authorship of the Book of Judges, no definite statement can be made. It was not written before the time of Samuel and probably at a time when Israel already had a king. The ancient tradition which names Samuel as the author may well be correct. The Jewish Talmud makes this assertion with great emphasis, and the vivid presentation seems to point to this prophet, for which reason modern critics have rarely called the statement into question. It may be added that the activity of the Judges is mentioned in both the Old and the New Testament, and that they have always been regarded as types of Christ, the eternal Redeemer of His people.[2]

---

[2] Cp. *Concordia Bible Class.* Mar., 1919, 35, 36; Fuerbringer, *Einleitung in das Alte Testament*, 27-29.

27

Judges 1

Political Conditions of the Period. OVERTHROW OF VARIOUS ENEMIES. — **V. 1. Now, after the death of Joshua,** which was related in the last chapter of the Book of Joshua, **it came to pass,** as the author states in taking up the thread of the narrative, **that the children of Israel asked the Lord,** through the Urim and Thummim of the high priest, Num. 27, 21, **saying, Who shall go up for us against the Canaanites first to fight against them?** Joshua had very emphatically enjoined upon them the extermination of the tribes of Canaan which still remained, and therefore the question of the representatives of the entire nation was who it was to be that should initiate the aggressive measures, to which tribe the leadership had been assigned in beginning the final conquest of the land. **V. 2. And the Lord said, Judah shall go up,** for this tribe had been made the leader and champion of Israel even by the blessing of Jacob, Gen. 49, 8-10; **behold, I have delivered the land into his hand.** As it pleased the Lord to receive the inquiry of the people in this manner, so He gave the promise of His divine assistance in the coming struggle. **V. 3. And Judah said unto Simeon, his brother,** the tribe having its cities in the midst of the possession of Judah, Josh. 19, 1.-9, **Come up with me into my lot,** share my lot with me, join forces with me in this undertaking, **that we may fight against the Canaanites; and I likewise will go with thee into thy lot,** join forces with him in conquering the cities allotted to him. **So Simeon went with him. V. 4. And Judah went up,** reinforced by the army of Simeon; **and the Lord delivered the Canaanites and the Perizzites,** who evidently had gained the necessary courage to join their forces at this time, with the purpose of ejecting the invaders, **into their hand; and they slew of them in Bezek,** a place not yet definitely identified, **ten thousand men. V. 5. And they found Adoni-bezek,** the leader of the heathen forces, **in Bezek;** they met his armies there, having been informed of their presence and of their hostile intention; **and they fought against him, and they slew the Canaanites and the Perizzites. V. 6. And Adoni-bezek fled; and they pursued after him, and caught him, and cut off his thumbs and great toes,** making it impossible for him to use his bow or to escape. **V. 7. And Adoni-bezek said, Threescore and ten kings, having their thumbs and their great toes cut off, gathered their meat under my table;** after mutilating them in this manner, he had forced them to pick up their food under his table, where he threw them scraps as he might have done to hungry dogs. **As I have done, so God hath requited me;** he realized and confessed that he was but receiving his just deserts, that the tribe of Judah simply recompensed him by the direction of God. **And they,** apparently his own servants, **brought him to Jerusalem,** for which reason some commentators think that this was his home, **and there he died,** under the just punishment of God. **V. 8. Now the children of Judah had fought against Jerusalem,** literally, "And there fought the sons of Judah against Jerusalem"; for they followed up the advantage which they had gained and attacked the city which sheltered Adoni-bezek, **and had taken it, and smitten it with the edge of the sword, and set the city on fire.** Thus the power of this king was definitely broken, although the army of Judah did not take, or retain possession of, the city at this time, probably because they expected the tribe of Benjamin to occupy the stronghold. **V. 9. And afterward,** after the taking of Jerusalem, **the children of Judah,** with their allies, **went down to fight against the Canaanites that dwelt in the mountain,** in the highland of Judah, **and in the south,** the steppes toward the southeast and south, **and in the valley,** the lowland in the west, including Philistia. **V. 10. And Judah went against the canaanites that dwelt in Hebron,** under the leadership of Caleb; **(now the name of Hebron before was Kirjath-arba;) and they slew Sheshai, and Ahiman, and Talmai,** the three sons of Anak; for after the first conquest of the city by Joshua the Anakim had reoccupied it. **V. 11. And from thence he went against the inhabitants of Debir,** a city some ten miles southwest of Hebron; **and the name of Debir before was Kirjath-sepher; v. 12. and Caleb said, He that smiteth Kirjath-sepher and taketh it, to him will I give Achsah, my daughter, to wife. V. 13. And Othniel, the son of Kenaz, Caleb's younger brother, took it; and he gave him Achsah, his daughter, to wife. V. 14. And it came to pass, when she came to him, that she moved him to ask of her father a field; and she lighted from off her ass; and Caleb said unto her, What wilt thou? V. 15. And she said unto him, Give me a blessing; for thou hast given me a south** land; give me also springs of water. And Caleb gave her the upper springs and the nether springs. This paragraph, which agrees exactly with Josh. 15, 14-19, is here repeated to make the zeal of Caleb, the unselfishness of Othniel, and the prudence of Achsah points of instruction. "The thing to be especially noted, however, is the firmness of Othniel in resisting his wife's enticement to make requests which it is more becoming in her to make. Not many men have so well withstood the ambitious and eagerly craving projects of their wives." (Lange.) V. 16. And the children of the Kenite, Moses' father-in-law, whom Moses had apparently persuaded to join Israel, Num. 10, 29-32, went up out of the city of palm trees, Jericho, Deut. 34, 3, with the children of Judah into the wilderness of Judah, which lieth in the south of Arad, a district about eight hours south of Hebron, whose king had attacked Israel during the march through the wilderness, Num. 21, 1; and they went and dwelt among the people, in the immediate neighborhood of Judah, with whom they were allied. V. 17. And Judah went with Simeon, his brother, according to the promise made v. 3, and they slew the Canaanites that inhabited Zephath, on the boundary of the desert, and utterly destroyed it. And the name of the city was called Hormah, a name sometimes given to it before, but now definitely connected with it, Num. 21, 2; 1 Sam. 30, 29. V. 18. Also Judah, carrying the campaign into the land of the Philistines, took Gaza with the coast thereof, and Askelon with the coast thereof, and Ekron with the coast thereof, three city-states with the smaller towns tributary to them. These the army of Judah took by storm, in a sudden onslaught, but did not garrison them and therefore soon lost them again. V. 19. And the Lord was with Judah, in this campaign of swift destruction; **and he drave out the inhabitants of the mountain,** where personal valor and strength were the chief factors in battle; **but could not drive out the inhabitants of the valley, because they had chariots of iron.** When it came to a contest with these engines of destruction, the faith of the soldiers of Judah failed them, causing them to abandon the duty of gaining entire mastery of the land. **V. 20. And they gave Hebron unto Caleb, as Moses said,** this taking place after the completion of the conquest, when the entire tribe entered upon its possessions; **and he expelled thence the three sons of Anak.** Thus the aged hero received the gift which had been promised him. Everyone who takes part in the suffering and in the fighting of the people of God will in the end take part in the glorious heritage of the children of God.

VARIOUS HEATHEN LEFT IN CANAAN. — **V. 21. And the children of Benjamin did not drive out the Jebusites that inhabited Jerusalem,** who returned to the city as soon as the armies of Judah and Simeon marched southward; **but the Jebusites dwell with the children of Benjamin in Jerusalem unto this day.** This notice is here inserted partly to show that the conquered city did not remain in the hands of Israel, partly to indicate that Judah had no intention of permanently occupying a city allotted to Benjamin. **V. 22. And the house of Joseph,** the Manassites and Ephraimite, **they also went up against Bethel,** a strongly fortified city, whose men had marched to the assistance of Ai, Josh. 8, 17; **and the Lord was with them. V. 23. And the house of Joseph sent to descry Bethel,** a scouting party. **(Now the name of the city before was Luz,** namely, in ancient times, when the country was still in the hands of the Canaanites.) "As Jebus indicated particularly the fortress, Jerusalem the city, -although the latter name also embraced both, -so a similar relation must be assumed to have existed between Bethel and Luz. Otherwise the border of Benjamin could not have run south of Luz, Josh. 18, 13, while nevertheless Bethel was reckoned among the cities of Benjamin, Josh. 18, 22." (Lange.) It was thus the old section of the city, the fortress part, against which the expedition was directed. **V. 24. And the spies saw a man come forth out of the city,** after they had vainly sought a suitable place for a successful assault, **and they said unto him, Show us, we pray thee, the entrance into the city,** some way of entering it unawares, **and we will show thee mercy,** spare him and his family as a reward for this assistance. **V. 25. And when he showed them the entrance into the city,** apparently some hidden passage, thus making it unnecessary to storm the city, **they smote the city,** all the inhabitants, **with the edge of the sword; but they let go the man and all his family;** he, like Rahab, saved the life of his entire family by his service to the army of the Lord. **V. 26. And the man went into the land of the Hittites,** very likely in the mountains of the north or in Phenicia, **and built a city, and called the name thereof Luz; which is the name thereof unto this day. V. 27. Neither did Manasseh drive out the inhabitants of Beth-shean and her towns,** on the border of the Jordan Valley, **nor Taanach and her towns,** farther to the west in the Plain of Esdraelon, **nor the inhabitants of Dor and her towns,** on the coast of the Mediterranean, **nor the inhabitants of Ibleam and her towns, nor the inhabitants of Megiddo and her towns,** these two also being located in the beautiful Plain of Jezreel; **but the Canaanites would dwell in that land,** accepting the proposals or conditions of the conquerors. **V. 28. And it came to pass, when Israel was strong, that they put the Canaanites**

to tribute, this being true of all the tribes in general, **and did not utterly drive them out.** The children of Israel disregarded the command to exterminate the Canaanites, even when they were in a position to carry it out. **V. 29. Neither did Ephraim drive out the Canaanites that dwelt in Gezer,** a town four or five miles east of the present Joppa or Jeffa; **but the Canaanites dwelt in Gezer among them. V. 30. Neither did Zebulun drive out the inhabitants of Kitron nor the inhabitants of Nahalol; but the Canaanites dwelt among them and became tributaries,** while they occupied their pastures and meadows. **V. 31. Neither did Asher drive out the inhabitants of Accho,** on the coast of the Mediterranean, north of Carmel, **nor the inhabitants of Zidon,** the ancient capital of Philistia, **nor of Ahlab, nor of Achzib, nor of Helbah, nor of Aphik, nor of Rehob,** all of these in the foothills of the Lebanon or on the Phenician coast; **v. 32. but the Asherites dwelt among the Canaanites, the inhabitants of the land; for they did not drive them out. V. 33. Neither did Naphtali drive out the inhabitants of Beth-shemesh nor the inhabitants of Beth-anath; but he dwelt among the Canaanites, the inhabitants of the land; nevertheless the inhabitants of Beth-shemesh and of Beth-anath became tributaries unto them. V. 34. And the Amorites,** in the lower part of the Plain of Sharon, along the Mediterranean, **forced the children of Dan into the mountain; for they would not su1fer them to come down to the valley; v. 35. but the Amorites would dwell in Mount Heres in Aijalon, and in Shaalbim,** since they were provided with all the appliances of military art and had resisted even Judah; **yet the hand of the house of Joseph prevailed,** rested very heavily upon the Amorites, **so that they became tributaries. V. 36. And the coast of the Amorites,** at the time of the conquest of the land, **was from the going up to Akrabbim, from the rock, and upward,** from the Scorpion-height in the southeast over to the extreme southwest, where the mountains arise that fringe the Wilderness of Zin. From this entire country they had been driven and now retained only a small part of the Mediterranean lowland, just north of Philistia. The history, as here presented, has many analogies in the spiritual field. Many a Christian who started out with a willing mind has become weary of the continual battle, has permitted the enemies to reoccupy lost territory, and so has lost everything he had gained.

28

Judges 2

The Changing Conditions.

THE REPROOF OF THE ANGEL OF THE LORD. — **V. 1. And an Angel of the Lord,** that is, the Angel of the Lord, who is equal to the Lord in essence, who had brought up Israel out of Egypt and led them to the Land of Promise, **came up from Gilgal,** where He had revealed Himself to Joshua as the Prince of the host of Jehovah, **to Bochim,** a place where the representatives of the people were assembled at that time, **and said, I made you to go up out of Egypt,** the speaker thus expressly identifying Himself with Jehovah, **and have brought you unto the land which I sware unto your fathers; and I said, I will never break My covenant with you,** Gen. 17, 7. **V. 2. And ye shall make no league with the inhabitants of this land,** never enter into entangling alliances with them; **ye shall throw down their altars,** utterly destroy all evidences of idolatry. **But ye have not obeyed My voice,** they had done just that against which they had been warned; **why have ye done this?** This is not merely a sorrowful exclamation, but a searching question, a call to repentance, a reproof because they had spared the Canaanites and had permitted their altars to remain. **V. 3. Wherefore I also said,** through the mouth of Joshua, Josh. 23, 13, **I will not drive them out from before you,** as a punishment of their disobedience, **but they shall be as thorns in your sides, and their gods shall be a snare unto you,** Ex. 23, 33. "Israel, in the conquest, has acted like a slothful gardener. It has not thoroughly destroyed the thorns and thistles of its fields. The consequence will be that sowing and planting and other field labors will soon be rendered painful by the presence of spiteful thorns. What will turn the Canaanites into stinging weeds and snares for Israel? The influence of habitual intercourse. Familiarity blunts aversion, smoothes away contrarieties, removes differences, impairs obedience. It induces forgetfulness of what one was, what one promised, and to what conditions one is subject. Familiar intercourse with idolaters will weaken Israel's faith in the invisible God." (Lange.) **V. 4. And it came to pass, when the Angel of the Lord spake these words unto all the children of Israel, that the people lifted up their voice and wept,** in deep alarm over their sin, with the bitter weeping of repentance. **V. 5. And they called the name of that place,** probably before Shiloh, where the people may have been assembled for one of the great festivals, **Bochim** (weepers); **and they sacrificed there unto the Lord,** sin-offerings and burnt offerings, for the purpose of obtaining forgiveness of their sins. After repentance and reconciliation comes sacrifice, also for a Christian who has so far forgotten himself as to seek the friendship of the world and has been brought to the realization of his sin.

THE CORRUPTION OF THE PEOPLE AND ITS PUNISHMENT. — **V. 6. And when Joshua had let the people go,** literally, "And Joshua sent away the people"; for here the narrative is continued from the last paragraph of the Book of Joshua, in almost the identical words, Josh. 24, 28-31, **the children of Israel went every man unto his inheritance to possess the land. V. 7. And the people served the Lord all the days of Joshua, and all the days of the elders that outlived Joshua,** literally, "that prolonged their days. after Joshua," **who had seen all the great works of the Lord that He did for Israel.** They were firm in their faith, and their example served to keep all the people on the right way. **V. 8. And Joshua, the son of Nun, the servant of the Lord, died, being an hundred and ten years old,** Josh. 24, 29. **V. 9. And they buried him in the border of his inheritance in Timnath-heres,** or Timnath-serah, the name Heres apparently having been borne by this whole division of the mountains of Ephraim, **in the mount of Ephraim, on the north side of the hill Gaash. V. 10. And also all that generation,** all the contemporaries of Joshua, **were gathered unto their fathers; and there arose another generation after them which knew not the Lord, nor yet the works which He had done for Israel.** They had not been witnesses of, they had not personally experienced, the miraculous revelations of divine power in giving the Land of Promise to the children of Israel. They did not feel their indebtedness to God, they were not conscious of the fact that victory and freedom and riches came to them from the Lord. **V. 11. And the children of Israel did evil in the sight of the Lord,** before His very eyes, **and served Baalim,** here said of all false gods, of the entire heathen worsip, for Baal was the chief male idol of all the Canaanitish nations. **V. 12. And they forsook the Lord God of their fathers,** the only true God, **which brought them out of the land of Egypt, and followed other gods, of the gods of the people that were round about**

them, principally Baal and Ashtaroth, the latter being the chief female deity of the heathen nations of Canaan, **and bowed themselves unto them,** in regular systematic worship, implying a conviction of the heart, **and provoked the Lord to anger,** deeply grieved Him. **V. 13. And they forsook the Lord,** the repetition of this statement serving to emphasize the heinousness of the transgression, **and served Baal and Ashtaroth.** There was no outright rejection of Jehovah, but a mingling of His worship with the Canaanitish nature cult. But this attitude is incompatible with the true religion; for since Jehovah is the only true God, beside and before whom there are no other gods, every mingling of His worship with the adoration of idols places Him on a level with these imaginary gods. That is the essence of all syncretism and unionism, not the elevation of falsehood to the dignity of truth, but the desecration of truth to the level of falsehood. **V. 14. And the anger of the Lord was hot,** was kindled, **against Israel, and He delivered them into the hands of spoilers that spoiled them, and He sold them into the hands of their enemies round about, so that they could not any longer stand before their enemies.** In abandoning the people to the resistless violence of their hostile neighbors, God took away from them the basis of their nationality and delivered them into the hands of nations that oppressed and robbed them at will. **V. 15. Whithersoever they went out, the hand of the Lord was against them for evil,** in not a single undertaking were they successful, **as the Lord had said, and as the Lord had sworn unto them,** Lev.26; Deut.28; **and they were greatly distressed,** they were put into tight places, severely oppressed. **V. 16. Nevertheless the Lord raised up judges, which delivered them out of the hand of those that spoiled them,** the purpose of this merciful manifestation being to cause them to return to the Lord in repentance and gratitude. **V. 17. And yet they would not hearken unto their judges,** namely, by desisting from idolatry which the judges tried to suppress, **but they went a-whoring after other gods,** for idolatry is spiritual adultery and immorality, **and bowed themselves unto them; they turned quickly out of the way which their fathers walked in, obeying the commandments of the Lord; but they did not so.** Even the presence of these men who were not the regular rulers, but extraordinary authorities, appointed directly by God, failed to work a permanent reformation in the people. **V. 18. And when the Lord raised them up judges, then the Lord was with the judge,** with every single one, **and delivered them out of the hand of their enemies all the days of the judge,** as long as he lived; **for it repented the Lord because of their groanings by reason of them that oppressed them and vexed them,** He always had sympathy with their sorry plight and turned back to them in kindness. **V. 19. And it came to pass, when the judge was dead, that they returned,** turned back to their former manner of thinking, and acting, **and corrupted themselves more than their fathers,** became guilty of the idolatrous customs of their fathers in a still higher degree, **in following other gods to serve them, and to bow down unto them; they ceased not from their own doings,** literally, they did not drop their peculiar manner of acting, **nor from their stubborn way.** Such was the ever-recurring story during the period of the Judges. **V. 20. And the anger of the Lord was hot against Israel; and He said, Because that this people hath transgressed My covenant which I commanded their fathers,** namely, to clear Canaan of the heathen nations and not to become guilty of idolatry, **and have not hearkened unto**

My voice, v. 21. I also will not henceforth drive out any from before them of the nations which Joshua left when he died; for Israel was still surrounded by a circle of heathen nations living within its promised borders, to say nothing of those who with their idolatry were tolerated in the territory actually subjugated; **v. 22. that through them I may prove Israel whether they will keep the way of the Lord to walk therein, as their fathers did keep it, or not.** Cp. Josh. 23, 13. Thus the divine plan of a gradual extermination of the Canaanitish nations still remaining was suspended, the punishment being intended to lead the people to repentance. **V. 23. Therefore the Lord left those nations, without driving them out hastily; neither delivered He them into the hand of Joshua.** Thus the historical and moral background of the entire book has been given in these two introductory chapters. Note: The Lord makes use of the same patience and mercy in dealing with men today, but when all His efforts are rejected time and again, He finally withdraws His hand in anger and delivers them to the results of their own stubbornness.

29

Judges 3

The Time of Othniel, Ehud, and Shamgar.

THE NATIONS WHICH REMAINED. — **V. 1. Now these are the nations which the Lord left to prove Israel by them,** to test their faithfulness to Him, **even as many of Israel as had not known all the wars of Canaan,** the younger generation which enjoyed the fruits of conquest, but did not estimate aright the greatness of the dangers endured by the fathers, and therefore did not sufficiently value the help of God; **v. 2. only that the generations of the children of Israel might know, to teach them war,** give them an idea, make them realize the great cost of the boon of freedom and material wealth which they were enjoying, **at the least such as before knew nothing thereof,** the final object being that they might learn humility and submission to the Law; **v. 3. namely, five lords of the Philistines,** those of the five city-states Gaza, Ashdod, Ashkelon, Gath, and Ekron, Josh. 13, 3, **and all the Canaanites,** chiefly along the coast of the Mediterranean Sea and in the Jordan Valley, **and the Sidonians,** the Phenicians, **and the Hivites that dwelt in**

mount Lebanon, from mount Baal-hermon, in the southern Anti-Lebanon, west of Damascus, **unto the entering in of Hamath,** in the valley of the Orontes. **V. 4. And they,** these heathen nations, **were to prove Israel by them, to know whether they would hearken unto the commandments of the Lord which He commanded their fathers by the hand of Moses.** By being oppressed by their enemies and thereupon delivered by the Lord through the medium of wars, Israel was both to be tested and strengthened in obedience to the Lord. **V. 5. And the children of Israel dwelt among the Canaanites, Hittites, and Amorites, and Perizzites, and Hivites, and Jebusites,** all of whom they permitted to live in their midst, making no serious effort to drive them out, chap; 1, 21-35. **V. 6. And they took their daughters to be their wives, and gave their daughters to their sons,** thus entering into the most intimate social relationship with them, **and served their gods,** the natural consequence of breaking down the barriers which the Lord had erected by His prohibition, Ex. 34, 16. 23. 24; Deut. 7, 3. 4. That is almost invariably the progress of apostasy: friendship with the world, marriages with infidels, rejection of the Lord.

OTHNIEL JUDGE OF ISRAEL. — **V. 7. And the children of Israel did evil in the sight of the Lord,** the usual formula introducing a chapter of oppression and deliverance, chap. 2, 11, **and forgot the Lord, their God, and served Baalim and the groves,** that is, Asherah, for in the heathen worship, the altar was consecrated to Baal, the pillar or treeidol to Astarte, or Ashtaroth, chap. 2, 13. **V. 8. Therefore the anger of the Lord was hot against Israel,** it was kindled, it flared up in an angry flame, **and He sold them into the hand of Chushan-rishathaim, king of Mesopotamia,** some mighty monarch toward the East; **and the children of Israel served Chushan-rishathaim eight years,** by being obliged to pay heavy tribute money. **V. 9. And when the children of Israel cried unto the Lord,** as they felt the severity of the oppression more and more, **the Lord raised up a deliverer to the children of Israel,** a man who was to save them from the tyrant, **who delivered them, even Othniel, the son of Xenaz, Caleb's younger brother,** the conqueror of Debir, chap. 1, 13; Josh. 15, 16. 17. **V. 10. And the Spirit of the Lord came upon him,** filling him with extraordinary military ability and valor, as well as the wisdom necessary to decide difficult cases according to the Law, **and he judged Israel,** restored justice and order, **and went out to war; and the Lord delivered Chushan-rishathaim, king of Mesopotamia, into his hand; and his hand prevailed against Chushan-rishathaim,** he defeated the oppressor and threw off the burden which was bearing Israel down. Thus the consciousness of God and of the duty toward Jehovah was restored in Israel. **V. 11. And the land had rest forty years,** the people being able to follow all the pursuits of peace without outside interference. **And Othniel, the son of Kenaz,** under whose blameless and happy rule the land had been restored to its former prosperity, **died.** Thus the children of Israel had received a lesson the force of which was to be impressed upon them for all times, for every proof of God's kindness is intended to make men cling to Him in firm trust.

EHUD AND THE MOABITES. SHAMGAR. — **V. 12. And the children of Israel did evil again in the sight of the Lord; and the Lord strengthened,** encouraged, **Eglon, the king of Moab,** the country southeast of the Dead Sea, **against Israel, because they had done evil in the sight of the Lord. V. 13. And he,** Eglon, who evidently combined shrewdness with energy, **gathered unto him the children of Ammon,** to the northeast, like those of Moab, inveterate enemies of Israel, Deut. 23, 3. 4, **and Amalek,** toward the southwest, also ancient enemies of the Lord's people, Ex. 17, 10-16, **and went and smote Israel, and possessed the city of palmtrees,** the fertile oasis in which the ruins of Jericho were located. Evidently not only the tribe of Benjamin, in whose territory the battle was fought, but all Israel, had grown careless, dull, and incapable. **V. 14. So the children of Israel served Eglon, the king of Moab, eighteen years,** by a regular payment of tribute, such as he chose to exact. **V. 15. But when the children of Israel cried unto the Lord,** being roused from their lethargy once more, **the Lord raised them up a deliverer,** as before, **Ehud, the son of Gera, a Benjamite, a man left-handed,** literally, "unpracticed, awkward, with the right hand," because the skill which other people have in their right hand he had in his left; **and by him the children of Israel sent a present unto Eglon, the, king of Moab,** he being the leader or spokesman of the delegation bearing the proof of their subjection. **V. 16. But Ehud,** before setting out on this humiliating mission, **made him a dagger which had two edges,** a very effective weapon for stabbing at short range, **of a cubit length** (about twenty inches); **and he did gird it under his raiment upon his right thigh,** out of sight and on the side from which he could immediately draw. **V. 17. And he brought the present unto Eglon, king of Moab,** who had made the oasis of Jericho his headquarters while he held the supremacy over Israel; **and Eglon was a very fat man,** extremely corpulent, even for an Oriental monarch. **V. 18. And when he, Ehud, had made an end to offer the present,** the audience giving him an opportunity to make the observations which he needed, **he sent away the people that bare the present,** for it was considered a mark of special respect to have a great many bearers for the tribute. **V. 19. But he himself turned again from the quarries,** or boundary-stones, **that were by Gilgal,** unto which point he had accompanied the rest of the delegation, returning to the quarters of the Moabite king, **and said, I have a secret errand unto thee, O king; who said, Keep silence,** thus bidding Ehud wait until the room was cleared before imparting his secret message, which Eglon naturally thought to be of value to him, especially since the return of Ehud alone seemed to indicate that he did not want his companions to know what he had to say. **And all that stood by him,** the usual attendants of the king, **went out from him,** at the king's signal indicating that he wished to be alone with the visitor. **V. 20. And Ehud came unto him,** approached nearer to him; **and he was sitting in a summer parlor,** an inner chamber, opening on an exposed balcony, his private chamber, and a cool retreat, **which he had for himself alone. And Ehud said, I have a message from God unto thee. And he arose out of his seat,** probably out of respect for this word. **V. 21. And Ehud put forth his left hand, and took the dagger from his right thigh, and thrust it into his** (Eglon's) **belly; v. 22. and the haft also went in after the blade; and the fat closed upon the blade,** holding it firmly inside the abdomen, **so that he,** Ehud, **could not draw the dagger out of his belly; and the dirt came out,** or, the point of the blade came out at the rear. **V. 23. Then Ehud went forth through the porch,** the open balcony, **and shut the doors of the parlor upon him, and locked them. V. 24. When he was gone out,** with a calmness intended to disarm every suspicion on the part of the king's attendants, **his servants came; and when** they saw that, **behold, the doors of the parlor were locked, they said, Surely he covereth his feet** (doeth his easement) **in his summer chamber. V. 25. And they tarried till they were ashamed,** these words adding the notion of displeasure and ill humor; **and, behold, he opened not the doors of the parlor; therefore they took a key,** another key, **and opened them,** the long silence having filled them with great uneasiness; **and, behold, their lord was fallen down dead on the earth. V. 26. And Ehud escaped while they tarried, and passed beyond the quarries,** or the boundary-stones, **and escaped unto Seirath,** in the foothills toward the northwest. **V. 27. And it came to pass, when he was come, that he blew a trumpet in the mountain of Ephraim,** this trumpet-blast being transmitted among the mountains, **and the children of Israel,** with whom he had evidently agreed upon this signal, **went down with him from the mount, and he before them,** as their leader. **V. 28. And he said unto them, Follow after me; for the Lord hath delivered your enemies, the Moabites, into your hand. And they went down after him, and took the fords of Jordan toward Moab, and suffered not a man,** namely, of the Moabites, **to pass over** and thus to escape. The Moabite army was therefore trapped between the Jordan and the mountains, with their leader dead. **V. 29. And they slew of Moab at that time,** in the battle which followed, **about ten thousand men, all lusty,** literally, "fat," in good physical condition, **and all men of valor; and there escaped not a man,** Moab was thoroughly vanquished. **V. 30. So Moab was subdued that day under the hand of Israel. And the land had rest fourscore years. V. 31. And after him,** following his example in the west, **was Shamgar, the son of Anath, which slew of the Philistines six hundred men with an ox goad,** a primitive, but effective instrument or weapon on account of the sharp iron prick at the end; **and he also delivered Israel,** apparently from a local subjugation. In these narratives both the righteousness and the goodness of the Lord is apparent. For God punishes transgressions of every kind, often with great severity, but when the transgressors turn to Him in true repentance He is glad to send them help and salvation. It is for us to keep our Savior in mind at all times and thus to avoid all wilful sins.

30

Judges 4

The Victory of Deborah and Barak.

THE PROPHETESS DEBORAH CALLS BARAK. — **V. 1. And the children of Israel again did evil in the sight of the Lord,** literally, "they added, or continued to do, wickedness," **when Ehud was dead;** for he had kept down the spirit of idolatry and maintained a successful defensive position against all enemies. **V. 2. And the Lord sold them into the hand of Jabin, king of Canaan, that reigned in Hazor,** evidently a very important city-state; for its king had stood at the head of a strong league of northern tribes in the time of Joshua, Josh. 11, 1. 10. 11, and the city had been rebuilt after its destruction by Israel; **the captain of whose host was Sisera, which dwelt in Harosheth of the Gentiles,** undoubtedly located in one of the valleys of Galilee, as Northern Canaan was later called. Jabin's scheme of keeping Israel in subjection by exerting pressure from two different points was apparently very successful, and the outlook seemed to favor his plan of regaining possession of the entire territory taken from his ancestors by Joshua. **V. 3. And the children of**

Israel cried unto the Lord; for he had nine hundred chariots of iron; and twenty years he mightily oppressed the children of Israel, making them feel the full weight and power of his might. **V. 4. And Deborah, a prophetess,** one possessing the prophetic gift from the Spirit of Jehovah, **the wife of Lapidoth, she judged Israel at that time,** exercising the functions of the supreme court in deciding difficult cases and thus being an acknowledged leader in the nation. **V. 5. And she dwelt under the palm-tree of Deborah,** which received its name from that fact, **between Ramah and Bethel,** in the territory of Benjamin, **in Mount Ephraim. And the children of Israel came up to her for judgment.** Deborah was a woman of fiery spirit, as the exact translation shows; she was like a torch for Israel, kindling their languid hearts, a capable and energetic woman, but no fanatic. **V. 6. And she sent and called Barak, the son of Abinoam, out of Kedeshnaphtali,** a city in the extreme north of the later Galilee, and not far from Razor, **and said unto him, Hath not the Lord God of Israel commanded, saying, Go and draw toward Mount Tabor,** southwest of the Sea of Galilee and north of the Plain of Esdraelon, **and take with thee ten thousand men of the children of Naphtali and of the children of Zebulun?** The plan of assembling, as suggested by the Lord through the mouth of the prophetess, was that of drawing the men from the two tribes down to Tabor gradually, in small squads, the movement thus escaping the notice of the oppressors. **V. 7. And I,** the Lord further says, **will draw unto thee, to the river Kishon, Sisera, the captain of Jabin's army, with his chariots and his multitude; and I will deliver him into thine hand.** It was a clear command, with a definite promise. **V. 8. And Barak said unto her, If thou wilt go with me, then I will go; but if thou wilt not go with me, then I will**

not go. Although Barak had no doubt concerning the truth of Deborah's words, he did not yet feel the divine enthusiasm for the battle, being conscious of his own inability to carry out the command of the Lord alone. **V. 9. And she said, I will surely go with thee; notwithstanding the journey that thou takest,** the expedition upon which he was now entering, **shall not be for thine honor,** Barak would not be hailed as the conqueror of Jabin and Sisera; **for the Lord shall sell Sisera into the hand of a woman,** namely, Jael, as the continuation of the story shows; for Deborah was speaking as a prophetess. **And Deborah arose and went with Barak to Kedesh.** It makes no difference to the Lord whether the men and the instruments at hand are strong or weak, He is able to carry out His will as He chooses.

THE DEFEAT OF SISERA. — **V. 10. And Barak called Zebulun and Naphtali to Kedesh,** as Deborah had suggested; **and he went up with ten thousand men at his feet,** on foot, infantry only, for they had neither chariots nor cavalry; **and Deborah went up with him.** With their number constantly growing, as new bands from the hills join them, they reach the designated place. **V. 11. Now Heber, the Kenite, which was of the children of Hobab, the father-in-law of Moses,** or brother-in-law, for the Hebrew word means simply a male relative by marriage, **had severed himself from the Kenites,** who had settled in the extreme southern part of Canaan, chap. 1, 16, **and pitched his tent,** taken up a homestead, **unto the Plain of Zaanaim, which is by Kedesh,** in the territory of Naphtali. **V. 12. And they showed Sisera,** some one brought him the tidings, **that Barak, the son of Abinoam, was gone up to Mount Tabor,** that the Israelites were preparing to throw off the yoke of Jabin. **V. 13. And Sisera gathered together,** assembled by sending out criers, **all his chariots,**

even nine hundred chariots of iron, and all the people that were with him, from Harosheth of the Gentiles unto the river of Kishon, for the Plain of Esdraelon, or Jezreel, at the headwaters of the Kishon was a ground on which his army could properly deploy. **V. 14. And Deborah said unto Barak, Up! For this is the day in which the Lord hath delivered Sisera into thine hand. Is not the Lord gone out before thee?** This was a prophetic and most vivid assurance of victory. **So Barak went down from Mount Tabor, and ten thousand men after him,** apparently in a sudden attack, before the terrible chariot-force had well arranged itself. **V. 15. And the Lord discomfited Sisera,** terrified him, threw him into confusion, **and all his chariots and all his host, with the edge of the sword before Barak,** for nothing could withstand the charge of the army of Israel, fired as it was with divine enthusiasm by Deborah, **so that Sisera lighted down off his chariot,** in a panic of terror, **and fled away on his feet,** seeking only to save his life in the general destruction. **V. 16. But Barak pursued after the chariots,** as their drivers turned in headlong flight, **and after the host,** the infantry of the enemy's army, **unto Harosheth of the Gentiles,** to the very gates of their stronghold; **and all the host of Sisera fell upon the edge of the sword,** in the terrible conflict in which the sword mowed them down on every hand; **and there was not a man left. V. 17. Howbeit Sisera fled away on his feet to the tent of Jael, the wife of Heber, the Kenite,** seeking refuge at the first place that seemed to promise him security; **for there was peace between Jabin, the king of Razor, and the house of Heber, the Kenite.** Thus the mighty enemies were overthrown by the power of the Lord, for it is a small matter for Him to deliver His people with a handful of men from the hands of the mightiest tyrant.

SISERA'S DEATH. — **V. 18. And Jael went out to meet Sisera,** after the manner of Oriental hospitality, her object being to coax him into the house, **and said unto him, Turn in, my lord, turn in to me; fear not.** She wanted to disarm all suspicions. **And when he had turned in unto her into the tent,** probably feeling safer in the women's apartments, **she covered him with a mantle,** with a close, ruglike covering. **V. 19. And he said unto her, Give me, I pray thee, a little water to drink; for I am thirsty,** for it was a rule of hospitality that whoever had eaten or drunk anything in the tent was received into the peace of the house. **And she opened a bottle of milk, and gave him drink, and covered him,** having effectually allayed all his suspicions. **V. 20. Again he said unto her, Stand in the door of the tent, and it shall be, when any man doth come and inquire of thee and say, Is there any man here? that thou shalt say, No.** He felt altogether secure, and lay down to sleep after giving Jael these instructions. **V. 21. And Jael, Heber's wife,** mindful of the fact that the man lying in her tent was a tyrant, a ruthless enemy of a nation with which her family was joined in the bonds of the closest relationship, **took a nail of the tent,** one of the tent-pins, **and took an hammer in her hand, and went softly unto him, and smote the nail into his temples, and fastened it into the ground; for he was fast asleep and weary,** from his long flight. **So he died. V. 22. And, behold, as Barak pursued Sisera, Jael came out to meet him, and said unto him, Come, and I will show thee the man whom thou seekest. And when he came into her tent, behold, Sisera lay dead, and the nail was in his temples.** Deborah's word that the Lord would sell Sisera into the hand of a woman had been literally fulfilled. **V. 23. So God subdued on that day Jabin, the king of Canaan, before the children of Israel,** by this complete defeat of his general and the entire army. **V. 24. And the hand of the children of Israel prospered,** they gained in power, **and prevailed against Jabin, the king of Canaan,** resting ever more heavily upon him, **until they had destroyed Jabin, king of Canaan.** The rule of this one king at least was definitely at an end. Note: Faith shows its power also in weak instruments, for it is the strength of God and not of men. Faith, which always keeps God's Word and promise before the eyes, is able to enter into battle at all times and to gain the victory. That is the victory which overcometh the world, even our faith.

31

Judges 5

The Song of Deborah and Barak.

THE GLORY AND POWER OF ISRAEL. — **V. 1. Then sang Deborah and Barak, the son of Abinoam, on that day,** the song having been composed by Deborah in celebration of the great victory, **saying, v. 2. Praise ye the Lord for the avenging of Israel, when the people willingly offered themselves,** literally, "for the free exhibition of warlike valor in Israel," namely, when the people with their leaders wholly devoted themselves to God. and hazarded their lives in the strength of this faith, "for the willing war-service of the people, praise Jehovah." To God alone all glory and honor shall ever be given. **V. 3. Hear, O ye kings; give ear, O ye princes,** namely, all those of the heathen nations round about; **I, even I, will sing unto the Lord; I will sing praise to the Lord God of Israel,** literally, "I to Jehovah, I will sing, will play to Jehovah, the God of Israel," her song demanding all the more attention since she is a prophetess filled with the, Spirit of God. After this inspiring introduction the singer reminds the hearers of some of the great deeds of God in the past. **V. 4.**

Lord, when Thou wentest out of Seir, when Thou marchedst out of the field of Edom, namely, when He prepared for the giving of the Law on Mount Sinai, His coming at that time being compared to the rising of a mighty thunderstorm in the East, in the highlands of Edom, **the earth trembled, and the heavens dropped, the clouds also dropped water.** Cp. Ex. 19, 16; Hab. 3, 10. **V. 5. The mountains melted from before the Lord,** flowed away, as it were, by reason of mighty earthquakes, **even that Sinai from before the Lord God of Israel,** for it was there that the disturbance was concentrated. Ps. 97, 5. After this rehearsal of God's wonderful majesty, Deborah pictures the distress of Israel before the victory just gained. **V. 6. In the days of Shamgar, the son of Anath,** who proved himself a hero in a local attack on the Philistines, chap. 3, 31, **in the days of Jael,** even though this heroic woman was then already living, yet Israel as a whole was in a miserable plight, **the highways were unoccupied,** the people of Israel had ceased to use them for fear of their enemies, **and the travelers walked through byways,** made use of hidden paths, often with crooked and zigzag courses, in order to escape the vigilance of their enemies. **V. 7. The inhabitants of the villages ceased,** the open, unfortified hamlets were deserted for fear of marauding bands, **they ceased in Israel, until that I, Deborah, arose, that I arose a mother in Israel,** to nurse and protect the people with motherly care. **V. 8. They,** the people of Israel, **chose new gods,** the cause of their downfall, the reason for their misery; **then was war in the gates,** as a result of their having forsaken the old, the everlasting God, Deut. 32, 17. **Was there a shield or spear seen among forty thousand in Israel?** There were no warriors left to protect the country against the fury of the enemies. **V. 9. My heart is toward the**

governors of Israel, she was with them heart and soul, she inspired them with hope and trust in Jehovah, **that offered themselves willingly among the people,** devoting themselves to the cause of conquering the Lord's enemies. **Bless ye the Lord. V. 10. Speak, ye that ride on white asses,** the nobles of the people should meditate upon the deeds of the Lord, **ye that sit in judgment,** on splendid rugs or mats such as were used on saddles, **and walk by the way,** for the simple wayfarers, the poor and lowly among the people, were also included in this admonition. **V. 11. They that are delivered from the noise of archers in the places of drawing water, there shall they rehearse the righteous acts of the Lord, even the righteous acts toward the inhabitants of His villages in Israel; then shall the people of the Lord go down to the gates.** This is a picture of peace times. Instead of the noise and shouting of those contending at the cisterns, anxious to get away before some band of the enemies might come along, they could now take their time and sound forth songs of praise to Jehovah for His deeds of righteousness, also in restoring freedom to the inhabitants of the open hamlets, for the people could now return without fear to the gates of their towns and cities, since the power of the oppressor was broken. **V. 12. Awake, awake, Deborah; awake, awake, utter a song;** there was need of her singing her most inspiring song in imparting enthusiasm to the soldiers whom she had bidden Barak assemble. **Arise, Barak, and lead thy captivity captive;** for by fighting and leading the enemy captive he would end the conflict, **thou son of Abinoam. V. 13. Then he made him that remaineth have dominion over the nobles among the people; the Lord made me have dominion over the mighty,** literally, "Then went down a remnant of the powerful, the people; Jehovah went down for me among the mighty." It was indeed only a small remnant of the powerful, a fraction of mighty Israel that went forth to battle with the tyrant, but the Lord was in their midst at the call of Deborah, and therefore they could freely risk the conflict. **V. 14. Out of Ephraim was there a root of them against Amalek;** for to this tribe belonged Joshua, the hero against the Amalekites, Ex. 17. **After thee, Benjamin, among thy people;** for it was Ehud of this tribe who had rendered Benjamin illustrious. **Out of Machir came down governors,** men who had proved themselves able leaders of the people, also in this campaign, **and out of Zebulun they that handle the pen of the writer,** or, "the staff of him who musters well," men distinguished for leadership. **V. 15. And the princes of Issachar were with Deborah,** although they brought no troops, their presence proved their interest in the campaign; **even Issachar, and also Barak; he was sent on foot into the valley,** he had only infantry under his command, but he made his furious, overwhelming attack nevertheless. **For the divisions of Reuben there were great thoughts of heart;** the tribe of Reuben, in its habitations along its brooks in the east country, reflected so long upon the necessity and the possibility of joining the army of Barak until it was too late. **V. 16. Why abodest thou among the sheepfolds to hear the bleatings of the flocks?** Because the Reubenites preferred the security of their homes, they are here addressed with bitter irony. **For the divisions of Reuben there were great searchings of heart;** they meditated and considered the matter well enough, but they were unable to arouse themselves to action. **V. 17. Gilead abode beyond Jordan,** both the tribes of Reuben and Gad seemed to consider their living east of Jordan sufficient excuse for not joining their brethren; **and why did Dan,** whose territory was so near, **remain in ships?** letting his own commercial interests take preference over the needs of his brethren. **Asher continued on the seashore,** dwelling securely in his harbors, **and abode in his breaches,** in the small bays on which the harbors were located. **V. 18. Zebulun and Naphtali were a people that jeoparded their lives unto the death in the high places of the field.** The men of Zebulun willingly offered their souls, their lives, for the liberation of their country, and those of Naphtali on the heights of their mountainous territory. Their praise, therefore, is sung in this hymn. The soldiers of the Lord who freely set forth to battle with the enemies of Christ, with the weapons of the Spirit, are to be commended, but those who remain idle while their brethren are engaged in campaigns which threaten the very existence of the Church, deserve to be severely reprimanded.

THE DEFEAT AND DEATH OF SISERA. — **V. 19. The kings came and fought,** said figuratively of the leaders of Jabin's army; **then fought the kings of Canaan in Taanach by the waters of Megiddo,** for the two cities are barely three miles apart, and the plain is watered by several small tributaries of the Kishon. **They took no gain of money,** they did not get so much as one piece of silver as booty nor one ounce of money to buy them off. **V. 20. They fought from heaven; the stars in their courses fought against Sisera,** literally, "From heaven fought the stars, from their courses they fought against Sisera"; by an extraordinary phenomenon the Lord sent confusion into the ranks of the enemy. **V. 21. The river of Kishon swept them away,** snatched them away, as they attempted to cross it in their headlong flight, **that ancient river, the river Kishon;** the very brook was an instrument of help against the foe. **O my soul, thou hast trodden down**

strength, or, "Step forth with strength," as Deborah urges herself onward in singing of the mighty defeat. **V. 22. Then were the horse-hoofs broken by the means of the prancings, the prancings of their mighty ones,** or, "Then stamped the hoofs of the horses from the rushing, the rushing of his champions," as the foe, panic-stricken before Israel, dashed away in furious flight. **V. 23. Curse ye: Meroz, said the Angel of the Lord, curse ye bitterly the inhabitants thereof, because they came not to the help of the Lord, to the help of the Lord against the mighty.** When they could have been of assistance to the army of Barak, in destroying the fleeing foes, they refused to help. **V. 24. Blessed above women shall Jael, the wife of Heber, the Kenite, be; blessed shall she be above women in the tent.** People of Meroz, members of the nation of Israel, refused to help, but Jael, though only a woman, though a mere dweller in tents and not of the descendants of Jacob, made use of the opportunity offered her. **V. 25. He asked water, and she gave him milk; she brought forth butter,** the very thickest, the most excellent cream, **in a lordly dish,** in a show-bowl, the finest vessel in the tent. **V. 26. She put her hand to the nail,** the tent-pin, **and her right hand to the workmen's hammer; and with the hammer she smote Sisera, she smote off his head, when she had pierced and stricken through his temples.** The very fierce and vivid description may be rendered: She swung it upon Sisera, she pierces his head, and she crashes and pounds through his temples. **V. 27. At her feet he bowed, he fell, he lay down; at her feet he bowed, he fell; where he bowed, there he fell down dead.** So the smitten chieftain drew himself together after the first blow was struck, sought to rise, and fell back. Twice more he writhed convulsively and then died. And now the last scene is pictured. **V. 28. The mother of Sisera looked out at a window, and cried through the lattice,** full of uneasiness and impatience over the delay of her son, otherwise so quick in returning with rich booty, **Why is his chariot so long in coming? Why tarry the wheels of his chariots?** If he himself is delayed, why does he not at least send word of the success of his enterprise? **V. 29. Her wise ladies answered her,** with the wisdom of pride that cannot conceive of a defeat for Sisera; **yea, she returned answer to herself, v. 30. Have they not sped? Have they not divided the prey,** thereby being detained so long; **to every man a damsel or two; to Sisera a prey of divers colors,** beautiful colored or purple robes, **a prey of divers colors of needlework, of divers colors of needlework on both sides, meet for the necks of them that take the spoi1,** color-embroidered vestments, two for his neck as booty? "The glowing heat of her prophetic enthusiasm shines through the irony with which she places the vain pride of unbelieving enemies over against the almighty power of God. It is not an irony of hatred, disfiguring the face with scornful smiles, but such as springs from the consciousness that God's wisdom and power are superior to all heroes and heathen." (Lange.) **V. 31. So let all thine enemies perish, O Lord,** fallen and brought to naught like Sisera; **but let them that love Him be as the sun when he goeth forth in his might.** The rising of the sun in his full strength is a fitting picture of the rising of Israel to an ever more glorious manifestation of power, according to the intention of the Lord. **And the land had rest forty years.**

32

Judges 6

The Call of Gideon.

THE OPPRESSION OF MIDIAN. — **V. 1. And the children of Israel did evil in the sight of the Lord,** after the forty years of rest; **and the Lord delivered them into the hand of Midian seven years.** The Midianites, descendants of Abraham and Keturah, occupied the rich steppes east of the territory of Moab and Ammon. After their decisive defeat at the hands of the children of Israel at the time of Moses, Num.31, they had again grown numerous enough to give vent to their ancient hatred for the people of God. **V. 2. And the hand of Midian prevailed against Israel,** rested heavily upon the people; **and because of the Midianites the children of Israel made them the dens which are in the mountains and caves and strongholds.** They made use of the natural grottoes and caves in the limestone, excavated others, made them habitable by digging air-holes from above, and fortified many, to serve not only for retreats in case of a raid, but also as places for the safe-keeping of their personal property. **V. 3. And so it was, when Israel had sown,** prepared the fields for harvest,

that the Midianites came up, and the Amalekites, the other tribe which was especially hostile to Israel, **and the children of the East,** desert tribes living by plunder and pillage, **even they came up against them; v. 4. and they encamped against them, and destroyed the increase of the earth,** by wantonly plundering and devastating the harvest-fields, **till thou come unto Gaza,** the raids thus extending across the entire land, to the Philistine country, **and left no sustenance for Israel, neither sheep, nor ox, nor ass. V. 5. For they,** the Midianites and their allies, **came up with their cattle and their tents,** fully supplied with all they needed; **and they came as grasshoppers,** locusts, **for multitude,** and also for voracity; **for both they and their camels were without number,** a very great multitude; **and they entered into the land to destroy it,** that was their avowed purpose, wantonly and ruthlessly to devastate the entire land, making it unfit for habitation. **V. 6. And Israel was greatly impoverished,** brought down very low, deeply distressed, **because of the Midianites; and the children of Israel cried unto the Lord,** they turned to Him in repentance. **V. 7. And it came to pass, when the children of Israel cried unto the Lord because of the Midianites, v. 8. that the Lord sent a prophet unto the children of Israel,** a man directly inspired by Him, **which said unto them, Thus saith the Lord God of Israel, I brought you up from Egypt, and brought you forth out of the house of bondage,** namely, as a people, Ex. 13, 3. 14; 20, 2; **v. 9. and I delivered you out of the hand of the Egyptians, and out of the hand of all that oppressed you, and drave them out from before you,** the nations of Canaan as they were defeated by Moses and Joshua, **and gave you their land; v. 10. and I said unto you, I am the Lord, your God; fear not the gods of the Amorites,** the name here standing for the

Canaanitish nations in general, **in whose land ye dwell; but ye have not obeyed My voice.** That was the explanation of their present plight. God does not suffer disobedience in His children to go unpunished. But in sending such punishment, His intention is to draw His children back to Him in true sorrow over their sins, that they plead for mercy and forgiveness.

THE ANGEL OF THE LORD APPEARS TO GIDEON. — **V. 11. And there came an Angel of the Lord,** the Angel in the extraordinary sense of the term, the Son of God, **and sat under an oak which was in Ophrah, that pertained unto Joash, the Abiezrite,** in the territory of Manasseh, apparently in the northwestern part of the plain, not far from the territories of Asher, Naphtali, and Zebulun; **and his son Gideon threshed wheat by the winepress,** the place where the grapes were pressed out, not an exposed threshing-floor, **to hide it from the Midianites,** bands of whose raiders might be expected at any time. **V. 12. And the Angel of the Lord appeared unto him,** Gideon, **and said unto him, The Lord is with thee, thou mighty man of valor.** The reference was not only to his physical strength, but to the determination and energy which was apparent in his entire appearance. **V. 13. And Gideon said unto him, O my Lord,** for he realized that this man was not a common man, **if the Lord be with us, why, then, is all this befallen us?** Cp. Deut. 31, 17. **And where be all His miracles which our fathers told us of, saying, Did not the Lord bring us up from Egypt?** These words did not arise from doubt and unbelief, but from a deep feeling of Israel's dishonor. **But now the Lord hath forsaken us, and delivered us into the hands of the Midianites.** It was the only conclusion which Gideon found possible. **V. 14. And the Lord looked upon him,** for He it was that appeared in the form of the Angel, **and said, Go** in this thy might, and thou shalt save Israel from the hand of the Midianites. **Have not I sent thee,** or, Do not I send thee? **V. 15. And he said unto Him, O my Lord, wherewith shall I save Israel?** acknowledging the speaker as the Lord God. **Behold, my family is poor in Manasseh,** my division of a thousand families is the lowliest in the tribe, **and I am the least in my father's house,** he occupied no position of influence and authority. **V. 16. And the Lord said unto him,** in taking away this objection, **Surely I will be with thee, and thou shalt smite the Midianites as one man;** their entire host would fall before him as though it consisted of but a single man. **V. 17. And he,** Gideon, **said unto Him, If now I have found grace in Thy sight, then show me a sign that Thou talkest with me,** literally, "whether thou art He who speaks with me," whether He had this divine authority thus to send him, in other words, whether He were God. **V. 18. Depart not hence, I pray Thee, until I come unto Thee and bring forth my present,** a sacrificial gift offered to God, from whose acceptance he would obtain evidence of the deity of the messenger, **and set it before thee.. And He said, I will tarry until thou come again. V. 19. And Gideon went in and made ready a kid,** preparing it for food, **and unleavened cakes of an ephod of flour** (almost twenty-six quarts). **The flesh he put in a basket, and he put the broth in a pot, and brought it out unto him under the oak and presented it,** set it down before his Visitor. **V. 20. And the Angel of God said unto him, Take the flesh and the unleavened cakes, and lay them upon this rock,** which He pointed out to him, **and pour out the broth,** namely, over the food. **And he did so. V. 21. Then the Angel of the Lord put forth the end of the staff that was in His hand, and touched the flesh and the unleavened cakes; and there rose up fire**

out of the rock, and consumed the flesh and the unleavened cakes. Then the Angel of the Lord departed out of his sight, disappearing as suddenly as He had come. **V. 22. And when Gideon perceived that He was an Angel of the Lord,** the Lord Himself, as He had revealed Himself to Abraham and to Joshua, **Gideon said, Alas, O Lord God!** an expression of dismay and of the fear of death, since he, a sinful human being, had spoken with Jehovah, **for because I have seen an Angel of the Lord face to face! V. 23. And the Lord said unto him,** no longer in visible form, but by the voice of the unseen God, **Peace be unto thee; fear not; thou shalt not die. V. 24. Then Gideon built an altar there unto the Lord, and called it Jehovah-shalom** ("The Lord is peace"); **unto this day it is yet in Ophrah of the Abiezrites.** This altar was not to serve for sacrifices, but as a memorial and witness of the theophany vouchsafed to Gideon, and of his expression that Jehovah did not desire to destroy Israel in His wrath, but had only thoughts of peace toward the people. The Son of God, Jesus Christ, has given us thousands of proofs that He is all-powerful, but also gracious and merciful. Therefore we should trust in His power and grace.

GIDEON GRANTED SPECIAL SIGNS. — **V. 25. And it came to pass the same night,** following this wonderful manifestation, **that the Lord said unto him, Gideon, Take thy father's young bullock, even the second bullock of seven years old, and throw down the altar of Baal that thy father hath,** for thus openly was idolatry practised in Israel, **and cut down the grove,** the Ashera pillar **that is by it,** the chief deities of the Canaanites being worshiped by the family of Abiezer; **v. 26. and build an altar unto the Lord, thy God, upon the top of this rock, in the ordered place,** on the grotto or fortification, the wood from the pillar of Ashera being intended to consume the burnt offering of Gideon, **and take the second bullock, and offer a burnt sacrifice with the wood of the grove which thou shalt cut down. V. 27. Then Gideon took ten men of his servants and did as the Lord had said unto him; and so it was, because he feared his father's household,** addicted to idolatry as they were, **and the men of the city that he could not do it by day, that he did it by night. V. 28. And when the men of the city arose early in the morning, behold, the altar of Baal was cast down, and the grove,** the wooden pillar erected in honor of Ashera, **was cut down that was by it, and the second bullock was offered upon the altar that was built,** for it was not yet fully consumed by the fire. **V. 29. And they said one to another, Who hath done this thing? And when they enquired and asked,** searching for the man who might be guilty, **they said,** either the searchers themselves upon strong suspicion, or men who knew of Gideon's exploit, **Gideon, the son of Joash, hath done this thing. V. 30. Then the men of the city said unto Joash, Bring out thy son that he may die, because he hath cast down the altar of Baal, and because he hath cut down the grove,** the wooden pillar, **that was by it. V. 31. And Joash said unto all that stood against him,** for he fully approved of the act of his son, **Will ye plead for Baal? Will ye save him?** The emphasis in either case is on the "ye," since Joash wanted to ridicule the idea of Baal's having need of men to defend him, if he were in truth god. **He that will plead for him, let him be put to death whilst it is yet morning; if he be a god, let him plead for himself, because one hath cast down his altar.** He demanded that his enraged townspeople wait till the morning, in order to give Baal time to avenge himself if he were able. Joash knew, and the people knew, that this settled the matter, for none of them seriously believed in the idol. It is one of the characteristic illusions of heathenism in all ages that it itself does not believe in that for which it appears to be so zealous. **V. 32. Therefore on that day he, Joash, called him,** Gideon, **Jerubbaal** ("Let Baal plead his case"), **saying, Let Baal plead against him, because he hath thrown down his altar.** This brought the incident to a close. **V. 33. Then all the Midianites and the Amalekites and the children of the East,** all the enemy allies, **were gathered together, and went over,** passed over Jordan from the east, **and pitched in the Valley of Jezreel,** in the upper reaches of the Kishon. **V. 34. But the Spirit of the Lord came upon Gideon,** clothing him like a garment or a coat of mail, **and he blew a trumpet,** to summon Israel against their enemies; **and Abiezer,** his own section of the tribe of Manasseh, **was gathered after him. V. 35. And he sent messengers throughout all Manasseh, who also was gathered after him; and he sent messengers unto Asher,** who had held back from Barak, **and unto Zebulun, and unto Naphtali; and they came up to meet them. V. 36. And Gideon said unto God,** in asking a further confirmation of the success of his undertaking, **If Thou wilt save Israel by mine hand, as Thou hast said, v. 37. behold, I will put a fleece of wool in the floor,** out in the open on the ground; **and if the dew be on the fleece only, and if it be dry upon all the earth beside, then shall I know that Thou wilt save Israel by mine hand, as Thou hast said.** He had such a humble opinion of himself and his influence that he felt the need of such a sign to establish his courage. **V. 38. And it was so; for he rose up early on the morrow, and thrust the fleece together, and wringed the dew out of the fleece, a bowl full of water,** while the ground round about was dry. **V. 39. And Gideon said unto God, let not Thine anger be hot against me, and I will speak but this**

once, requiring one more sign, in which all explanations on natural principles would be excluded; **let me prove, I pray Thee, but this once with the fleece; let it now be dry only upon the fleece,** which has a tendency to absorb the slightest moisture, **and upon all the ground let there be dew. V. 40. And God did so that night; for it was dry upon the fleece only, and there was dew on all the ground,** as Gideon had asked. His request did not flow from unbelief, but from the weakness of his flesh, which causes even the servants of God to be anxious for the future. But God is rich in kindness; He has compassion with our weakness, and comes to our assistance even with extraordinary blessings and miraculous manifestations.

33

Judges 7

The Overthrow of the Midianites.

THE ARMY REDUCED. –V. l. Then Jerubbaal, who is Gideon, and all the people that were with him, rose up early, and pitched beside the well of Harod, in the southwestern foothills above the plain, **so that the host of the Midianites were on the north side of them, by the hill of Moreh, in the valley,** where their outposts commanded a free view of the valley. **V. 2. And the Lord said unto Gideon, The people that are with thee are too many for Me to give the Midianites into their hands** (there were about 32,000 soldiers of Israel against 135,000 of the enemy), **lest Israel vaunt themselves against Me, saying, Mine own hand hath saved me.** This danger the Lord wanted to remove by a radical measure. **V. 3. Now, therefore, go to, proclaim in the ears of the people, saying, Whosoever is fearful and afraid, let him return and depart early from Mount Gilead,** Deut. 20, 8. The name Gilead was not confined to the country east of Jordan, but was also applied to a region between Ephraim and Manasseh. The tremblers were dismissed from this place, for they would only have been a hindrance in battle. **And there returned of the people twenty and two thousand; and there remained ten thousand. V. 4. And the Lord said unto Gideon, The people are yet too many,** and there was still danger of their vaunting themselves in case of a victory; **bring them down unto the water, and I will try them,** put them to a test, **for thee there; and it shall be that of whom I say unto thee, This shall go with thee, the same shall go with thee; and of whomsoever I say unto thee, This shall not go with thee, the same shall not go.** The entire region is well watered, there being no lack of brooks. **V. 5. So he brought down the people unto the water; and the Lord said unto Gideon, Every one that lappeth of the water with his tongue,** not taking the time to kneel down, but quickly scooping up some water with the hollow hand and drinking from its cuplike curve, **as a dog lappeth, him shalt thou set by himself,** in one division; **likewise every one that boweth down upon his knees to drink.** They were here under no constraint of any kind, and would show their natural characteristics very plainly. **V. 6. And the number of them that lapped, putting their hand to their mouth, were three hundred men,** such as showed their natural readiness, their alertness, disregarded their comfort; **but all the rest of the people bowed down upon their knees to drink water,** preferring to be comfortable rather than keenly watchful. **V. 7. And the Lord said unto Gideon, By the three hundred men that lapped,** sipping the water from their cupped hands, **will I save you, and deliver the Midianites into thine hand,** the ratio being one to four hundred and fifty; **and let all the other people go every man unto his place,** return home. **V. 8. So the people took victuals in their hand,** rather, they, the three hundred, took the people's food, which had been prepared for the campaign, **and their trumpets; and he sent all the rest of Israel every man unto his tent,** back to his own dwelling, **and retained those three hundred men. And the host of Midian was beneath him in the valley.** Gideon had only one advantage, that of location; every other consideration was against him. God has His own ways of ruling the world and of waging His wars, and the believers must simply learn to trust in Him.

THE DEFEAT OF THE MIDIANITES. –V. 9. **And it came to pass the same night that the Lord said unto him,** Gideon, **Arise, get thee down unto the host,** in a sudden night attack upon the enemy; **for I have delivered it into thine hand. V. 10. But if thou fear to go down,** to make the attack at once, **go thou with Phurah, thy servant, down to the host,** on a scouting expedition; **v. 11. and thou shalt hear what they say,** find out the state, disposition, and attitude of the enemy; **and afterward shall thine hands be strengthened to go down unto the host,** the information obtained on the first expedition would give him the courage to proceed with his night attack at once. **Then went he down with Phurah, his servant, unto the outside of the armed men that were in the host,** he proceeded to the very line of the vanguard of the camp, right among the outposts. **V. 12. And the Midianites and the Amalekites and all the children of the East lay along in the valley,** in their camp, **like grasshoppers for multitude; and their camels were without number, as the sand by the seaside for multitude;** countless numbers and vast resources against the handful of Gideon's men. **V. 13. And when Gideon was come,** as he crept up as near as he dared, **behold, there was a man that told a dream unto his fellow and said, Behold, I dreamed a dream, and,**

lo, a cake of barley-bread tumbled into the host of Midian, rolling down from the mountains, **and came unto a tent, and smote it that it fell, and overturned it, that the tent lay along,** upside down. The meaning is obvious, namely, this, that the oppressed and despised Israelites, the eaters of barley-bread, had descended from the mountains, the tent of the dream standing collectively for the entire encampment. **V. 14. And his fellow answered and said, This is nothing else save the sword of Gideon, the son of Joash, a man of Israel; for into his hand hath God delivered Midian and all the host.** Thus the Lord, through this dream and its correct interpretation, filled the hearts of the enemy with fear, while He strengthened His servant for the task awaiting him. **V. 15. And it was so, when Gideon heard the telling of the dream and the interpretation thereof,** which showed him the mood, the condition of mind of the enemies, **that he worshiped,** thanking God for this encouragement, **and returned into the host of Israel and said, Arise; for the Lord hath delivered into your hand the host of Midian.** Being assured of this fact, he was eager to make the charge. **V. 16. And he divided the three hundred men into three companies,** of a hundred men each, **and he put a trumpet in every man's hand, with empty pitchers,** earthen vessels, **and lamps,** torches, **within the pitchers,** where they were concealed until needed. **V. 17. And he said unto them, Look on me and do likewise; and, behold, when I come to the outside of the camp, it shall be that, as I do, so shall ye do. V. 18. When I blow with a trumpet, I and all that are with me, then blow ye the trumpets also on every side of all the camp and say, The sword of the Lord and of Gideon,** for that was the battle-cry. By attacking the camp of the Midianites from three sides at once and sounding with all possible noise, the enemy would be deceived concerning the size of the army of Israel and thrown into confusion. **V. 19. So Gideon, and the hundred men that were with him, came unto the outside of the camp in the beginning of the middle watch,** just about midnight, the time of the soundest sleep; **and they had but newly set the watch,** the sentinels having just been changed; **and they blew the trumpets, and brake the pitchers that were in their hands,** at the same time holding aloft the flaming torches. **V. 20. And the three companies blew the trumpets, and brake the pitchers, and held the lamps in their left hands, and the trumpets in their right hands to blow withal; and they cried, The sword of the Lord and of Gideon. V. 21. And they stood every man in his place round about the camp,** without advancing to a hand-to-hand encounter; **and all the host ran, and cried, and fled;** for they were seized with the alarm of panic when without warning the trumpets sounded, the pitchers crashed, the thundering battle-cry broke out. "It tells the Midianites that the sword of the God, whose people and faith they have oppressed, and of the man whose insignificance they have despised, whose family they have injured, and who through God becomes their conqueror, is about to be swung over their heads." (Lange.) **V. 22. And the three hundred blew the trumpets, and the Lord set every man's sword** among the host of the enemies, **against his fellow even throughout all the host,** as a result of their headless panic; **and the host fled to Bethshittah in Zererath,** toward Zererah, **and to the border of Abel-meholah, unto Tabbath,** in three different scattered columns toward the southeast, all in the attempt to reach the fords of the Jordan. **V. 23. And the men of Israel,** the enemy thus being engaged in headless flight, **gathered themselves** together out of Naphtali and out of Asher and out of all Manasseh, and pursued after the Midianites. V. 24. And Gideon, in the hope of cutting off the fleeing Midianites before they reached the safety of their own country, sent messengers throughout all Mount Ephraim, saying, Come down against the Midianites, and take before them the waters unto Beth-barah and Jordan, the purpose being to hold all the fords as far south as Beth-barah, and thus, if possible, to prevent the enemy even from reaching the Jordan in its lower passages. Then all the men of Ephraim gathered themselves together, and took the waters unto Beth-barah and Jordan. V. 25. And they, the Ephraimites, took two princes of the Midianites, Oreb and Zeeb (raven and wolf); and they slew Oreb upon the rock Oreb, and Zeeb they slew at the wine-press of Zeeb, both of these places receiving their names from these events, and pursued Midian, and brought the heads of Oreb and Zeeb to Gideon on the other side Jordan, where he had gone in pursuit of the fleeing enemy. Note: Much greater than the victory of Gideon is that of Christ, who delivered us from the oppression of Satan, not with swords and the power of earthly weapons, but by His almighty strength, and who makes known this victory in the Gospel, by which we become partakers of the redemption gained through His blood.

34

Judges 8

The End of the Campaign against Midian.

DIFFICULTIES WITH EPHRAIM AND THE CITIES SUCCOTH AND PENUEL. — **V. 1. And the men of Ephraim,** who had not been included in the order to mobilize their forces, chap. 6, 35, **said unto him,** Gideon, **Why hast thou served us thus, that thou calledst us not when thou wentest to fight with the Midianites?** They demanded an explanation for having been slighted by Gideon, as they supposed. **And they did chide with him sharply,** attacked him in a vehement quarrel. **V. 2. And he said unto them, What have I done now in comparison with you?** It was a diplomatic retort, for it placed the exploit of the Ephraimites in capturing the princes Oreb and Zeeb above the defeat of the entire army by Gideon's band. **Is not the gleaning of the grapes of Ephraim better than the vintage of Abiezer?** They had, indeed, had the gleaning of the battle, but this achievement, as Gideon intimates, is to be valued more highly than the victory of the three hundred men whom he called according to the name of his family, Abiezer. **V. 3. God hath**

delivered into your hands the princes of Midian, Oreb and Zeeb; and what was I able to do in comparison of you? As a real hero Gideon was truly humble and thereby, above all, gained his object, that of keeping peace in Israel. **Then their anger was abated toward him, when he had said that.** They were appeased, their pride and vanity was satisfied, but their jealousy was afterward rebuked most sharply by the deeds of Gideon. **V. 4. And Gideon came to Jordan, and passed over, he and the three hundred men that were with him, faint, yet pursuing them.** Their pursuit of the enemy had rendered them weak and faint, yet they continued on their way in order to complete the overthrow of the oppressors. **V. 5. And he said unto the men of Succoth,** near. which city, not far from the mouth of the Jabbok, he had forded the Jordan, **Give, I pray you, loaves of bread unto the people that follow me; for they be faint,** chiefly from hunger, for they had exhausted their small stock of provisions, **and I am pursuing after Zebah and Zalmunna, kings of Midian.** He and his band were risking their lives for all Israel, including the men of Gad, whom he was here addressing, and therefore his request was by no means unreasonable. **V. 6. And the princes,** the rulers or magistrates, **of Succoth said, Are the hands of Zebah and Zalmunna now in thine hand that we should give bread unto thine army?** Since bread costs money, their covetous hearts referred to the small band of Gideon as a host, and their sneering reference to the fists or arms of the Midianitish kings implied that they first wanted to see the enemy bound before them. Here was utter lack of charity combined with cowardice and even treason. **V. 7. And Gideon said, Therefore, when the Lord hath delivered Zebah and Zalmunna into mine hand, then I will tear your flesh with the thorns of the wilderness and with briers,** using these as threshing-flails on their backs. **V. 8. And he went up thence to Penuel,** a city some tell miles up the Jabbok, on its north bank, **and spake unto them likewise; and the men of Penuel answered him as the men of Succoth had answered him,** with the same exhibition of selfishness. **V. 9. And he spake also unto the men of Penuel, saying, When I come again in peace, I will break down this tower,** the strongest part of the city's fortification, upon which they relied. Lack of courage and selfishness are the chief dangers threatening the Church of Christ from within, for they make men unwilling to fight and sacrifice for the Lord.

THE END OF ZEBAH AND ZALMUNNA. — **V. 10. Now Zebah and Zalmunna were in Karkor,** near the headwaters of the Jabbok, **and their hosts with them, about fifteen thousand men, all that were left of all the hosts of the children of the East; for there fell an hundred and twenty thousand men that drew sword,** namely, in the battle in the Plain of Jezreel and in the pursuit. **V. 11. And Gideon went up by the way of them that dwelt in tents on the east of Nobah and Jogbehah,** the easternmost cities of Gad, **and smote the host,** attacking, apparently, from the northeast, from which direction the enemy did not expect an assault; **for the host was secure. V. 12. And when Zebah and Zalmunna fled, he pursued after them, and took the two kings of Midian, Zebah and Zalmunna, and discomfited all the host;** terror seized upon them, so that they offered no resistance, and the army surrendered. **V. 13. And Gideon, the son of Joash, returned from battle before the sun was up,** or, from the ascent or pass of Hecheres, in the hills east of Succoth, **v. 14. and caught a young man of the men,** the inhabitants, **of Succoth, and enquired of him,** in order to find out certain facts about the city; **and he described unto**

him the princes of Succoth and the elders thereof, wrote down their names for Gideon, **even threescore and seventeen men. V. 15. And he,** Gideon, **came unto the men of Succoth and said, Behold Zebah and Zalmunna,** whom he led along with him captive, **with whom ye did upbraid me,** concerning whom they had spoken to him in a jeering manner, **saying, Are the hands of Zebah and Zalmunna now in thine hand that we should give bread unto thy men that are weary? V. 16. And he took the elders of the city, and thorns of the wilderness and briers, and with them he taught the men of Succoth,** by giving them a well-deserved flogging he taught all the inhabitants of the city a lesson, especially concerning the penalties of treasonable selfishness. **V. 17. And he beat down the tower of Penuel, and slew the men of the city,** in a just punishment of their faithlessness and treason. **V. 18. Then said he unto Zebah and Zalmunna,** after his return to his own tribe, **What manner of men were they whom ye slew at Tabor?** He wanted a description of their face and form, their general appearance. **And they answered, As thou art, so were they; each one resembled the children of a king.** This was in reference to a raid which had been made by the Midianites before Gideon had been called to enter upon this campaign of vengeance. **V. 19. And he said, They were my brethren, even the sons of my mother,** the very nearest blood-relatives. **As the Lord liveth, if ye had saved them alive, I would not slay you,** he would have been inclined to spare their lives, but this one cruel action made it impossible for him to do so. **V. 20. And he said unto Jether, his first-born,** apparently still a lad, **Up, and slay them. But the youth drew not his sword; for he feared, because he was yet a youth,** not yet accustomed to slaying men. **V. 21. Then Zebah and Zalmunna**

said, Rise thou and fall upon us; for as the man is, so is his strength; their execution was a task, not for a weak lad, but for a full-grown man. **And Gideon arose and slew Zebah and Zalmunna, and took away the ornaments,** little moon-shaped pendants, **that were on their camels' necks.** In this way was the just punishment of God upon the oppressors put into execution.

THE CONSEQUENCES OF THE CAMPAIGN. — V. **22. Then the men of Israel said unto Gideon, Rule thou over us, both thou and thy son, and thy son's son also,** they wanted to establish a hereditary kingdom with their great deliverer at their head, as the founder of a royal dynasty; **for thou hast delivered us from the hand of Midian. V. 23. And Gideon said unto them, I will not rule over you, neither shall my son rule over you; the Lord shall rule over you.** Gideon did not feel himself called upon to found a royal dynasty in Israel, but considered the direct government of the Lord (theocracy) sufficient for the needs of the people. **V. 24. And Gideon said unto them, I would desire a request of you, that ye would give me every man the earrings of his prey,** the various rings, especially those worn in the nose and in the ears, which the soldiers of Israel had taken from the captives and slain in the recent battle. **(For they had golden earrings, because they were Ishmaelites.)** The enemies, members of nomad tribes as they were, had possessed a wealth of gold in the form of ornaments. **V. 25. And they answered, We will willingly give them,** they were very glad to comply with his request. **And they spread a garment, and did cast therein every man the earrings of his prey,** whatever booty he had gained in the form of gold ornaments and other precious possessions. **V. 26. And the weight of the golden earrings** that he requested was a thousand and seven hundred shekels of gold (more than $16,000 worth); **beside ornaments, and collars,** ear-pendants made of pearls and precious stones, **and purple raiment that was on the kings of Midian, and beside the chains that were about their camels' necks,** made up of moon shaped pendants. **V. 27. And Gideon made an ephod thereof,** a copy of that worn by the high priest at Shiloh, Ex. 28, **and put it in his city, even in Ophrah,** intending it as an act of worship to God, in accordance with his declaration that Jehovah alone was to be honored; **and all Israel went thither,** instead of to Shiloh, **a-whoring after it,** com mitting idolatry with the ephod of Gideon, perverting even faith into superstition; **which thing became a snare unto Gideon and to his house,** for he set aside the Aaronic priesthood and lowered the respect in which it was held by the people. **V. 28. Thus was Midian subdued before the children of Israel, so that they lifted Up their heads no more;** they were effectually overthrown. **And the country was in quietness forty years in the days of Gideon,** for his powerful influence kept the enemies in fear and the people from idolatry. **V. 29. And Jerubbaal, the son of Joash, went and dwelt in his own house,** retired to the outward position of a private person. **V. 30. And Gideon had threescore and ten sons of his body begotten; for he had many wives.** He had everything that made for fame and happiness in Israel, power and influence, peace, riches, and many sons. **V. 31. And his concubine that was in Shechem, she also bare him a son, whose name he called,** or, "and called his name," **Abimelech** ("My father is king"). It seems that this concubine from the beginning had great plans for the son of Gideon and taught him a false ambition from the start. **V. 32. And Gideon, the son of Joash, died in a**

good old age, untroubled by even the shadow of events which transpired after his death, **and was buried in the sepulcher of Joash, his father, in Ophrah of the Abiezrites,** a king in the estimation of the grateful Israelites, if not in deed. **V. 33. And it came to pass, as soon as Gideon was dead, that the children of Israel turned again, and went a-whoring after Baalim,** in all the idolatry of the Canaanites, **and made Baal-berith their god,** considering him as one with whom they had made a covenant. **V. 34. And the children of Israel remembered not the Lord, their God, who had delivered them out of the hands of all their enemies on every side; v. 35. neither showed they kindness to the house,** the children, the family, **of Jerubbaal, namely, Gideon, according to all the goodness which he had showed unto Israel.** They deliberately set out to forget everything that might have reminded them of repentance. Unbelief and ingratitude go hand in hand, for the heart of men is unreliable. Even great benefactors, through whom the Lord brings blessings upon His people, are soon forgotten.

35

Judges 9

The Reign of Abimelech.

ABIMELECH BECOMES KING. — **V. 1.** **And Abimelech, the son of Jerubbaal,** by his concubine, chap. 8, 31, **went to Shechem unto his mother's brethren,** all her nearest relatives, **and communed with them and with all the family of the house of his mother's father, saying,** **v. 2.** **Speak, I pray you, in the ears of all the men of Shechem, Whether is better for you, either that all the sons of Jerubbaal, which are threescore and ten persons, reign over you, or that one reign over you?** He presumes that the position of judge in Israel is hereditary, and craftily suggests that it would be of advantage to have only one man in that office rather than many. **Remember also that I am your bone and your flesh,** for he, through his mother, was a blood-relative of the citizens of Shechem. These two points he wanted them to consider carefully. **V. 3. And his mother's brethren,** acting upon the suggestion of Abimelech, **spake of him in the ears of all the men of Shechem all these words;** **and their hearts,** those of all the Shechemites, **inclined to**

follow Abimelech; for they said, He is our brother. They permitted themselves to be led astray by his perversion of the facts. **V. 4. And they gave him threescore and ten pieces of silver** (barely $45) **out of the house of Baal-berith,** for as idolaters they were opposed to Jerubbaal and his family, who had abolished idolatry wherever his influence extended, **wherewith Abimelech hired vain and light persons,** a body-guard from the idle rabble, the town-bums, easily enough converted into thugs, **which followed him. V. 5. And he went unto his father's house at Ophrah, and slew his brethren, the sons of Jerubbaal, being threescore and ten persons, upon one stone,** dragging them forth for a formal slaughter; **notwithstanding yet Jotham, the youngest son of Jerubbaal, was left; for he hid himself. V. 6. And all the men of Shechem,** after this bloody deed, **gathered together, and all the house of Millo,** the name of the fort or citadel of Shechem, **and went and made Abimelech king by the plain of the pillar that was in Shechem,** at the great stone, set up by Joshua under the oak, Josh. 24. 25. 26. Thus the followers of Baal, thugs and murderers, had triumphed over the followers of the true God. It is always a heavy chastisement in both Church and State if the enemies of the Lord obtain the power.

THE PARABLE OF JOTHAM. — **V. 7. And when they told it,** the entire story concerning the election of Abimelech, **to Jotham, he went and stood in the top of Mount Gerizim,** overlooking Shechem from the south, **and lifted up his voice, and cried and said unto them, Hearken unto me, ye men of Shechem, that God may hearken unto you,** a summons after the manner of the prophets. Now follows his parable. **V. 8. The trees went forth on a time to anoint a king over them,** no special reason being given for this desire; **and they said** unto the olive-tree, Reign thou over us. V. 9. But the olive tree said unto them, Should I leave my fatness, wherewith by me they honor God and man, have I lost my oil, have I become worthless, and go to be promoted over the trees, waving back and forth in an uncertain rule, an honor which may be taken from him at any time, by the fickleness of the subjects V. 10. And the trees said to the fig-tree, Come thou and reign over us. V. 11. But the fig-tree said unto them, Should I forsake my sweetness and my good fruit, and go to be promoted over the trees? V. 12. Then said the trees unto the vine, a symbol of government, as that which gives peace and comfort, Come thou and reign over us. V. 13. And the vine said unto them, Should I leave my wine, which cheereth God and man, a proverbial saying signifying that wine cheers all persons, even the highest and noblest, and go to be promoted over the trees? So all these trees rightly considered their calling of bearing precious fruits for the use of mankind of more importance than the uncertain honor of an elective kingship. V. 14. Then said all the trees unto the bramble, the thorn-bush, Come thou and reign over us. V. 15. And the bramble said unto the trees, If in truth, a fact which she could as yet hardly believe, ye anoint me king over you, then come and put your trust in my shadow, words which contain a cutting irony, as the Shechemites soon found out to their sorrow; and if not, let fire come out of the bramble, the despised and dangerous weed, also on account of its combustibility, and devour the cedars of Lebanon, the noblest trees in the country. Jotham now himself makes the application of his parable. V. 16. Now, therefore, if ye have done truly and sincerely in that ye have made Abimelech, that dangerous thorn-bush, king, and if ye have dealt well with Jerubbaal, who refused royal honors in Israel, **and his house, and have done unto him according to the deserving of his hands,** if it was such treatment which they had really deserved at the hands of the Shechemites or of all Israel; **v. 17. (for my father fought for you, and adventured his life far, and delivered you out of the hand of Midian; v. 18. and ye are risen up against my father's house this day, and have slain his sons, threescore and ten persons, upon one stone, and have made Abimelech, the son of his maid-servant,** for that was the actual position of Gideon's concubine, the mother of Abimelech, **king over the men of Shechem, because he is your brother;)** all these facts having been duly considered by them, **v. 19. if ye, then, have dealt truly and sincerely,** in faithfulness and uprightness, **with Jerubbaal and with his house this day, then rejoice ye in Abimelech, and let him also rejoice in you,** an expression of bitter scorn over their murderous faithlessness; **v. 20. but if not, let fire come out from Abimelech, and devour the men of Shechem, and the house,** the inhabitants, **of Millo; and let fire come out from the men of Shechem and from the house of Millo, and devour Abimelech.** So both the sinful trees and their tyrannical king were destined to be consumed. **V. 21. And Jotham ran away,** before the men of the city could recover from their surprise, **and fled, and went to Beer, and dwelt there, for fear of Abimelech, his brother,** for Abimelech was a tyrant and might put him to death, if he caught him. The government of tyrants and godless persons always brings misfortune upon a people and especially upon the Church.

THE DEFEAT OF GAAL. — **V. 22. When Abimelech had reigned, held sway, three years over Israel,** over as many of the people as acknowledged his rule, **v. 23. then God sent an evil spirit between Abimelech and the men of Shechem,** sowing the seeds of discord and treason between them; **and the men of Shechem dealt treacherously with Abimelech,** they rebelled against him; **v. 24. that the cruelty,** the violence, **done to the threescore and ten sons of Jerubbaal might come, and their blood be laid, upon Abimelech, their brother, which slew them, and upon the men of Shechem which aided him in the killing of his brethren.** The vengeance of God was to strike both the tyrant and those who had strengthened him in his wicked plans, as both were equally guilty. **V. 25. And the men of Shechem set liers-in-wait for him in the top of the mountains,** men in ambush for the purpose of bringing discredit upon Abimelech, who evidently did not live in Shechem, **and they robbed all that came along that way by them,** thus making it appear either that he was not able to keep the criminals at bay, or that they were operating with his consent, that he himself was a robber and a highwayman; **and it was told Abimelech,** his eyes thus being opened to the real state of affairs. **V. 26. And Gaal, the son of Ebed, came with his brethren,** apparently the leader of a roving band, **and went over to Shechem; and the men of Shechem put their confidence in him,** believing him to be the very man for their purpose, namely, to lead the rebellion against Abimelech. **V. 27. And they went out into the fields, and gathered their vineyards, and trode the grapes, and made merry,** arranged a great banquet or sacrificial meal, **and went into the house of their god,** Baal-berith, **and did eat and drink, and cursed Abimelech. V. 28. And Gaal, the son of Ebed,** apparently a true adventurer, **said, Who is Abimelech, and who is Shechem, that we should serve him? Is not he the son of Jerubbaal,** the enemy and destroyer of their god? **and Zebul his officer?** The ruler or prefect of the city was Abimelech's representative, according to Gaal's idea, the tyrant's tool. **Serve the men of Hamor, the father of Shechem,** the original heathen owners of the city; **for why should we serve him? V. 29. And would to God this people were under my hand! Then would I remove Abimelech.** His drunken boast was that if he but had as much authority as Zebul, he would soon disclaim allegiance to the tyrant and put him out of the way. **And he said to Abimelech,** a boastful challenge, as though the latter had been present in person, **Increase thine army and come out,** namely, to make war upon rebellious Shechem. **V. 30. And when Zebul, the ruler of the city, heard the words of Gaal, the son of Ebed,** when they were brought to his attention, **his anger was kindled. V. 31. And he sent messengers unto Abimelech privily,** or, to Tormah, **saying, Behold, Gaal, the son of Ebed, and his brethren be come to Shechem; and, behold, they fortify the city against thee. V. 32. Now, therefore, up by night, thou and the people that is with thee,** for Abimelech evidently was in the midst of his army, on some expedition, **and lie in wait in the field,** remain in ambush till the morning; **v. 33. and it shall be that in the morning, as soon as the sun is up, thou shalt rise early, and set upon the city,** move upon it to give battle; **and, behold, when he and the people that is with him come out against thee, then mayest thou do to them as. thou shalt find occasion. V. 34. And Abimelech rose up, and all the people that were with him, by night,** following the plan outlined by Zebul, **and they laid wait against Shechem in four companies. V. 35. And Gaal, the son of Ebed, went out, and stood in the entering of the gate of the city,** for he considered himself the ruler of the town; **and Abimelech rose up, and the people that were with him, from lying in**

wait, making ready for the attack on the city. **V. 36. And when Gaal saw the people,** the approaching forces, **he said to Zebul,** whose position as prefect made his presence in the gate necessary, **Behold, there come people down from the top of the mountains,** the higher hills in the distance. **And Zebul,** in order to deceive him and to prevent his gathering a full force for the defense of the city, **said unto him, Thou seest the shadow of the mountains as if they were men. V. 37. And Gaal spake again and said, See, there come people down by the middle of the land**, over the hills in the middle distance. **and another company come along by the Plain of Meonenim,** the Magicians' Grove, a dark woods against the near horizon. There could no longer be any doubt that an attacking force was moving upon the city. **V. 38. Then said Zebul unto him, Where is now thy mouth wherewith thou saidst, Who is Abimelech that we should serve him? Is not this the people that thou hast despised? Go out, I pray now, and fight with them.** Here was a chance to make good his boasting, if he were really such a great hero. **V. 39. And Gaal,** goaded on by this biting remark of Zebul, **went out before the men of Shechem,** in the presence of the heathen nobility of the city, **and fought with Abimelech, V. 40. And Abimelech chased him, and he fled before him,** escaping both death and capture, **and many were overthrown and wounded, even unto the entering of the gate. V. 41, And Abimelech,** instead of following up his advantage that day, **dwelt at Arumah,** went into camp at this small town near by; **and Zebul thrust out Gaal and his brethren, that they should not dwell in Shechem,** he once more became a rover. **V. 42. And it came to pass on the morrow that the people went out into the field,** pursuing their work in the fields and vineyards with the idea that Abimelech was satisfied with the banishment of Gaal; **and they,** scouts or sentinels, **told Abimelech. V. 43, And he took the people,** his army, **and divided them into three companies, and laid wait in the field, and looked, and, behold, the people were come forth out of the city; and he rose up against them, and smote them,** in the manner which is now explained. **V. 44, And Abimelech, and the company that was with him, rushed forward,** in a sudden charge, **and stood in the entering of the gate of the city,** thus cutting off the retreat of the men in the fields; **and the two other companies ran upon all the people that were in the fields, and slew them, V. 45. And Abimelech,** having held the gate until his forces had finished their gruesome work outside, **fought against the city all that day; and he took the city, and slew the people that was therein, and beat down the city,** leveling it to the ground, **and sowed it with salt,** to signify that the city was to remain a desert of salt forever (but it was afterward rebuilt. 1 Kings 12, 25).

THE END OF ABIMELECH. — **V. 46, And when all the men of the tower of Shechem,** probably the same as Beth-Millo, the fortress of the city, **heard that, they entered into an hold of the house of the god Berith,** thinking they would be safe in the sanctuary, **V. 47. And it was told Abimelech that all the men of the tower of Shechem were gathered together. V. 48. And Abimelech gat him up to Mount Zalmon,** so called from its wooded heights, **he and all the people that were with him; and Abimelech took an ax in his hand, and cut down a bough from the trees, and took it, and laid it on his shoulder,** all this being told with the details noted by an eye-witness,. **and said unto the people that were with him, What ye have seen me do, make haste and do as I have done. V. 49. And all**

the people, in obedience to his command. **likewise cut down every man his bough, and followed Abimelech, and put them to the hold,** which the men of the tower had considered a refuge, **and set the hold on fire upon them, so that all the men of the tower of Shechem died also, about a thousand men and women,** suffocated by the smoke and consumed by the flames. **V. 50. Then went Abimelech to Thebez,** evidently not far from Shechem, **and encamped against Thebez, and took it,** the city proper. **V. 51. But there was a strong tower within the city, and thither fled all the men and women and all they of the city, and shut it to them,** locked and barred it securely, **and gat them up to the top of the tower. V. 52. And Abimelech came unto the tower, and fought against it, and went hard unto the door of the tower to burn it with fire,** thereby stepping closely to the wall. **V. 53. And a certain woman cast a piece of a millstone,** the upper stone, known as the runner, **upon Abimelech's head, and all to** (wholly) **brake his skull,** crushing its bones. **V. 54. And he called hastily unto the young man, his armor-bearer, and said unto him, Draw thy sword and slay me, that men say not of me, A woman slew him.** Thus he was fierce and warlike to the end, determined not to have appearances against him. **And his young man thrust him through, and he died. V. 55. And when the men of Israel saw that Abimelech was dead, they departed every man unto his place.** The siege was raised and the dead chieftain forsaken. **V. 56. Thus God rendered the wickedness of Abimelech which he did unto his father in slaying his seventy brethren; v. 57. and all the evil of the men of Shechem did God render upon their heads; and upon them came the curse of Jotham, the son of Jerubbaal.** God often pursues that course, punishing wicked people by wicked people, overthrowing rebels by rebels. His avenging hand finds both the seducers and the seduced.

36

Judges 10

Israel's Further Apostasy and Punishment.

THE JUDGESHIP OF TOLA AND JAIR. — **V. 1. And after Abimelech there arose to defend,** that is, to save, to deliver, **Israel Tola, the son of Puah, the son of Dodo, a man of Issachar; and he dwelt in Shamir in Mount Ephraim,** in its northern ranges. **V. 2. And he judged Israel twenty and three years,** his work consisting chiefly in deciding difficult cases and in opposing every tendency of the people toward idolatry, whereby he also saved them from oppression by hostile nations; **and died, and was buried in Shamir. V. 3. And after him arose Jair, a Gileadite,** a man whose home was in Gilead, on the east side of Jordan, **and judged Israel twenty and two years. V. 4. And he had thirty sons that rode on thirty ass colts, and they had thirty cities, which are called Havoth-jair,** the villages of Jair, from the original Jair, Deut. 3, 14, **unto this day, which are in the land of Gilead.** The number of towns included in this designation was afterward increased to sixty. **V. 5. And Jair died, and was buried in Camon,** evidently one of the thirty cities referred to above.

Although both Tola and Jair waged no wars for Israel, their rule was beneficial nevertheless, for they kept the worship of Jehovah before the nation.

THE OPPRESSION OF THE PHILISTINES AND AMORITES. — **V. 6. And the children of Israel did evil again in the sight of the Lord,** this being some fifty years after the death of Gideon, **and served Baalim and Ashtaroth,** the male and female deities of the Canaanites, whose service Gideon had overthrown, **and the gods of Syria,** or Aram, whose king had been defeated by Othniel, **and the gods of Zidon,** or Phenicia, **and the gods of Moab,** whom Ehud had smitten, **and the gods of the children of Ammon, and the gods of the Philistines, and forsook the Lord, and served not Him,** preferring, instead, Baal in his various forms, Ashtaroth, Astarte, Camos, Milcom, or Moldch, and Dagon, as the idols of these heathen were called. The service of these false gods was often connected with the most revolting immorality, the most unnatural rites, not the least of which was the sacrifice of children. **V. 7. And the anger of the Lord was hot against Israel,** kindled to a consuming flame, **and He sold them into the hands of the Philistines,** who oppressed them from the west, **and into the hands of the children of Ammon,** who made their raids from the east. **V. 8. And that year,** when the Lord first delivered Israel into their hands, **they vexed and oppressed,** broke and crushed, **the children of Israel,** but that was merely the beginning of the punishment; **eighteen years, all the children of Israel that were on the other side Jordan in the land of the Amorites, which is in Gilead.** So the two and one half tribes were the chief sufferers in this oppression at the hands of the children of Ammon. **V. 9. Moreover, the children of Ammon passed over Jordan to fight also against Judah,** the powerful tribe which had, till now, practically been spared, **and against Benjamin and against the house of Ephraim, so that Israel was sore distressed,** powerless before the robbing of their harvests, the plundering of their villages, the exacting of tribute. **V. 10. And the children of Israel,** brought to their senses at last, **cried unto the Lord, saying, We have sinned against Thee, both because we have forsaken our God,** whose worship naturally had fallen into decay, **and also served Baalim. V. 11. And the Lord said unto the children of Israel,** very likely through the high priest then in office, for their representatives had undoubtedly come to Shiloh to make their confession of guilt, **Did not I deliver you from the Egyptians,** Ex. 1-14, **and from the Amorites,** Num. 21, **from the children of Ammon,** chap. 3, 13, **and from the Philistines,** chap. 3, 31? **V. 12. The Zidonians also,** who were allies of Jabin, chap. 4, 2, **and the Amalekites,** Ex. 17, **and the Maonites,** who were allies of the Amalekites, **did oppress you; and ye cried to Me, and I delivered you out of their hand.** His kindness toward them had been untiring, His goodness unparalleled. **V. 13. Yet ye have forsaken Me and served other gods; wherefore I will deliver you no more.** Cp. Deut. 32, 37. 38. They had chosen their gods; let these gods help them; this was a just punishment. **V. 14. Go and cry unto the gods which ye have chosen; let them deliver you in the time of your tribulation.** If a person has repeatedly experienced God's help and yet has time and again turned back to sin, God will finally refuse to hear his pleading. **V. 15. And the children of Israel,** truly repentant and fully conscious of their utter helplessness, **said unto the Lord, We have sinned; do Thou unto us whatsoever seemeth good unto Thee,** anything in the line of a direct punishment; **deliver us only, we pray Thee, this day. V. 16. And they put away**

the strange gods, introduced among them by the strange, the heathen nations, **from among them and served the Lord,** thus giving evidence of their sincere repentance; **and His soul was grieved for the misery of Israel,** literally, "it became too short," the misery of the penitent people now lasted too long for Him, He no longer felt anger against them. **V. 17. Then the children of Ammon were gathered together and encamped in Gilead,** in the part of Gilead occupied by them. **And the children of Israel,** at least the tribes concerned in the present oppression, if not the entire nation, **assembled themselves together and encamped in Mizpeh,** that is, Ramoth in Gilead, some ten miles west of Jordan. **V. 18. And the people and princes of Gilead,** all the nobles and rulers of the tribes east of Jordan, together with all their hosts, **said one to another, What man is he that will begin to fight against the children of Ammon,** the advantage being on the side of the aggressor? **He shall be head over all the inhabitants of Gilead,** not king, but leader, whom they would gladly follow as the man selected by God. God is rich in grace, patience, and mercy. He who seeks Him in earnest repentance is accepted by Him and delivered from all his afflictions.

37

Judges 11

Jephthah's Vow and Victory.

JEPHTHAH CHOSEN AS LEADER AGAINST AMMON. —
V. 1. Now Jephthah, the Gileadite, was a mighty man of valor, distinguished for courage and energy, **but he was the son of an harlot,** born outside of wedlock; **and Gilead,** one of the prominent men of the tribe, **begat Jephthah,** afterwards acknowledging him and rearing him in his house. **V. 2. And Gilead's wife bare him sons; and his wife's sons grew up, and they thrust out Jephthah,** expelled him from the home as not on the same level with them, **and said unto him, Thou shalt not inherit in our father's house; for thou art the son of a strange woman,** of one who was not properly a wife, even in the sense of a concubine, the stain resting upon his birth excluded him from the rights of a child in the family. **V. 3. Then Jephthah,** unable to find support among the elders of Gilead, **fled from his brethren,** an outcast of society, **and dwelt in the land of Tob,** a region toward the northeast, on the boundary of Syria; **and there were gathered vain men,** idle adventurers, **to Jephthah, and went out with him,** on

expeditions of war and plunder, after the manner of the Bedouins. **V. 4. And it came to pass in process of time that the children of Ammon made war against Israel,** as related in the preceding chapter. **V. 5. And it was so, that when the children of Ammon made war against Israel, the elders of Gilead went to fetch Jephthah out of the land of Tob,** for they believed him, with his qualities of valor and sagacity, with his military ability, to be the very man in this emergency; **v. 6. and they said unto Jephthah,** who had meanwhile acquired fame, rest, a family, and possessions, and was a worshiper of the true God, **Come and be our captain, that we may fight with the children of Ammon. V. 7. And Jephthah said unto the elders of Gilead,** in reminding them of the former harsh treatment which he had received at their hands, **Did not ye hate me and expel me out of my father's house,** namely, by not taking his part against the jealous brothers of his family? **And why are ye come unto me now, when ye are in distress?** So many years they had permitted the wrong to be unrighted, but now that they were in trouble they could find him. **V. 8. And the elders of Gilead said unto Jephthah, Therefore we turn again to thee now, that thou mayest go with us and fight against the children of Ammon and be our head over all the inhabitants of Gilead.** That was their way of acknowledging the wrong they had done and trying to atone for it. **V. 9. And Jephthah said unto the elders of Gilead, If ye bring me home again to fight against the children of Ammon and the Lord deliver them before me, shall I be your head?** It is a condition rather than a question: If you bring me back, and then stand united to fight Ammon and Jehovah finds you worthy of His blessing, then I will be your head. **V. 10. And the elders of Gilead said unto Jephthah,** with a solemn oath, **The Lord be witness between us if we do**

not so according to thy words. Not only in their obedience toward him, but also in their behavior toward Jehovah they were willing to be guided by his instruction and direction. **V. 11. Then Jephthah went with the elders of Gilead, and the people made him head and captain over them,** leader in both peace and war; **and Jephthah uttered all his words before the Lord in Mizpeh,** he repeated the conditions under which he would accept the office, and stated the obligations which devolved upon both him and the people. Thus Jephthah forgave and forgot the past insults in his willingness to serve Jehovah.

JEPHTHAH'S MESSAGE TO THE AMMONITES. — **V. 12. And Jephthah sent messengers unto the king of the children of Ammon,** for he intended to remove every suspicion as though he had ruthlessly violated the Lord's command not to molest the children of Ammon, Deut. 2, 5. 9. 19, **saying, What hast thou to do with me,** what matter should cause us to wage war against each other, **that thou art come against me to fight in my land? V. 13. And the king of the children of Ammon answered unto the messengers of Jephthah, Because Israel took away my land when they came up out of Egypt, from Arnon even unto Jabbok and unto Jordan,** for a part of the land of Sihon, king of the Amorites, had originally been in the hands of Moab and Ammon, Num. 21, 26. **Now, therefore, restore those lands again peaceably. V. 14. And Jephthah sent messengers again unto the king of the children of Ammon, v. 15. and said unto him, Thus saith Jephthah, Israel took not away the land of Moab nor the land of the children of Ammon; v. 16. but when Israel came up from Egypt and walked through the wilderness unto the Red Sea, and came to Kadesh,** Num. 14, 25; 13, 26, **v. 17. then Israel sent messengers unto the king of Edom, saying, Let me, I pray**

thee, pass through thy land; but the king of Edom would not hearken thereto, Num. 20, 18.21. **And in like manner they sent unto the king of Moab; but he would not consent; and Israel abode in Kadesh.** This was at the time when the children of Israel were on the western side of the mountains of Seir. **V. 18. Then they went along through the wilderness,** marching south to the Elanitic Gulf, and thence east into the desert, **and compassed the land of Edom and the land of Moab, and came by the east side of the land of Moab,** Num. 21, 11, **and pitched on the other side of Arnon,** on the south side, **but came not within the border of Moab,** to the territory actually occupied by the Moabites; **for Arnon was the border of Moab. V. 19. And Israel sent messengers unto Sihon, king of the Amorites, the king of Heshbon; and Israel said unto him, Let us pass, we pray thee, through thy land into my place. V. 20. But Sihon trusted not Israel to pass through his coast; but Sihon gathered all his people together, and pitched in Jahaz, and fought against Israel. V. 21. And the Lord God of Israel delivered Sihon and all his people into the hand of Israel, and they smote them; so Israel possessed all the land of the Amorites, the inhabitants of that country. V. 22. And they possessed all the coasts of the Amorites, from Arnon even unto Jabbok, and from the wilderness even unto Jordan.** This account agrees exactly and almost verbally with Num. 21, 21-25. Jephthah relates the history as it concerned the children of Israel and shows the false pretense of the king of Ammon. **V. 23. So now the Lord God of Israel hath dispossessed the Amorites from before His people Israel,** by a war of extermination, **and shouldest thou possess it?** For Ammon had not conquered Sihon and his host. **V. 24. Wilt not thou possess that which Chemosh, thy god, giveth thee**

to possess? They would surely consider such a procedure as just and fair, if they believed their war-god to have given them the victory in battle. **So whomsoever the Lord, our God, shall drive out from before us, them will we possess,** for Israel was surely entitled to the same consideration. **V. 25. And now art thou anything better than Balak, the son of Zipper, king of Moab,** namely, at the time when Israel conquered the land east of Jordan? **Did he ever strive,** enter into litigation, **against Israel, or did he ever fight against them,** although he might have claimed an interest in the land with greater right than the Ammonites, Num. 21,26, **v. 26. while Israel dwelt in Heshbon and her towns, and in Aroer and her towns, and in all the cities that be along by the coasts of Arnon, three hundred years? Why, therefore,** if so sure of their ownership, **did ye not recover them within that time?** Possession, so long undisputed, could not be called in question at this late day. **V. 27. Wherefore I,** Israel, **have not sinned against thee, but thou doest me wrong to war against me;** the Ammonites were using their supposed claim to the land as a pretext for attacking Israel. **The Lord, the Judge, be judge this day between the children of Israel and the children of Ammon.** Jephthah placed his case in the hands of Jehovah as the righteous Judge, who would render His decision by bestowing victory upon the righteous cause. **V. 28. Howbeit the king of the children of Ammon hearkened not unto the words of Jephthah which he sent him;** he refused to change his plans. The fact that God occasionally suffers the wickedness of the enemies to continue as a punishment upon His people does not change the fact that their doing is still wickedness before Him.

JEPHTHAH, AFTER HIS VICTORY, KEEPS HIS VOW. — **V. 29. Then the Spirit of the Lord came upon Jephthah, and**

he passed over Gilead and Manasseh, through the entire country east of Jordan, in order to muster as large an army as possible, **and passed over Mizpeh of Gilead,** to Remote in Gilead, with his entire army, to join that already assembled in camp at that place, **and from Mizpeh of Gilead he passed over unto the children of Ammon,** he attacked them in battle. **V. 30. And Jephthah vowed a vow unto the Lord and said, If Thou shalt without fail,** most assuredly, **deliver the children of Ammon into mine hands, v. 31. then it shall be that whatsoever cometh forth of the doors of my house to meet me when I return in peace from the children of Ammon,** after having gained the victory over them, **shall surely be the Lord's, and I will offer it up for a burnt offering. V. 32. So Jephthah passed over unto the children of Ammon to fight against them; and the Lord delivered them into his hands. V. 33. And he smote them from Aroer,** the northern city of this name, **even till thou come to Minnith,** a city not far from Heshbon, **even twenty cities, and unto the plain of the vineyards,** Abel Keramim, whose location is not known, **with a very great slaughter. Thus the children of Ammon were subdued before the children of Israel.** Jephthah's victory was a deed of faith. **V. 34. And Jephthah came to Mizpeh unto his house, and, behold, his daughter came out to meet him with timbrels,** castanets, **and with dances,** an expression of highest joy, a springing and leaping for happiness; **and she was his only child; beside her he had neither son nor daughter,** he lavished upon her as his pet, the darling of his household, all the affection and devotion of a heart that had long been lonely. **V. 35. And it came to pass, when he saw her, that he rent his clothes,** as a sign of deep distress and mourning, **and said, Alas, my daughter! thou hast brought**

me very low, and thou art one of them that trouble me, literally, "Deeply hast thou caused me to bow, and thou alone art distressing me," unwittingly causing him the depest agony; **for I have opened my mouth unto the Lord, and I cannot go back,** he could not make his vow unsaid. **V. 36. And she said unto him,** in a most beautiful and, at the same time, a most profoundly pathetic manner, **My father, if thou hast opened thy mouth unto the Lord, do to me according to that which hath proceeded out of thy mouth; forasmuch as the Lord hath taken vengeance for thee of thine enemies, even of the children of Ammon.** Jehovah had hearkened to Jephthah in giving him the victory, and so he must, in return, unfailingly keep his vow. The entire narrative is full of delicate and tender touches. **V. 37. And she said unto her father, Let this thing be done for me: let me alone two months,** so long he should delay the paying of his vow, **that I may go up and down upon the mountains,** far from the haunts of men, **and bewail my virginity, I and my fellows,** for by the vow of her father she was destined to perpetual virginity, one of the saddest lots that could befall a daughter of Israel, the only child, moreover, through which the house of her father could be continued. **V. 38. And he said, Go. And he sent her away for two months; and she went with her companions and bewailed her virginity upon the mountains. V. 39. And it came to pass at the end of two months that she returned unto her father, who did with her according to his vow which he had vowed,** by consecrating her to the service of the Lord, Ex. 13, 1. 2 ; Num. 18, 15, as one of the women serving at the door of the Tabernacle, Ex. 38, 8; 1 Sam. 2, 22; **and she knew no man,** the vow of her father denied her the married estate, and she had agreed to that vow. **And it was a custom**

in Israel v. 40. that the daughters of Israel went yearly to lament the daughter of Jephthah, the Gileadite, four days in a year, celebrating her in songs, in a festival, of which nothing further is known. That, then, was the sacrifice of Jephthah's daughter: she had to leave the house of her father and was deprived of the right to marry, her fate being at that time unparalleled in Israel. It should be noted that this story affords no basis of proof for the unnatural system in vogue in convents, especially since the motive was entirely different.[3]

---

3 Cp. *Lehre und Wehre*, Dec., 1916; Stoeckhardt, *Biblische Geschichte des Alten Testaments*, 190.

38

Judges 12

Civil War in Israel.

THE DEFEAT OF THE EPHRAIMITES. — **V. 1. And the men of Ephraim gathered themselves together and went northward,** or, marched Zaphon, a town in the tribe of Gad, on the eastern side of the Jordan Valley, **and said unto Jephthah, Wherefore passedst thou over to fight against the children of Ammon,** to attack them in battle, **and didst not call us to go with thee?** It was not zeal for fighting the Lord's battles which prompted this outburst, but a presumptuous jealousy, because the Ephraimites had not shared in the booty and in the results of success. **We will burn thine house upon thee with fire.** It was the same overbearing pride which they had shown with Gideon, but tile threat which they added in this case showed that they were even more presumptuous at this time than before. **V. 2. And Jephthah,** in an endeavor to make the situation clear to the arrogant meddlers, **said unto them, I and my people were at great strife with the children of Ammon,** literally, "A man of war was I, I and my people, and the children of Ammon [on the other side] very"; he and his fellow-citizens were engaged in a severe struggle with the invaders; **and when I called you,** this fact being omitted in chapter 11, because it had been unsuccessful, **ye delivered me not out of their hands.** The Ephraimites had probably refused to take part in the campaign because Jephthah had been chosen leader without their consent. **V. 3. And when I saw that ye delivered me not, I put my life in my hands,** he staked the most precious possession which he had, **and passed over against the children of Ammon,** in a bold attack upon their army, **and the Lord delivered them into my hand; wherefore, then, are ye come unto me this day to fight against me?** Although speaking in the name of all the Gileadites, he placed his own person in the foreground, because the enmity was directed chiefly against his person. **V. 4. Then Jephthah gathered together,** mobilized for immediate military duty, **all the men of Gilead and fought with Ephraim,** not only in self-defense, but as the judge of the nation putting down rebellion with force of arms; **and the men of Gilead,** of the entire country east of Jordan, **smote Ephraim because they said, Ye Gileadites are fugitives of Ephraim among the Ephraimites and among the Manassites,** thus heaping upon them the insult that their army was really a pack of deserters, a set of fugitives, a bunch of dissatisfied loafers from west of Jordan, a statement which deeply affected their tribal honor. **V. 5. And the Gileadites took the passages of Jordan before the Ephraimites,** the fords which led to the country of Ephraim; **and it was so, that when those Ephraimites which were escaped,** who had not been killed in battle, **said, Let me go over, that the men of Gilead said unto him, Art thou an Ephraimite?** For they did not want to slay any innocent persons. **If he said, Nay; v. 6. then said they unto him, Say**

now shibboleth (stream, flood); **and he said Sibboleth; for he could not frame** (was not able) **to pronounce it right.** It was a difference in dialect, and the Ephraimites simply could not get the sound right; their pronunciation betrayed them. **Then they took him,** every Ephraimite who was thus exposed, **and slew him at the passages of Jordan; and there fell at that time,** in the entire campaign, **of the Ephraimites forty and two thousand.** Thus the rebellious arrogance of Ephraim was punished. **V. 7. And Jephthah judged Israel six years,** his jurisdiction apparently extending chiefly over the country east of Jordan. **Then died Jephthah, the Gileadite, and was buried in one of the cities of Gilead.** Rebellions take place also in the midst of God's. people, the Church of Christ, and in more than one case the defenders of the truth have made a certain statement of Scripture a Shibboleth. in order to make a distinction between friends. and enemies. But the weapons of our warfare are spiritual.

THE JUDGESHIPS OF IBZAN, ELON, AND ABDON. — V. 8. **And after him** (Jephthah) **Ibzan of Bethlehem judged Israel.** This Bethlehem was that in the tribe of Zebulun, and Ibzan's jurisdiction seems to have extended over the northern tribes only. **V. 9. And he had thirty sons and thirty daughters, whom he sent abroad,** saw them well provided for in marriage, **and took in thirty daughters from abroad for his sons. And he judged Israel seven years,** living in princely and happy state in the midst of the people. **V. 10. Then died Ibzan, and was buried at Bethlehem. V. 11. And after him Elon, a Zebulonite,** in the same part of Cavnaan, **judged Israel; and he judged Israel ten years. V. 12. And Elon, the Zebulonite. died,** also after a peaceful and happy judgeship, **and was buried in Aijalon, in the country of Zebulun. V. 13. And after him**

Abdon, the son of Hillel, a Pirathonite, in the country of Ephraim, **judged Israel. V. 14. And he had forty sons and thirty nephews** (grandsons), **that rode on threescore and ten ass colts,** in itself a mark of princely authority; **and he judged Israel eight years,** keeping the people in discipline and in obedience to God. **V. 15. And Abdon, the son of Hillel, the Pirathonite, died, and was buried in Pirathon in the land of Ephraim, in the mount of the Amalekites,** that section of the mountains formerly occupied by this heathen tribe. If the teachers and rulers called by God will at all times follow the rule of God's Word, they will be able to lead even the weak in knowledge the right way.

39

Judges 13

The Birth of Samson.

THE FIRST APPEARANCE OF THE ANGEL. — **V. 1. And the children of Israel did evil again in the sight of the Lord,** they fell back into their former ways of idolatry, adding to the transgression of their fathers; **and the Lord delivered them into the hand of the Philistines forty years,** the tribes most concerned in this oppression being Dan and Judah with Simeon. **V. 2. And there was a certain man of Zorah,** Josh. 19, 41, **of the family of the Danites,** the tribes nearest to the territory of the Philistines, **whose name was Manoah; and his wife was barren and bare not,** a fact which was regarded as a painful visitation of the Lord, if not as a distinct curse. **V. 3. And the Angel of the Lord,** He who is equal with God in essence, who always revealed Himself when help and salvation was needed, **appeared unto the woman and said unto her, Behold, now, thou art barren and bearest not; but thou shalt conceive and bear a son,** an announcement much like that made to Abraham, to Zacharias, and to Mary. **V. 4. Now, therefore, beware, I pray thee, and drink not**

wine nor strong drink, the latter being a very intoxicating beverage usually made of barley, dates, and honey, **and eat not any unclean thing,** Lev. 11; Deut. 14; **v. 5. for, lo, thou shalt conceive and bear a son. And no razor shall come on his head; for the child shall be a Nazarite unto God from the womb,** from his birth to his death, Num. 6, 5. **And he shall begin to deliver Israel out of the hands of the Philistines.** It was only a beginning which he made, for his victories were not full and final, the complete deliverance being effected later. **V. 6. Then the woman came and told her husband, saying, A man of God came unto me,** the word used for a prophet or for one in the most intimate relation toward God, **and his countenance,** his appearance, **was like the countenance of an angel of God,** that is, the special Angel, in whom the invisible God reveals Himself to men, this fact being well known among the children of Israel, **very terrible,** inspiring the greatest awe and reverence; **but I asked him not whence he was,** not daring to ask for this information, **neither told he me his name; v. 7. but he said unto me, Behold, thou shalt conceive and bear a son; and now drink no wine nor strong drink, neither eat any unclean thing; for the child shall be a Nazarite to God from the womb to the day of his death.** As a man set apart to God by a vow, consecrated to His service, the son who was to be born should lead his entire life. The children of Christian parents are also consecrated to the Lord, even before their birth, and should spend their entire life in His service.

THE SECOND APPEARANCE OF THE ANGEL. — **V. 8. Then Manoah intreated the Lord and said, O my Lord, let the man of God which Thou didst send come again unto us and teach us what we shall do unto the child that shall be born.** He was not unbelieving, but he desired a confirmation of his wife's statements and further instructions as to their manner of conducting themselves. **V. 9. And God hearkened unto the voice of Manoah,** for He has respect to the scruples of His weak children if they but turn to Him in childlike trust. **And the Angel of God came again unto the woman as she sat in the field; but Manoah, her husband, was not with her. V. 10. And the woman made haste, and ran, and showed her husband,** announced the fact of the Angel's coming to her husband, **and said unto him, Behold, the man hath appeared unto me that came unto me the other day.** Her language was again that which implied that she believed the visitor to be the Angel of the Lord. **V. 11. And Manoah arose,** from the work which he just then had in hand, **and went after his wife,** who ran ahead in her eagerness, **and came to the man and said unto him, Art thou the man that spakest unto the woman? And He said, I am. V. 12. And Manoah said, Now let thy words come to pass. How shall we order the child, and how shall we do unto him?** When this happy event would take place, he wanted to be sure of treating the boy in a manner which would accord entirely with God's plans. **V. 13. And the Angel of the Lord said unto Manoah, Of all that I said unto the woman let her beware;** she had sufficient instructions concerning her conduct. **V. 14. She may not eat of anything that cometh of the vine,** not even the tendrils and leaves, **neither let her drink wine or strong drink, nor eat any unclean thing; all that I commanded her let her observe,** the responsibility was naturally laid on the mother, because a holy and pure consecration was to rest on him whom she was to bring forth. **V. 15. And Manoah said unto the Angel of the Lord, I pray Thee, let us detain Thee until we shall have made ready a kid for Thee.** This reminds us of the manner in which Gideon wanted to show hospitality to the Angel of the Lord, chap. 6, 18–21. **V. 16. And the Angel of the Lord said unto Manoah, Though thou detain Me, I will not eat of thy bread,** of the meal prepared for Him; **and if thou wilt offer a burnt offering, thou must offer it unto the Lord,** literally, "But if thou wilt offer a burnt sacrifice to Jehovah, offer it"; that is, He would not hinder Manoah, he might go ahead with his preparations. **For Manoah knew not that He was an Angel of the Lord,** the Angel of the Lord in the very special sense of the word. **V. 17. And Manoah said unto the Angel of the Lord, What is Thy name, that, when Thy sayings come to pass, we may do Thee honor?** namely, by sending presents. **V. 18. And the Angel of the Lord said unto him, Why askest thou thus after My name, seeing it is secret?** The great name of the heavenly Visitor was *Peli*, that is, Wonderful, the God of wonders, Is. 9, 6 (5) A miracle He performed here before Manoah and his wife, but a far greater miracle was to be performed in the future, when He whose name is Wonderful would be born of a virgin. **V. 19. So Manoah,** still not knowing the identity of the visitor, **took a kid with a meat-offering, and offered it upon a rock unto the Lord,** as a burnt offering; **and the Angel did wondrously,** performed a miracle with it before their eyes; **and Manoah and his wife looked on. V. 20. For it came to pass, when the flame went up toward heaven from off the altar,** evidently in a manner similar to that related in the case of Gideon, chap. 6, 21, for the flame seems to have come out of the rock, **that the Angel of the Lord ascended in the flame of the altar,** thereby revealing His identity. **And Manoah and his wife looked on it and fell on their faces to the ground,** in worshipful adoration at the presence of God. **V. 21. But the Angel of the Lord did no more appear to Manoah and to his wife,** He did not present Himself in visible form again. **Then Manoah knew,** he finally understood and was convinced, **that he was an Angel of the Lord. V. 22. And Manoah said unto his wife, We shall surely die because we have seen God.** Cp. Gen. 16, 13; Ex. 33, 20. **V. 23. But his wife,** whose faith was more childlike, but also firmer, **said unto him, If the Lord were pleased to kill us, He would not have received a burnt offering and a meat-offering at our hands, neither would He have showed us all these things;** the acceptance of their sacrifice, together with the miraculous revelation, showed that the Lord was not angry with them; **nor would as at this time have told us such things as these,** He would not have given them the promise of a son at a stated time if He had planned to put them to death. **V. 24. And the woman,** the wife of Manoah, in due time **bare a son and called his name Samson; and the child grew, and the Lord blessed him.** Cp. 1 Sam. 2, 21. **V. 25. And the Spirit of the Lord began to move him at times in the camp of Dan between Zorah and Eshtaol.** This statement serves as an introduction to the following chapters, with their narration of Samson's exploits, for in every case the Spirit of Jehovah took hold on him and impelled him to perform special deeds of valor against the Philistines. Samson is clearly a type of Christ, whose conception and birth was far more miraculous, however. And Christ was always and in extraordinary measure filled with the Holy Ghost, for He was, even in His human existence, united with the Father in the most intimate relationship. And as Samson was a savior of his people, so Christ, again in a measure beyond compare, is the Redeemer of all His people, of the whole world, from the oppression of death and the devil.

40

Judges 14

Samson's Wedding-Feast.

THE PRELIMINARY ARRANGEMENTS. — **V. 1. And Samson went down to Timnath,** in the region where the highlands of Judah merge into the plains of Philistia, **and saw a woman in Timnath of the daughters of the philistines,** who were therefore encroaching pretty far upon the territory of the Israelites. **V. 2. And he came up,** to the hilly country where the home of his parents was, **and told his father and his mother, and said, I have seen a woman in Timnath of the daughters of the Philistines; now, therefore, get her for me to wife.** The act of giving children in marriage is clearly the prerogative of the parents according to the plain doctrine of God's Word. A young man may state his preference and, in most cases, urge his suit successfully, but first with his own parents, for unless he sets forth with their blessing, or at least with their express consent, the serious business of taking a wife may prove disastrous to him. **V. 3. Then his father and his mother said unto him, Is there never a woman among the daughters of thy brethren,** of his own tribe, **or among**

all my people, in all Israel, **that thou goest to take a wife of the uncircumcised Philistines,** for the rite of circumcision was a distinction which Israel had above all heathen nations as a sign of God's covenant. The objection of Manoah and his wife was founded upon Ex. 34, 16 and Deut. 7, 3. 4, for, although the philistines are not expressly named in the list of heathen nations with whose members marriage was not to be consummated, yet the principle of the prohibition excluded the Philistines as well as all others. Mixed marriages are dangerous at all times, and parents will best perform their duty if they prevent the union between their children and unbelievers, and also false believers, from the start. **And Samson said unto his father, Get her for me; for she pleaseth me well.** It may have been only a temporary attachment which Samson felt, but he was insistent, and his parents finally consented. **V. 4. But his father and his mother knew not that it was of the Lord,** that Jehovah had so arranged matters, **that he sought an occasion against the Philistines,** a valid ground for a quarrel and for an attack upon them; **for at that time the Philistines had dominion over Israel,** the Lord had delivered Israel into their hand to be oppressed by them, chap. 13, 1. **V. 5. Then went Samson down, and his father and his mother, to Timnath,** the young man evidently preceding his parents in his eagerness to press his suit with the woman of his choice, **and came to the vineyards of Timnath,** to the hills which bordered upon a more desolate section of country; **and, behold, a young lion,** fierce and bloodthirsty, **roared against him,** rushed upon him with all evidences of bloodthirstiness. **V. 6. And the Spirit of the Lord came mightily upon him,** urging him on with great force, **and he rent him as he would have rent a kid,** taking hold of the beast with his bare hands and slaughtering him with the greatest ease, **and he had nothing in his hand,** no weapon of any kind; **but he told not his father or his mother what he had done,** he was conscious for the first time that the strength which he possessed was an unusual power, and he felt diffident about discussing it even with his parents, all the more so because they would have been startled by the account of the danger in which he had been. **V. 7. And he went down and talked with the woman,** with the idea of finding out more of her character and suitability by a conversation with her; **and she pleased Samson well,** the impression which he had first gained was confirmed. **V. 8. And after a time he returned to take her,** coming down once more with his parents to celebrate the nuptials, **and he turned aside to see the carcass of the lion,** for the heat of the dry season is so great as to take up all the moisture from a dead body before decay sets in; **and, behold, there was a swarm of bees and honey in the carcass of the lion,** the wild bees had lost no time in using the dry carcass as a hive. **V. 9. And he took thereof in his hands,** drawing it out with his fingers as the only spoons available and using his hands as vessels, **and went on eating,** munched of the honey as he went along, **and came to his father and mother, and he gave them, and they did eat,** also relishing the delicacy; **but he told not them that he had taken the honey out of the carcass of the lion,** for that would have brought out the story of the encounter with the lion. This incident gave Samson the suggestion for the riddle which he proposed during the week of feasting. A greater than Samson, Christ, the almighty God, has overcome the roaring lion, Satan, and this victory is the source of peace, salvation, and life for all men.

THE RIDDLE AT THE WEDDING-FEAST. — **V. 10. So his father went down unto the woman,** to signify his parental approval of the match and to attend the wedding; **and Samson made there a feast,** intending to live in Timnath and not take his bride to the city of his parents; **for so used the young men to do,** that was the custom at that time, that the bridegroom provided the entertainment. **V. 11. And it came to pass, when they,** the parents and relatives of the bride, **saw him, that they brought thirty companions,** attendants of the groom, "sons of the bride-chamber," **to be with him,** for Samson had neglected to provide himself with these very necessary witnesses, with this retinue of merrymakers. **V. 12. And Samson said unto them,** evidently as soon as the festivities began, **I will now put forth a riddle unto you,** announce or propose it to them; **if ye can certainly declare it me,** give its solution, **within the seven days of the feast, and find it out, then I will give you thirty sheets,** ordinary garments, **and thirty change of garments,** dresses of state, to be worn on festival occasions; **v. 13. but if ye cannot declare it me, then shall ye give me thirty sheets and thirty change of garments. And they said unto him,** feeling sure of their ability to gain the prize held out before them, **Put forth thy riddle that we may hear it. V. 14. And he said unto them, Out of the eater came forth meat, and out of the strong came forth sweetness,** literally, "Out of the feeder, consumer [German, *Fresser*], came forth food, and out of the powerful one something sweet." **And they could not in three days expound the riddle,** for so long they attempted to get the solution honestly. **V. 15. And it came to pass on the seventh day that they said unto Samson's wife, Entice thy husband that he may declare unto us the riddle,** she was to manage in some way to get him to reveal the solution or at least a key to its understanding, **lest we burn thee and thy father's house with fire; have ye called,** invited,

us to take that we have, to impoverish, to plunder them? **Is it not so?** They implied that the riddle was merely a pretense, a scheme, to make them pay, although they had willingly agreed to the terms stated by Samson. Their threat shows their callous brutality, their miserable covetousness. **V. 16. And Samson's wife wept before him and said, Thou dost but hate me, and lovest me not,** the easiest and handiest reproach in the circumstances; **thou hast put forth a riddle unto the children of my people and hast not told it me.** Her speech shows that the woman, in a choice between her husband and her people, inclined to the Philistines, the usual result in the case of mixed marriages. **And he said unto her, Behold, I have not told it my father nor my mother,** who might, till now, have expected him to share his secrets with them, **and shall I tell it thee? V. 17. And she wept before him the seven days,** for her curiosity had prompted her to badger him from the very first day, **while their feast lasted; and it came to pass on the seventh day that he told her, because she lay sore upon him,** she was unbearably importunate in her pleading; **and she told the riddle to the children of her people,** thus betraying the confidence of her husband. **V. 18. And the men of the city said unto him on the seventh day before the sun went down,** before the time as fixed by him had expired, **What is sweeter than honey? And what is stronger than a lion? And he said unto them, If ye had not plowed with my heifer, ye had not found out my riddle,** a proverbial expression which, at the same time, indicated his contempt for the method employed by them. **V. 19. And the Spirit of the Lord came upon him, and he went down to Ashkelon,** a city of the Philistines on the coast of the Mediterranean, **and slew thirty men of them, and took their spoil,** their attire, of which the fallen were usually stripped, **and gave change of garments unto them which expounded the riddle.** "It is in harmony with the dramatic course of the action that Samson flung to his treacherous friends, as the price of their deception, garments snatched from their own countrymen." (Lange.) **And his anger was kindled,** in a flame of bitter resentment against the entire Philistine nation, **and he went up to his father's house,** leaving his wife at Timnath. **V. 20. But Samson's wife,** for such the woman now was before all the world, **was given to his companion,** to his chief attendant at the wedding festival, to his "best man," **whom he had used as his friend.** Cp. John 3, 29. This action on the part of the woman's parents shows the low state of morals in their nation, and the fact that the woman added infidelity to treason characterizes her as well; hers was a mean and small soul. Note: It was the Spirit of God who urged Samson to slay the Philistines. The same Spirit today is full of zeal against all godlessness and impels the believers to use the weapons of the Word in combating every form of unchristian doctrine and conduct.

41

Judges 15

Samson's Heroic Deeds.

SAMSON'S REVENGE ON THE PHILISTINES. — **V. 1. But it came to pass within a while after,** it may have been a matter of six weeks or two months later, **in the time of wheat harvest,** which usually begins in the first part of May in Palestine, **that Samson visited his wife with a kid,** coming with a present to show that he bore her no personal grudge; **and he said, I will go in to my wife into the chamber,** the inner apartment of the house, which the women occupied. **But her father would not suffer him to go in,** he barred his way. **V. 2. And her father said, I verily thought that thou hadst utterly hated her,** the first excuse which popped into his mind, suggested by his anxiety and fear; **therefore I gave her to thy companion. Is not her younger sister fairer than she? Take her, I pray thee, instead of her.** The offer to let his other daughter be Samson's wife was made with the idea of placating the wronged husband, especially as he held up the beauty of this daughter as an added attraction; another glimpse of the low moral state of the Philistines. **V. 3. And**

Samson said concerning them, literally, "to them," either the father of his former wife and those present, or to his own family and neighbors, **Now shall I be more blameless than the Philistines, though I do them a displeasure;** they would not really be able to blame him for his conduct in doing them evil. He turned his personal wrong into an occasion of a national exploit against the enemy of his people as a whole, for he regarded the act of his father-in-Law as a manifestation of the Philistine hatred against the children of Israel. **V. 4. And Samson went and caught three hundred foxes,** small jackals, which are very plentiful in that neighborhood to this day, **and took firebrands,** torches, **and turned tail to tail,** tying the jackals together by twos, **and put a firebrand in the midst between two tails. V. 5. And when he had set the brands on fire, he let them go into the standing corn,** the grain-fields, **of the Philistines, and burned up both the shocks,** where the grain was already stacked, **and also the standing corn,** which was not yet cut, **with the vineyards and olives,** for the three hundred animals, almost crazed by the flaming torches that wrapped their tails in fire, sped first through the lowlands and then up the hillsides, through the vineyards and olive plantations. **V. 6. Then the Philistines said, Who hath done this? And they,** men acquainted with the facts, **answered, Samson, the son-in-law of the Timnite, because he had taken his wife and given her to his companion. And the Philistines came up and burned her and her father with fire,** probably by setting fire to their house and burning it with all the inmates. It was an act of the most brutal cruelty. **V. 7. And Samson said unto them, Though ye have done this, yet will I be avenged of you, and after that I will cease,** he would most certainly not rest until he had taken revenge in full upon the Philistines for this new act of brutality, which was directed also against him. **V. 8. And he smote them hip and thigh,** with a destruction involving everything, said of unmerciful warfare, in which no quarter is given, **with a great slaughter; and he went down and dwelt in the top of the rock Etam,** in a cleft or cave on the border of the Philistine country, a standing menace to the Philistines. The believers must never grow lax in their warfare against all their spiritual enemies, since their soul's salvation is at stake.

SAMSON'S LONE VICTORY. — **V. 9. Then the Philistines,** in order to take revenge for the slaughter inflicted upon them by Samson, **went up,** taking the field against Israel, **and pitched in Judah,** encamped in the territory of this tribe, **and spread themselves in Lehi,** probably on the road leading to the highlands of Judah from the southwest. **V. 10. And the men of Judah said, Why are ye come up against us? And they answered, To bind Samson are we come up, to do to him as he hath done to us,** that is, to put him to death. **V. 11. Then three thousand men of Judah,** blind to the fact that they had, in Samson, a leader of incomparable strength and energy, under whose leadership they might easily have thrown off the bondage of the Philistines, **went to the top of the rock Etam and said to Samson,** in a statement which laid bare the cowardliness of their hearts, bound in idolatry as they were, **Knowest thou not that the Philistines are rulers over us? What is this that thou hast done unto us?** They rebuked him for a reckless fool, who was bringing trouble upon all their heads. **And he said unto them, As they did unto me, so have I done unto them.** He found it necessary to apologize for his conduct to his own brethren, who refused to recognize in him their deliverer. **V. 12. And they said unto him, We are come**

down to bind thee, that we may deliver thee into the hand of the Philistines, an act of betrayal by which they hoped to save their lives and fortunes. **And Samson said unto them, Swear unto me that ye will not fall upon me yourselves,** namely, for the purpose of putting him to death; for matters had reached a stage where this was not beyond the bounds of possibility, and Samson was powerless in that case, since he would not soil his hands with the blood of his countrymen. **V. 13. And they spake unto him, saying, No; but we will bind thee fast and deliver thee into their hand; but surely we will not kill thee.** They gave Samson the assurance which he needed for his plans. **And they bound him with two new cords and brought him up from the rock,** into the camp of the Philistines. **V. 14. And when he came unto Lehi,** where the headquarters of the enemy were, **the Philistines shouted against him,** their jubilant shouts met him, for they believed that he was now in their power. **And the Spirit of the Lord came mightily upon him,** filled him with invincible, superhuman strength, **and the cords that were upon his arms became as flax that was burned with fire,** like tow singed by the action of the flame. **and his bands loosed from off his hands.** literally, "melted or flowed from his hands," as though turned to a liquid. **V. 15. And,** looking about for any kind of a weapon, **he found a new jawbone of an ass,** of one but recently fallen on the field, whose bones still had great elasticity, **and put forth his hand, and took it, and slew a thousand men therewith,** for the enemies, seized with a panic of terror, were utterly unable to defend themselves. It was a remarkable victory. **V. 16. And Samson said,** shouting out his song of triumph, **With the jawbone of an ass, heaps upon heaps, with the jaw of an ass, have I slain a thousand men.** It is a stanza of poetic ecstasy:

With the jawbone of an ass
  I slew two armies;
With the jawbone of an ass
  I took vengeance on a thousand.

V. 17. And it came to pass, when he had made an end of speaking, when he had uttered his song of victory, **that he cast away the jawbone out of his hand and called that place Ramath-lehi** (hill of the jawbone). **V. 18. And he was sore athirst,** for the battle and the pursuit of the enemies had been strenuous work, and it was in the midst of summer, **and called on the Lord, and said, Thou hast given this great deliverance into the hand of Thy servant,** for Samson was conscious of the fact that he was fighting the battles of Jehovah for His people; **and now shall I die for thirst, and fall into the hands of the uncircumcised,** the enemies of the divine covenant, the Philistines? **V. 19. But God clave an hollow place that was in the jaw,** He opened a mortarlike cleft in the rock at Lehi, **and there came water thereout,** a miracle in answer to the prayer of Samson; **and when he had drunk, his spirit came again, and he revived; wherefore he called the name thereof En-hakkore** (well of him that cried), **which is in Lehi unto this day,** the miraculous spring was still to be seen when this book was written. **V. 20. And he,** Samson, **judged Israel in the days of the Philistines twenty years.** His activity as judge is purposely referred to, for it was due to his efforts that the true God was once more worshiped in Israel. Note: In the power of the Lord it is possible also for us to tear asunder all bands, to overcome all obstacles, and to conquer the hostile world. For the Lord Himself strengthens and revives us in the battle which we are obliged to wage in this world.

42

Judges 16

The Last Deeds and the Death of Samson.

SAMSON AT GAZA. — **V. 1. Then went Samson to Gaza,** on the Mediterranean, in Southwestern Philistia, one of the chief strongholds of his enemies, **and saw there an harlot,** a public prostitute, **and went in unto her,** thus becoming guilty of fornication. Samson is a type of the entire Israelitish nation at that time; for as long as he clung to the Lord and followed His direction, He was a hero and champion against the enemies of Israel, but when he forsook Jehovah's commandments and indulged in sensuality, the disapproval of the Lord rested upon him, just as it did upon the spiritual adultery, the idolatry, of his people. **V. 2. And it was told the Gazites, saying, Samson is come hither. And they compassed him in,** setting watchmen all about the harlot's house, **and laid wait for him all night in the gate of the city,** men charged with taking him as soon as he should attempt to leave, **and were quiet all the night,** lest they should reveal their plans to Samson, **saying, In the morning, when it is day, we shall kill him.** With the coming of the dawn, when it would become light outside, they would have the courage to attack their enemy. **V. 3. And Samson lay till midnight, and arose at midnight,** the watchmen apparently having settled down so quietly that they did not notice his coming, **and took the doors of the gate of the city and the two posts,** wrenching them from their foundations, **and went away with them, bar and all,** as it had been locked in place to prevent his escape, **and put them,** the heavy gates with the posts, **upon his shoulders, and carried them up to the top of an hill that is before Hebron,** calmly making that trip to the mountains toward the east with the immense load resting upon him. The humiliation inflicted upon the Philistines was all the greater since the gates of a city symbolized its civic and national strength. It is not stated here that the Spirit of the Lord urged Samson to perform this deed, but he followed his own idea, making a show of his great physical strength. It is the beginning of severe transgression for a believer to put his trust in his own ability; for pride cometh before a fall.

SAMSON AND DELILAH. — **V. 4. And it came to pass after-ward,** some time after this exploit, **that he loved a woman in the valley of Sorek whose name was Delilah.** This was not very far from his home place, and he entered into an unlawful union with this woman, whose name is purposely mentioned, for she, by her sinful fascination, debilitated his strength. **V. 5. And the lords of the Philistines,** well acquainted with the power of voluptuousness, **came up unto her and said unto her, Entice him, and see wherein his great strength lieth,** by making use of every possible allurement she was to find out the secret of his great strength, **and by what means we may prevail against him, that we may bind him to afflict him,** to get him into their power and permanently to subdue him;

and we will give thee, everyone of us, eleven hundred pieces of silver, a sum totaling between 3,000 and 3,500 dollars, frankly bribe money. As a true daughter of Philistia the woman agreed to sell the man who trusted her so foolishly. **V. 6. And Delilah said to Samson,** feigning a flattering reverence for his great strength, **Tell me, I pray thee, wherein thy great strength lieth, and wherewith thou mightest be bound to afflict thee,** so that some one might get him into his power. **V. 7. And Samson said unto her, If they bind me with seven green withes,** seven cords of animal tendons not yet stretched, **that were never dried, then shall I be weak and be as another man,** endowed with only the normal strength of the average man. **V. 8. Then the lords of the Philistines brought up to her seven green withes which had not been dried,** ropes made of fresh tendons, **and she bound him with them,** very likely with an air of playfulness. **V. 9. Now there were men lying in wait,** in ambush, **abiding with her in the chamber,** for she had permitted a Philistine spy to conceal himself in the inner apartment. **And she said unto him, The Philistines be upon thee, Samson. And he,** momentarily brought back to his senses by her cry of treason, **brake the withes as a thread of tow is broken when it toucheth the fire,** when it is brought near enough to feel the fire's heat. **So his strength was not known. V. 10. And Delilah said unto Samson,** "with the brazen effrontery characteristic of women whose charms are great and whose hearts are bad," **Behold, thou hast mocked me and told me lies; now tell me, I pray thee, wherewith thou mightest be bound. V. 11. And he said unto her, If they bind me fast with new ropes that never were occupied,** that had never been used for any kind of work, **then shall I be weak and be as another man. V. 12. Delilah therefore took new ropes**

and bound him therewith, again as unconcerned as possible, **and said unto him, The Philistines be upon thee, Samson. And there were liers-in-wait abiding in the chamber;** she had again permitted a Philistine spy to conceal himself in the inner apartment. **And he brake them from off his arms like a thread. V. 13. And Delilah said unto Samson,** her avarice and vexation goading her on, **Hitherto thou hast mocked me and told me lies; tell me wherewith thou mightest be bound.** She is past cajolery and now demands to know. **And he said unto her,** coming ever nearer to the full truth, **If thou weavest the seven locks of my head with the web,** namely, that on the loom standing in her apartment, as common, in those days, as a spinning-wheel was at later periods in other countries. **V. 14. And she,** acting upon his suggestion, wove the long hair of his head into her web as woof, and then **fastened it with the pin,** the batten which is used to beat up the weft, thus clamping his hair securely to the loom, **and said unto him, The Philistines be upon thee, Samson. And he awaked out of his sleep,** for he had fallen asleep while she was operating the loom, **and went away with the pin of the beam, and with the web,** he wrenched his hair loose and left the disappointed woman with her loom. **V. 15. And she said unto him,** at his next visit, **How canst thou say, I love thee, when thine heart is not with me?** She reproached him with the insincerity of his regard for her, since real affection would have no secrets from her. **Thou hast mocked me these three times and hast not told me wherein thy great strength lieth. V. 16. And it came to pass, when she pressed him daily with her words and urged him,** ceaselessly teasing and boring him to death, **so that his soul was vexed unto death,** plagued with impatience with her and so weary that the freshness and keenness of his mind were gone from him, **v. 17. that he told her all his heart,** he unfolded to her the innnermost secrets of his heart, **and said unto her, There hath not come a razor upon mine head; for I have been a Nazarite unto God from my mother's womb. If I be shaven, then my strength will go from me, and I shall become weak and be like any other man. V. 18. And when Delilah saw,** judging from his entire attitude, **that he had told her all his heart, she sent and called for the lords of the Philistines,** who had evidently become doubtful as to results, **saying, Come up this once, for he hath showed me all his heart. Then the lords of the Philistines came up unto her and brought money in their hand,** for Delilah would undoubtedly not have gone ahead with her betrayal of her lover unless she had had the definite assurance that the money which she coveted would be forthcoming. **V. 19. And she made him,** Samson, **sleep upon her knees; and she called for a man,** one of those concealed in ambush in her apartment, **and she caused him to shave off the seven locks of his head; and she began to afflict him,** she, the weak woman, was strong enough to manage him, **and his strength went from him. V. 20 And she said, The Philistines be upon thee, Samson. And he awoke out of his sleep and said, I will go out as at other times before and shake myself,** thus freeing himself from the fetters and from the hands of the Philistines. **And he wist not that the Lord was departed from him,** with the clipping of his hair, with the end of his Nazarite state, Jehovah had gone from him. **V. 21. But the Philistines took him,** laid hold on him in avenging hatred, **and put out his eyes, and brought him down to Gaza, and bound him with fetters of brass,** as a safeguard against his escaping; **and he did grind in the prison-house,** condemned to the lowest work of female slaves. That is the invariable result if men love the lusts of the world, especially such sins against the Sixth Commandment. He who yields to the temptation several times will become weaker with every attack made upon him, until he becomes a slave of sin.

THE END OF SAMSON. — **V. 22. Howbeit the hair of his head began to grow again after he was shaven,** literally, as when he was shaven. for it came out again in a very short while, and the Philistines did not remember the significance of this. **V. 23. Then the lords of the Philistines gathered them together for to offer a great sacrifice unto Dagon, their god, and to rejoice,** as over a great victory, to be celebrated with a general feast of thanksgiving; **for they said, Our god hath delivered Samson, our enemy, into our hand.** Dagon was the chief idol of the Philistines, being worshiped not only at Gaza, but also at Ashdod; he was usually represented with the body of a fish, but with human head and hands. **V. 24. And when the people saw him,** as Samson was led forth, **they praised their god,** in a foolish burst of idolatry; **for they said, Our god hath delivered into our hands our enemy and the destroyer of our country,** for such he was by his having set their fields and orchards afire, **which slew many of us. V. 25. And it came to pass, when their hearts were merry,** in the course of the feasting and carousing, **that they said, Call for Samson that he may make us sport,** be the object of ribald jesting and cutting mockery. **And they called for Samson out of the prison-house; and he made them sport,** he made a fine target for all the mean and mocking sayings which they could think of as their tongues were loosened by wine; **and they set him between the pillars,** those of the house or temple in which the feast was being celebrated. **V. 26. And Samson said unto the lad that held him by the hand,** who led him from one place to another on account of his blindness, **Suffer me that I may feel the pillars whereupon the house standeth, that I may lean upon them.** The building was put up in such a manner as to have not only the lower part, but also the upper open galleries resting principally upon two mighty pillars, which supported the chief beams of the vast building. **V. 27. Now the house was full of men and women; and all the lords of the Philistines were there,** the more distinguished visitors occupying the lower part of the house; **and there were upon the roof,** the open gallery above, surrounded by open trellis-work, **about three thousand men and women, that beheld while Samson made sport. V. 28. And Samson,** who had repented of his deep fall, **called unto the Lord and said, O Lord God, remember me, I pray thee, and strengthen me, I pray thee, only this once, O God, that I may be at once avenged of the Philistines for my two eyes.** He no longer placed his trust in himself nor in his hair, but only and entirely in Jehovah, the true God. In revenging himself for the loss of his eyes, he would at the same time inflict a terrible punishment upon the enemies of Israel. **V. 29. And Samson took hold of the two middle pillars upon which the house stood,** its entire weight being concentrated there, **and on which it was borne up,** he pressed steadily and firmly against them, **of the one with his right hand and of the other with his left. V. 30. And Samson said, Let me,** literally, my soul, **die with the Philistines. And he bowed himself with all his might,** pulling the pillars down with him; **and the house fell upon the lords and upon all the people that were therein,** the entire building toppled over and crashed down upon itself, burying the merrymakers under its ruins. **So the dead which he,** Samson, **slew at his death were more than they which he slew in his life. V. 31. Then his brethren,** the members of his own people, **and all the house of his father came down, and took him, and brought him up,** in a funeral procession which gave him more honor in death than he had gotten in life, **and buried him between Zorah and Eshtaol in the burying place of Manoah, his father,** who had not lived to see the shame of his great son. The Philistines, terrified by the evidence of God's almighty power in the catastrophe which had befallen them, permitted the body of Samson to be removed without objection. Their princes were dead, their power, for the time being, broken. **And he judged Israel twenty years.** Thus Samson died with a prayer to the true God upon his lips. And so He raises up His children from their transgressions, leads them to repentance, and helps them to obtain the end of faith, their soul's salvation.

43

Judges 17

The Idolatry of Micah.

THE MAKING OF THE IMAGE. — **V. 1. And there was a man of Mount Ephraim whose name was Micah.** The fine meaning of this man's name, "who is like Jehovah," does not change the fact that the evils of the period were growing, that the decay of the priesthood had set in, that there was a general prevalence of discord and immorality, not to speak of idolatry, in Israel. **V. 2. And he said unto his mother,** evidently a widow to whom her husband had left a considerable sum of money, **The eleven hundred shekels of silver** (about $700) **that were taken from thee, about which thou cursedst and spakest of also in mine ears, behold, the silver is with me; I took it.** So the awful curse spoken upon the unknown thief by his mother caused Micah to return the money to her, since he feared the effect of the curses in his case. "As one shakes off rain, so he would free himself of this curse-laden money." **And his mother said,** in an effort to save her son from the effects of her terrible malediction, **Blessed be thou of the Lord, my son!** She praised him for his confession, although her own religion does not seem to have been any too pure any more. **V. 3. And when he had restored the eleven hundred shekels of silver to his mother, his mother said, I had wholly dedicated the silver unto the Lord from my hand for my son to make a graven image and a molten image; now, therefore, I will restore it unto thee.** The money which her son handed back to her, after having taken it secretly, she immediately consecrated to the Lord for the purpose of equipping the sanctuary which Micah had planned. **V. 4. Yet he restored the money unto his mother,** still from fear of the curse which she had uttered; **and his mother took two hundred shekels of silver** (about $128), her ardor for Jehovah having evidently cooled since she actually had the money in her hands once more, **and gave them to the founder,** to the silversmith, **who made thereof a graven image and a molten image,** image and cast-work, the pedestal probably being cast, and the picture, apparently an ox or calf, being carved or chiseled; **and they were in the house of Micah,** they were added to the equipment of his private sanctuary. **V. 5. And the man Micah had an house of gods,** a place where he worshiped, **and made an ephod,** a garment like that worn by the high priest, with the Urim and Thummim, Ex. 39, **and teraphim,** small household gods, oracle gods, **and consecrated one of his sons,** filled his hand, made him his priest, Lev. 7, 37, **who became his priest.** It was a peculiar situation which obtained in the house of Micah: he and his mother had not openly broken with the worship of Jehovah, -they rather prided themselves upon their being members of His people, -but their hearts were not wholly with the true God, as the maintaining of this private sanctuary shows. The situation has its parallel in our days, when thousands of men claim for themselves the Christian name and protest their belief in the true God, while still setting up their own private gods, whom they then designate with some high-sounding name to dupe themselves and to deceive others. **V. 6. In those days there was no king in Israel, but every man did that which was right in his own eyes.** This note is added by the author in order to give one reason for such conditions as here described, namely, the absence of a central civil authority. The sin of Micah is committed throughout the length and breadth of the so-called civilized countries, both by gross and by fine idolatry.

A LEVITE MADE THE IDOL'S PRIEST. — **V. 7. And there was a young man out of Bethlehem-judah,** later the birthplace of the Savior, **of the family of Judah, who was a Levite, and he sojourned there,** he lived there for a while as a stranger. **V. 8. And the man departed out of the city from Bethlehem-judah to sojourn where he could find a place.** Many of the cities which had been allotted to the Levites being still in the hands of the Canaanites, this man had no real home, and so traveled from the territory of Judah toward the north, in the hope of finding some place that would please him. **And he came to Mount Ephraim, to the house of Micah, as he journeyed,** the place evidently being on the main highway between the northern and southern parts of the country. **V. 9. And Micah said unto him, Whence comest thou? And he said unto him, I am a Levite of Bethlehem-judah, and I go to sojourn where I may find a place. V. 10. And Micah said unto him, Dwell with me, and be unto me a father and a priest,** to be treated with all reverence and honor, **and I will give thee ten shekels of silver by the year** (about $6.40 cash) **and a suit of apparel,** the necessary clothing, **and thy victuals,** his board was thus also included. **So the Levite went in,** forgetting entirely that he was consecrated to the service of Jehovah alone. **V. 11. And the Levite was content to dwell with the man,** he made up his mind to stay; **and the young man was unto him as one of his sons,** he took care of him in the same manner as he did his sons. **V. 12. And Micah consecrated the Levite,** filled his hand, the standing expression for ordaining a priest, for inducting him into office, taken from the ceremony of laying the offerings required at the consecration of a priest upon his hands; **and the young man became his priest and was in the house of Micah. V. 13. Then said Micah, Now know I that the Lord will do me good, seeing I have a Levite to my priest.** It was a peculiar blindness which caused Micah to look for blessings to Jehovah against whom he was sinning with his image worship. The mere fact that the man belonged to the tribe of Levi and was really under obligation to serve at the altar of Jehovah only could never change the fact of the mortal sin which was being committed in his house day by day, for the Levite himself did wrong in permitting himself to be hired. When men who have been called to be preachers of the Gospel become chaplains in antichristian societies, in which the honor of the Savior is set aside, they are committing the same sin as the Levite of Micah.

44

Judges 18

M**icah's Idolatry Transplanted to Laish-Dan.** THE DANITES SEEK A NEW LOCATION. — **V. 1. In those days there was no king in Israel,** this fact being noted here again to explain the behavior of the Danites and to register the author's disapproval of their action; **and in those days the tribe of the Danites sought them an inheritance to dwell in; for unto that day all their inheritance had not fallen unto them among the tribes of Israel.** Dan had indeed been given an allotment, in Northern Philistia, in the foothills and in the plain along the Mediterranean, Josh. 19, 40-48, but their territory had been insufficient for their needs from the beginning, chiefly because they could not summon the necessary courage and warlike valor to force out the heathen inhabitants of that country, chap. 2, 34. **V. 2. And the children of Dan sent of their family five men from their coasts,** men specially qualified for that purpose, selected from their whole tribe, **men of valor, from Zorah, and from Eshtaol,** two cities in the eastern part of their territory, **to spy out the land and to search it;**

and they said unto them, Go, search the land, namely, for a place where they might settle without great trouble; **who when they came to Mount Ephraim,** on that great highway from the south to the north, **to the house of Micah, they lodged there,** in some part of Micah's great establishment. **V. 3. When they were by the house of Micah,** probably on the next morning, when they passed the apartments of the family, **they knew the voice of the young man, the Levite,** they recognized the dialect of his speech, which differed from that of the Ephraimites, or they heard the sound of the bells on his priestly garments; **and they turned in thither,** their curiosity having been aroused, **and said unto him, Who brought thee hither? And what makest thou in this place? And what hast thou here?** The situation seemed so strange to them that they demanded a detailed explanation. **V. 4. And he said unto them, Thus and thus dealeth Micah with me,** giving an outline of his history, **and hath hired me, and I am his priest. V. 5. And they,** also so weak in their religious convictions and knowledge that they found no fault with the man for his action, **said unto him, Ask counsel, we pray thee, of God, that we may know whether our way which we go shall be prosperous;** the Levite's oracle was to give them information concerning the probable success of their undertaking. **V. 6. And the priest,** after having made a great show with his copy of the priest's ephod and his teraphim, **said unto them, Go in peace; before the Lord is your way wherein ye go.** The answer, "Your way is in the sight of Jehovah," was thoroughly ambiguous, but they chose to explain it in a manner favorable to their enterprise, as the Levite intended them to do. **V. 7. Then the five men departed,** continuing their scouting expedition, **and came to Laish,** in the extreme northern part of Canaan, east of the headwaters of Jordan, **and saw the people that were therein,** who belonged to the Canaanitish tribes of Northern Palestine, **how they dwelt careless, after the manner of the Zidonians,** to whom they were probably related, **quiet and secure,** concerned chiefly with commercial interests and not given to warlike enterprises; **and there was no magistrate in the land that might put them to shame in any thing,** no hereditary ruler to oppress them in any respect, no conqueror, no tyrant, bothered them; **and they were far from the Zidonians,** their city may have been a colony of Zidon, but they were so far from the coast of the Mediterranean that assistance from there could hardly be expected, **and had no business with any man,** they had entered neither into an offensive nor a defensive alliance with any of the neighboring cities. They hurt no man, and therefore did not expect to be hurt by any one, although they belonged to the nations whom the children of Israel had been commanded to exterminate. **V. 8. And they,** the spies, **came unto their brethren to Zorah and Eshtaol,** they returned with their report; **and their brethren said unto them, What say ye? V. 9. And they said, Arise, that ye may go up against them; for we have seen the land, and, behold, it is very good; and are ye still?** The Danites were sitting there inactive, while they had such a fine opportunity to gain this city. **Be not slothful to go, and to enter to possess the land. V. 10. When ye go, ye shall come unto a people secure,** living in careless security, and therefore easily overcome, **and to a large land,** with room for expansion on all sides; **for God hath given it into your hands; a place where there is no want of anything that is in the earth,** with all the wealth and attractiveness which distinguished the rest of Canaan. **V. 11. And there went**

from thence of the family of the Danites, out of Zorah and out of Eshtaol, six hundred men appointed with weapons of war, fully armed for battle, each man with his family. **V. 12. And they went up, and pitched in Kirjath-jearim, in Judah,** on the northern boundary of Judah, **wherefore they called that place Mahaneh-dan** (camp of Dan) **unto this day; behold, it is behind Kirjath-jearim.** An expedition for the purpose of planting a colony in this manner was at that time such an extraordinary event that the name of the camp was ever afterward remembered. But the entire undertaking was a self-appointed task on the part of Dan and was not commanded by God. It is God's will that we remain in our station and take its burdens upon us, until He Himself shows us another way. Then His mercy and blessings will be with us.

THE PRIEST OF MICAH TAKEN TO LAISH. — **V. 13. And they passed thence unto Mount Ephraim,** along the way taken by the spies, **and came unto the house of Micah. V. 14. Then answered the five men that went to spy out the country of Laish, and said unto their brethren,** giving in advance the information which the members of their tribe would presently ask for, **Do ye know that there is in these houses an ephod, and teraphim, and a graven image, and a molten image,** a carved and chased idol with its molten pedestal? **Now, therefore, consider what ye have to do,** the suggestion of the spies being that the Danites should not overlook this opportunity to provide themselves with a worship of their own. **V. 15. And they,** acting upon the hint received, **turned thitherward, and came to the house of the young man, the Levite,** where this private sanctuary was, fully equipped with everything needed in such an institution, **even unto the house of Micah, and saluted him,** they greeted the priest most kindly. **V. 16. And the six hundred men appointed with their weapons of war, which were of the children of Dan, stood by the entering of the gate,** at the entrance to the enclosure, near the sanctuary. **V. 17. And the five men that went to spy out the land went up, and came in thither,** being familiar with the location of everything from their previous visit, **and took the graven image, and the ephod, and the teraphim, and the molten image,** all the equipment of the sanctuary, the objects used in worship by Micah; **and the priest stood in the entering of the gate with the six hundred men that were appointed with weapons of war.** This strange behavior of the priest in permitting the robbery of the sanctuary for whose care he was hired is now explained, for this paragraph is here entered, although the event took place before the Levite deserted his post. **V. 18. And these went into Micah's house, and fetched the carved image, the ephod, and the teraphim, and the molten image. Then said the priest unto them,** it was then that he had tried to interfere, **What do ye? V. 19. And they said unto him, Hold thy peace,** be absolutely quiet; **lay thine hand upon thy mouth, and go with us, and be to us a father and a priest,** the position which he had occupied in the house of Micah, chap. 17, 10. **Is it better for thee to be a priest unto the house of one man, or that thou be a priest unto a tribe and a family in Israel?** That was the argument which had appealed to the Levite's ambitious and avaricious heart and caused him to turn his back when the five spies plundered Micah's sanctuary. **V. 20. And the priest's heart was glad, and he took the ephod, and the teraphim, and the graven image, and went in the midst of the people,** where he was safe. **V. 21. So they turned and departed, and put the little ones and the cattle and the carriage,** all their most valuable possessions, **before them,** to have them safe in case they should be attacked by Micah and his men. **V. 22. And when they were a good way from the house of Micah, the men that were in the houses near to Micah's house,** both those belonging to his own establishment and those of the village which arose near the sanctuary, **were gathered together and overtook the children of Dan. V. 23. And they cried unto the children of Dan,** hailed them, bidding them stop. **And they turned their faces, and said unto Micah, What aileth thee that thou comest with such a company?** They feigned ignorance of any happening concerning Micah. **V. 24. And he said, Ye have taken away my gods which I made, and the priest, and ye are gone away; and what have I more?** He no longer tries to deceive himself and others that it was really Jehovah's worship which he was carrying on in his house, but calls his sin by the right name, confessing his idolatry. **And what is this that ye say unto me, What aileth thee? V. 25. And the children of Dan said unto him,** depending upon their superior power and holding that might makes right, **Let not thy voice be heard among us, lest angry fellows,** men bitter of soul, of a fierce disposition, **run upon thee, and thou lose thy life with the lives of thy household,** any rash act on his part would cause not only his own death, but that of his entire family. **V. 26. And the children of Dan,** having bullied Micah into silence, **went their way; and when Micah saw that they were too strong for him, he turned and went back unto his house.** He was a sadder and a wiser man, who, strictly speaking, had no redress, as he had sinned against Jehovah and could not appeal to the Lord of Israel for revenge. **V. 27. And they took the things which Micah had made, and the priest which he had, and came unto Laish, unto a people that** were at quiet and secure, v. 7; **and they smote them with the edge of the sword,** in a sudden attack, **and burned the city with fire. V. 28. And there was no deliverer,** as the spies had rightly reported, **because it was far from Zidon, and they had no business with any man; and it was in the valley that lieth by Beth-rehob,** extending to that city, along the valley of the upper Jordan. **And they built a city and dwelt therein. V. 29. And they called the name of the city Dan, after the name of Dan, their father,** their progenitor, **who was born unto Israel; howbeit the name of the city was Laish,** or Leshem, Josh. 19, 47. 48, **at the first. V. 30. And the children of Dan set up the graven image,** for idolatrous purposes; **and Jonathan, the son of Gershom, the son of Manasseh,** rather, the descendant of Moses, for that, apparently, was the name of the idolatrous priest, **he and his sons were priests to the tribe of Dan until the day of the captivity of the land,** namely, when the Philistines captured the Ark of the Covenant and became masters of the entire country, 1 Sam. 4, 21. 22. **V. 31. And they set them up Micah's graven image, which he made, all the time that the house of God was in Shiloh.** Mark: Idolatry in every form, false doctrine, quickly and easily finds adherents and is hard to eradicate when once established. He that is guilty of introducing false doctrine not only deceives himself, but also gives occasion to others to fall. The harm usually extends to many generations and destroys many souls.

45

Judges 19

The Infamous Deed of the Men of Gibeah.

THE LEVITE AND HIS CONCUBINE. — **V. 1. And it came to pass in those days, when there was no king in Israel,** when so many things happened which would not have taken place if there had been some one to enforce law and order in Israel, **that there was a certain Levite sojourning on the side of Mount Ephraim,** living outside of a Levitical city, in the more distant parts of this range, **who took to him a concubine out of Bethlehem-judah,** a secondary wife in addition to his real wife, this in itself indicating a decay of the priesthood. **V. 2. And his concubine played the whore against him,** beyond him, she became unfaithful to the man whom she had willingly followed, **and went away from him unto her father's house to Bethlehem-judah,** probably for fear of punishment, Deut. 22, 22, **and was there four whole months,** literally, some time, about four months. **V. 3. And her husband arose,** he set out from home, **and went after her, to speak friendly unto her,** to speak to her heart, to show her that he carried no grudge against her, **and to bring her again,**

having his servant with him and a couple of asses, one for the woman to return on; **and she,** having permitted herself to be assured of his entire friendliness, **brought him into her father's house,** for only then would he accept his father-in-law's hospitality; **and when the father of the damsel saw him, he rejoiced to meet him. V. 4. And his father-in-law, the damsel's father, retained him,** kept him from returning home by the exercise of an uncommon, exaggerated hospitality which may have been prompted to some extent by a feeling of guilt for not having returned the Levite's concubine sooner; **and he abode with him three days; so they did eat and drink and lodged there. V. 5. And it came to pass on the fourth day, when they arose early in the morning, that he rose up to depart; and the damsel's father said unto his son-in-law, Comfort thine heart with a morsel of bread,** a true Oriental exaggeration of humility, for they were continually feasting, **and afterward go your way. V. 6. And they sat down, and did eat and drink both of them together,** the women not being permitted to eat together with the men; **for the damsel's father had said unto the man, Be content, I pray thee,** he asked that favor of him, **and tarry all night, and let thine heart be merry. V. 7. And when the man rose up to depart,** with an uneasy feeling that he really ought to be at home, **his father-in-law urged him; therefore he lodged there again. V. 8. And he arose early in the morning on the fifth day to depart; and the damsel's father,** still with the same excess of hospitality, **said, Comfort thine heart, I pray thee. And they tarried until afternoon,** literally, till the day declined, till past noon, **and they did eat, both of them. V. 9. And when the man rose up to depart, he and his concubine and his servant, his father-in-law, the damsel's father, said unto**

him, Behold, now the day draweth toward evening, literally, the day sinks down, **I pray you tarry all night; behold, the day groweth to an end,** the pitching time of the day was near. **Lodge here that thine heart may be merry; and tomorrow get you early on your way that thou mayest go home.** The Levite's experience was that of all weak and vacillating people: first, unnecessary delay and then overstrained hurry. **V. 10. But the man would not tarry that night, but he rose up and departed, and came over against Jebus, which is Jerusalem,** for the road from Bethlehem to the north passed by Jerusalem; **and there were with him two asses saddled; his concubine also was with him. V. 11. And when they were by Jebus, the day was far spent,** it was late afternoon; **and the servant said unto his master, Come, I pray thee, and let us turn in into this city of the Jebusites,** for the city was still in the hands of the heathen at that time, **and lodge in it. V. 12. And his master said unto him, We will not turn aside hither into the city of a stranger, that is not of the children of Israel,** for the Benjamites had not yet taken the city, chap. 1, 21, and he feared to be plundered by the Jebusites; **we will pass over to Gibeah,** about as far north of Jerusalem as Bethlehem was south. **V. 13. And he said unto his servant, Come and let us draw near to one of these places to lodge all night, in Gibeah or in Ramah,** another town near by. **V. 14. And they passed on and went their way,** having still some six or eight miles to travel. **And the sun went down upon them when they were by Gibeah, which belongeth to Benjamin. V. 15. And they turned aside thither, to go in and to lodge in Gibeah; and when he went in, he sat him down in a street of the city,** in the open place or square of the city, where they expected some resident of the city to invite them into his house, according to ancient usage; **for there was no man that took them into his house to lodging,** no one invited the traveler to the shelter of his roof. **V. 16. And, behold, there came an old man from his work out of the field at even, which was also of Mount Ephraim; and he sojourned in Gibeah,** he was not a citizen of the town; **but the men of the place were Benjamites. V. 17. And when he had lifted up his eyes, he saw a wayfaring man in the street of the city,** feeling the lack of hospitality in this city of Israel; **and the old man,** mindful of the love toward the stranger enjoined in the Law, Deut. 10, 19, **said, Whither goest thou? And whence camest thou?** This was said, either in true hospitable interest, or in surprise that a man should not have heard of the inhospitable disposition of this town. **V. 18. And he said unto him, We are passing from Bethlehem-judah toward the side of Mount Ephraim; from thence am I; and I went to Bethlehem-judah. But I am now going to the house of the Lord,** that is, his walk in life, his occupation was at the house of Jehovah, the Levite thus mentioning his order; **and there is no man that receiveth me to house,** probably because they knew his occupation and were hostile to everything that reminded them of the true religion and of purity of life. **V. 19. Yet there is both straw and provender for our asses; and there is bread and wine also for me, and for thy handmaid, and for the young man which is with thy servants; there is no want of anything;** they were not looking for charity, but only for shelter for the night. **V. 20. And the old man said, Peace be with thee; howsoever, let all thy wants lie upon me,** he would care for all the needs of the travelers; **only lodge not in the street. V. 21. So he brought him into his house, and gave provender unto the asses; and they washed their feet, and did eat and drink,** enjoying the hospitality of the old man.

True hospitality is a virtue which cannot be practiced too often, for thereby some have entertained angels unawares, Heb. 13, 2.

THE SHAMEFUL ACT OF THE MEN OF GIBEAH. — **V. 22. Now, as they were making their hearts merry,** as they became better acquainted during the evening meal, **behold, the men of the city, certain sons of Belial,** worthless, profitless, vicious fools, among whom, apparently, were also the leaders of the city, **beset the house round about,** to prevent escape, **and beat at the door,** becoming more insistent right along, **and spake to the master of the house, the old man, saying, Bring forth the man that came into thine house that we may know him.** They wanted to commit the same revolting crime of Sodomy or pederasty upon the Levite which had brought destruction upon Sodom, Gen. 19, 6-8. **V. 23. And the man, the master of the house, went out unto them,** as Lot had done in the same situation, **and said unto them, Nay, my brethren, nay, I pray you, do not so wickedly; seeing that this man is come into mine house,** being protected by the ancient rules of hospitality, **do not this folly. V. 24. Behold, here is my daughter, a maiden, and his concubine; them I will bring out now, and humble ye them,** in making them objects of their lust, **and do with them what seemeth good unto you; but unto this man do not so vile a thing,** in committing an act of infamous immorality. **V. 25. But the men would not hearken to him,** for even ordinary fornication did not satisfy their depraved desires; **so the man took his concubine, and brought her forth unto them,** hoping thereby to save himself, to prevent one sin by committing another; **and they,** turning their wantonness upon the woman, since no other victim seemed available, **knew her, and abused her all the night**

until the morning, in an orgy of devilish lust; **and when the day began to spring,** at the first dawn of morning, **they let her go. V. 26. Then came the woman in the dawning of the day,** just as it was getting light, **and fell down at the door of the man's house where her lord,** her husband, **was, till it was light,** deprived of her life by the beastly treatment accorded her by the mob. **V. 27. And her lord rose up in the morning, and opened the doors of the house, and went out to go his way,** considering the idea of ever recovering his concubine as being utterly hopeless in this den of iniquity; **and, behold, the woman, his concubine, was fallen down at the door of the house, and her hands were upon the threshold,** her arms stretched out, as though seeking help. **V. 28. And he said unto her, Up, and let us be going. But none answered.** His wife was dead. **Then the man took her up upon an ass, and the man rose up and gat him unto his place. V. 29. And when he was come into his house, he took a knife, and laid hold on his concubine, and divided her, together with her bones,** divided after the manner of slaughtered animals, **into twelve pieces, and sent her into all the coasts of Israel,** messengers going forth to explain the meaning of their gruesome burden, according to an ancient custom of inviting men to join in wreaking vengeance upon the perpetrators of such a beastly act. **V. 30. And it was so, that all that saw it said, There was no such deed done nor seen from the day that the children of Israel came up out of the land of Egypt unto this day. Consider of it, take advice, and speak your minds;** they were to think over the case, to take counsel one with another, and get ready to act in the matter, for it was out of the question that such a horrible deed should go unpunished. That is the result when men forget and forsake the living God – every form of uncleanness and immorality, the most unnatural horrors: Let the heart of every man be firm in the fear of the Lord, lest he take part in deeds of darkness and become a slave of the Prince of Darkness.

46

Judges 20

War of the Other Tribes against Benjamin.
THE BENJAMITES REFUSE TO DELIVER UP
THE GUILTY. — **V. 1. Then all the children of
Israel went out,** all housefathers or able-bodied men leaving
their homes, **and the congregation was gathered together
as one man,** they assembled as a congregation, with the
full consciousness of organic union, **from Dan,** the most
northern town, **even to Beersheba,** the most southern city,
the expression thus denoting a most general participation of
the men of Israel, **with the land of Gilead,** the country east
of Jordan, **unto the Lord,** with the Lord's approval, knowing
that their assembly was well-pleasing to Him, **in Mizpeh,**
near the western boundary of Benjamin. **V. 2. And the chief
of all the people, even of all the tribes of Israel, presented
themselves in the assembly of the people of God,** all the
officers of the civic organization, of the government, heads
of a community of warriors, **four hundred thousand footmen
that drew sword.** That was the strength of the army of Israel
at that time. **V. 3. (Now, the children of Benjamin heard**

267

that the children of Israel were gone up to Mizpeh.) They knew of the meeting, had probably been invited to attend, but neither sent representatives, nor did they give any token of horror or indignation over the infamous deed committed in their midst. **Then said the children of Israel,** in an effort to determine the facts of the case, **Tell us, how was this wickedness?** The question was directed to the entire assembly, everyone who knew anything of the matter being requested to give the information which he possessed. **V. 4. And the Levite, the husband of the woman that was slain,** at whose instigation the assembly had convened, **answered and said, I came into Gibeah that belongeth to Benjamin, I and my concubine, to lodge. V. 5. And the men of Gibeah,** the lords of the city, for they were guilty with their whole city, since they had not prevented the excess, **rose against me, and beset the house round about upon me by night, and thought to have slain me.** The crime which the men of Gibeah had intended was really worse than murder, and it would probably have resulted in the Levite's death; he may have been ashamed to speak of the crime by its right name. **And my concubine have they forced that she is dead,** a victim of their bestial lusts. **V. 6. And I took my concubine, and cut her in pieces, and sent her throughout all the country of the inheritance of Israel; for they have committed lewdness,** a most unnatural immoral deed, **and folly in Israel,** a most revolting wickedness, a crime against the entire people. **V. 7. Behold, ye are all children of Israel,** familiar with the Lord's condemnation of such wickedness; **give here your advice and counsel,** they should decide upon a course of action after having passed sentence upon the guilty. **V. 8. And all the people arose as one man,** with energetic unanimity, **saying, We will not any**

of us go to his tent, return home, **neither will we any of us turn into his house,** for even a short stay, until this crime had been avenged. **V. 9. But now, this shall be the thing which we will do to Gibeah: we will go up by lot against it,** in such a manner that the lot should decide which warriors should be actively engaged in the expedition; **V. 10. and we will take ten men of an hundred throughout all the tribes of Israel and an hundred of a thousand and a thousand out of ten thousand,** ten per cent. of the entire army, **to fetch victual for the people,** to provide food and equipment for the expedition, **that they may do, when they come to Gibeah of Benjamin, according to all the folly that they have wrought in Israel,** punishing them in the measure which they deserved for their crime. **V. 11. So all the men of Israel were gathered against the city, knit together,** a unit in fellowship, **as one man,** firmly resolved to see this thing through to an end which would please Jehovah and remove the stain from Israel. **V. 12. And the tribes of Israel sent men through all the tribe,** the families of the tribe, **of Benjamin, saying, What wickedness is this that is done among you? V. 13. Now, therefore, deliver us the men, the children of Belial, which are in Gibeah, that we may put them to death, and put away evil from Israel.** By the punishment of the criminals, delivered up to justice by the Benjamites, the requirements of the Law would have been satisfied, and Benjamin itself would have been vindicated. **But the children of Benjamin would not hearken to the voice of their brethren, the children of Israel,** thus becoming partakers in the sin of the citizens of Gibeah. Israel here proved itself to be a congregation of the Lord, in letting itself be ruled and directed by the Lord's Word and will. A true congregation will be zealous for the name and honor of

God, also by fighting against all sinful acts and by removing the leaven of wickedness and uncleanness from its midst.

THE REVERSES OF ISRAEL. — **V. 14. But the children of Benjamin gathered themselves together out of the cities,** namely, those of the entire tribe, **unto Gibeah,** thus placing themselves under the leadership of its wicked chiefs, **to go out to battle against the children of Israel. V. 15. And the children of Benjamin were numbered at that time out of the cities,** out of their entire territory, **twenty and six thousand men that drew sword,** able-bodied warriors, **beside the inhabitants of Gibeah, which were numbered seven hundred chosen men. V. 16. Among all this people there were seven hundred chosen men left-handed,** literally, "deprived of the use of their right hand"; **everyone could sling stones at an hair breadth, and not miss.** Since the Benjamites at first took up their stand on the heights, these skilful slingers were of special value to them in repelling the attacks of the Israelites. **V. 17. And the men of Israel, beside Benjamin,** with the exception of this one tribe, **were numbered four hundred thousand men that drew sword; all these were men of war. V. 18. And the children of Israel arose and went up to the house of God,** to Bethel, where the ark had probably been brought for the duration of this expedition, **and asked counsel of God,** through the Urim and Thummim of the high priest, **and said, Which of us shall go up first to the battle against the children of Benjamin? And the Lord said, Judah shall go up first,** to fight in the vanguard of the army, to open the battle, as the champion of the nation. **V. 19. And the children of Israel rose up in the morning and encamped against Gibeah,** they set themselves in battle array. **V. 20. And the men of Israel went out to battle against Benjamin; and the men** of Israel put themselves in array to fight against them at Gibeah. V. 21. And the children of Benjamin came forth out of Gibeah, in a sudden, desperate thrust, and destroyed down to the ground of the Israelites that day, both by slaying and by disabling, twenty and two thousand men. It was a case of overconfidence, of self-righteous assurance on the part of Israel. V. 22. And the people, the men of Israel, encouraged themselves, they invested themselves with new strength, and set their battle again in array in the place where they put themselves in array the first day, anxious to wipe out the disgrace of the first defeat. V. 23. (And the children of Israel went up and wept before the Lord until even, truly sorrowful over their display of sinful self-confidence, and asked counsel of the Lord, saying, Shall I go up again to battle against the children of Benjamin, my brother? The question implies some doubts concerning the justice of their cause. And the Lord said, Go up against him.) V. 24. And the children of Israel came near against the children of Benjamin the second day, they advanced in a rapid attack. V. 25. And Benjamin went forth against them out of Gibeah the second day, and destroyed down to the ground of the children of Israel again, by slaying, wounding, and disabling eighteen thousand men; all these drew the sword, the tenth part of their army had thus been slaughtered or put out of commission. V. 26. Then all the children of Israel, the soldiers, and all the people, the non-combatants that had come along with the army, went up, and came unto the house of God, apparently again to Bethel, and wept, and sat there before the Lord, and fasted that day until evening, in deep sorrow over their own sins, for they felt that these defeats were placed upon them in the nature of a chastisement, in order to teach them humility and trust in God alone, **and offered burnt offerings and peace-offerings before the Lord,** sacrifices intended to plead for God's merciful assistance. **V. 27. And the children of Israel enquired of the Lord, (for the Ark of the Covenant of God was there in those days, v. 28. and Phinehas, the son of Eleazar, the son of Aaron, stood before it in those days,** so these events happened not long after the death of Joshua,) **saying, Shall I yet again go out to battle against the children of Benjamin, my brother, or shall I cease? And the Lord,** whose object of teaching the Israelites repentance and humility had been attained, **said, Go up; for tomorrow I will deliver them into thine hand.** This was not a mere permission, but a definite command, with a promise attached to it. Chastisements, such as the Lord laid upon Israel in this instance, are always beneficial to His children, for they make them realize their absolute dependence upon God and remind them of their many lapses in faithfulness and obedience toward Jehovah.

THE BENJAMITES DEFEATED AND ALMOST EXTERMI-NATED. — **V. 29. And Israel set liers-in-wait round about Gibeah;** they no longer relied upon superior force, but made use of strategic arts in placing various details of soldiers in ambush. **V. 30. And the children of Israel went up against the children of Benjamin on the third day,** moving forward to attack the city, **and put themselves in array against Gibeah as at other times. V. 31. And the children of Benjamin,** in total ignorance of the ambush in their rear, **went out against the people, and were drawn away,** torn away, severed, **from the city; and they began to smite of the people and kill,** to wound, disable, and slay, **as at other times, in the highways,** at the intersection of two roads, **of which one goeth up to**

the house of God, to Bethel, **and the other to Gibeah in the field,** to the fields near the city, **about thirty men of Israel. V. 32. And the children of Benjamin said, They are smitten down before us, as at the first. But the children of Israel,** relying upon their ambuscade, said, **Let us flee, and draw them from the city unto the highways,** as just related. **V. 33. And all the men of Israel rose up out of their place,** they relinquished their advanced position, **and put themselves in array,** forming a new line of battle, **at Baal-tamar** (place of palms); **and the liers-in-wait of Israel came forth out of their places, even out of the meadows of Gibeah,** a slope near the city denuded of forest growth, but probably covered with bushes which offered sufficient shelter to the men in ambush. **V. 34. And there came against Gibeah ten thousand chosen men out of all Israel,** that being the sum total of the men who had been placed in ambush, **and the battle was sore; but they,** the Benjamites, **knew not that evil was near them,** that misfortune had overtaken them. **V. 35. And the Lord smote Benjamin before Israel,** this fact being brought out here with great emphasis; **and the children of Israel destroyed of the Benjamites that day twenty and five thousand and an hundred men; all these drew the sword. V. 36. So the children of Benjamin saw that they were smitten,** they had thought, when they rushed forward to attack the invading army that the Israelites were once more overcome; **for the men of Israel gave place to the Benjamites, because they trusted unto the liers-in-wait, which they had set beside Gibeah. V. 37. And the liers-in-wait hasted and rushed upon Gibeah,** all these details being added here in a description of the battle; **and the liers-in-wait drew themselves along,** they moved forward steadily, **and smote all the city with the edge**

of the sword. **V. 38. Now there was an appointed sign,** one which both the attacking party and the ambush had agreed upon, **between the men of Israel and the liers-in-wait, that they should make a great flame with smoke,** a mighty pillar which could not be overlooked, **rise up out of the city. V. 39. And when the men of Israel retired in the battle, Benjamin began to smite and kill of the men of Israel about thirty persons,** as related above, v. 31. **for they said, Surely they are smitten down before us as in the first battle. V. 40. But when the flame began to arise up out of the city with a pillar of smoke,** the whole city, apparently, going up in smoke, **the Benjamites looked behind them, and, behold, the flame of the city ascended up to heaven,** literally, "there went up the whole of the city heavenward." **V. 41. And when the men of Israel turned again,** making a sudden firm stand after their apparent flight, **the men of Benjamin were amazed,** filled with terror; **for they saw that evil was come upon them. V. 42. Therefore they turned their backs before the men of Israel unto the way of the wilderness,** trying to escape toward the northeast; **but the battle overtook them; and them which came out of the cities they destroyed in the midst of them,** literally, "and they out of the cities destroyed them in their midst," that is, wherever the fugitives came, the inhabitants of the cities fell upon them and slew them, for the feeling again et Benjamin was bitter everywhere. **V. 43. Thus they inclosed the Benjamites round about,** completely surrounding them, **and chased them, and trode them down with ease,** or, from Menuchah, **over against Gibeah toward the sun-rising. V. 44. And there fell of Benjamin,** in this part of the battle, **eighteen thousand men; all these were men of valor. V. 45. And they turned,** trying to escape in another direction, **and fled toward**

the wilderness unto the rock of Rimmon, about fifteen miles north of Jerusalem; **and they,** the Israelites, **gleaned of them,** killed in this running skirmish after the main battle, **in the highways five thousand men; and pursued hard after them unto Gidom,** in the direction toward Rimmon, **and slew two thousand men of them. V. 46. So that all which fell that day of Benjamin were twenty and five thousand men that drew the sword; all these were men of valor.** This is a round number, the exact number included one hundred men more, v. 35. In addition, there were evidently a thousand men who had fallen in the first battles, making the total of the slain Benjamites twenty-six thousand and one hundred. **V. 47. But six hundred men turned and tied to the wilderness unto the rock Rimmon,** they effected their escape and fortified themselves in the fastnesses of this rocky wilderness, **and abode in the rock Rimmon four months. V. 48. And the men of Israel,** in a fury which knew no mercy, **turned again upon the children of Benjamin,** on the defenseless part of the population, old people, women, and children, **and smote them with the edge of the sword, as well the men of every city as the beast, and all that came to hand,** whatever living thing they happened to strike; **also they set on fire all the cities that they came to.** It was a campaign of extermination much more savage than any undertaken against any of the heathen nations. But it was the punishment of God upon the tribe which had taken the part of the criminals of Gibeah; for the holiness of God cannot bear the abominations of the heathen in the midst of His people. All those who know His command and truth, and still persist in doing according to the manner of the heathen, should be excluded from the company of the believers, eventually to be punished by the wrath of Him who is a jealous God.

47

Judges 21

The Tribe of Benjamin Rebuilt.
THE EXPEDITION AGAINST JABESH-GILEAD. — **V. 1. Now the men of Israel had sworn in Mizpeh,** at the time of the great assembly, chap. 20, 1, when the embittered feeling against Benjamin ran high, **saying, There shall not any of us give his daughter unto Benjamin,** to any member of that tribe, **to wife,** man for man they had promised that. **V. 2. And the people,** after the close of the war of vengeance, **came to the house of God,** to Bethel, where the Ark of the Covenant remained till the end of the campaign, **and abode there till even before God, and lifted up their voices, and wept sore,** realizing the extent of their passionate outburst and its effects, for it had been to punish the guilty, not to destroy a tribe, that Israel had taken the field; **v. 3. and said, O Lord God of Israel, why is this come to pass in Israel, that there should be today one tribe lacking in Israel?** The fierceness of civil war had had its usual consequences, but the complaint of the people included, at the same time, the prayer that God might show them ways and means of averting the

entire destruction of the tribe of Benjamin. **V. 4. And it came to pass on the morrow that the people rose early, and built there an altar,** large enough for their purpose, **and offered burnt offerings and peace-offerings,** for they realized that the plans which they had could not be realized without a full reconciliation with the Lord, which meant, of course, a full return to the fellowship of His mercy. **V. 5. And the children of Israel said,** realizing that there might be a way out of their difficulty, **Who is there among all the tribes of Israel that came not up with the congregation unto the Lord,** to take part in this campaign of vengeance? **For they had made a great oath,** which included the threat of death upon every one that did not appear, **concerning him that came not up to the Lord at Mizpeh, saying, He shall surely be put to death. V. 6. And the children of Israel** (had) **repented them,** they had been filled with deep sympathy and care for the rebuilding of the tribe of Benjamin, **for Benjamin, their brother, and said, There is one tribe cut off from Israel this day. V. 7. How shall we do for wives for them that remain,** whence and how could wives be provided for them, **seeing we have sworn by the Lord that we will not give them of our daughters to wives?** These two factors, that of the oath and that of the possible non-appearance of some part of the tribes, having been set forth, the author continues his narrative. **V. 8. And they said, What one is there of the tribes of Israel that come not up to Mizpeh to the Lord? And, behold,** when they made careful inquiry, a thing which they had neglected to do in their first indignation and zeal, **there came,** had come, **none to the camp from Jabesh-gilead,** a city of the valley east of Jordan, about midway between the Sea of Galilee and the Dead Sea, **to the assembly. V. 9. For the people were numbered,** to make sure that this report was true, **and, behold, there were none of the inhabitants of Jabesh-gilead there. V. 10. And the congregation sent thither twelve thousand men of the valiantest,** especially renowned among men known for their valor, and commanded them, **saying, Go and smite the inhabitants of Jabesh-gilead with the edge of the sword,** as a punishment for their neglect in joining the congregation of the Lord in this important enterprise, **with the women and the children. V. 11. And this is the thing that ye shall do, Ye shall utterly destroy every male, and every woman that hath lain by man,** in carnal intercourse. **V. 12. And they,** the men of the expedition, **found among the inhabitants of Jabesh-gilead four hundred young virgins, that had known no man by lying with any male; and they brought them unto the camp to Shiloh,** where it had been removed, now that the campaign had been brought to a close, **which is in the land of Canaan,** to distinguish it from Jabesh in Gilead. **V. 13. And the whole congregation sent some,** envoys, **to speak to the children of Benjamin that were in the rock Rimmon, and to call peaceably unto them,** to assure them of their peaceful intentions. **V. 14. And Benjamin came again at that time,** the six hundred men that had escaped returned to the land of their inheritance; **and they,** the congregation **gave them wives which they had saved alive of the women of Jabesh-gilead,** the four hundred virgins; **and yet so they sufficed them not,** for there were still two hundred men to be supplied. One step had been taken for the restoration of the tribe, but there was still more to be done.

WIVES FOR THE REMAINING BENJAMITES FROM THE DAUGHTERS OF SHILOH. — **V. 15. And the people repented them,** they were again filled with anxious care, **for Benjamin,**

because that the Lord had made a breach in the tribes of Israel, since this one tribe had been almost exterminated. **V. 16. Then the elders of the congregation said,** in discussing other possibilities of securing wives for the remaining Benjamites, **How shall we do for wives for them that remain, seeing the women are destroyed out of Benjamin?** So far as the members of their tribe were concerned, there were no women for them. **V. 17. And they said, There must be an inheritance for them that be escaped of Benjamin,** ways and means had to be found to that end, **that a tribe be not destroyed out of Israel. V. 18. Howbeit we may not give them wives of our daughters; for the children of Israel have sworn, saying, Cursed be he that giveth a wife to Benjamin. V. 19. Then they said,** as an expedient was finally suggested to them, **Behold, there is a feast of the Lord in Shiloh yearly,** year after year, **in a place which is on the north side of Bethel, on the east side of the highway that goeth up from Bethel to Shechem and on the south of Lebonah,** this detailed description being added for the sake of the Benjamites, who might thus reach the designated locality without attracting attention. **V. 20. Therefore they commanded the children of Benjamin, saying, Go and lie in wait in the vineyards; v. 21. and see, and, behold, if the daughters of Shiloh come out to dance in dances,** at the designated time, probably the festival of the Passover, **then come ye out of the vineyards, and catch you every man his wife of the daughters of Shiloh,** the virgin which he intended to make his wife, **and go to the land of Benjamin. V. 22. And it shall be, when their fathers or their brethren come unto us to complain,** to make this robbery of the virgins a court case, **that we will say unto them, Be favorable unto them for our sakes, because we**

reserved not to each man his wife in the war; for ye did not give unto them at this time, that ye should be guilty. This has been transcribed as follows: "Be quiet and gentle; give the maidens kindly to us. You know that we did not take them in war, as booty, as, for instance, at Jabesh. We have indeed allowed them to betaken (for which no grudge is to be held against Benjamin); but in peace, not for injury; and as you did not give them, no guilt attaches to you." (Lange.) **V. 23. And the children of Benjamin did so, and took them wives, according to their number, of them that danced, whom they caught,** a total of two hundred virgins; **and they went and returned unto their inheritance, and repaired the cities,** which had been burned down, **and dwelt in them. V. 24. And the children of Israel,** all those who had been engaged in the campaign of punishment against Benjamin, **departed thence at that time, every man to his tribe and to his family, and they went out from thence every man to his inheritance. V. 25. In those days there was no king in Israel; every man did that which was right in his own eyes,** a notice once more inserted by the author, in order to intimate that such things would probably not have happened if there had been a strong central government dispensing justice in the entire nation. Just as the congregation of Israel accepted the remaining Benjamites after they had been punished and acknowledged their wrong, so a Christian congregation will remit the sins of the penitent sinners when they apply for readmission to the Lord's assembly.

III

The Book of Ruth

48

Introduction

This short book, "the idyl of David's great-grandmother," tells the charming story of Ruth the Moabitess, who lived in the days when the Judges ruled in Israel, a more exact fixing of the time being almost impossible. "One of the sweetest stories in the Bible, showing that even in the blackest period God has men and women who love and serve Him. In Boaz we have the model rich man of his age; every act and word shows his deep faith in God. In Ruth we have an example of modesty and patience, coupled with a remarkable belief in the true God. In Naomi we have a specimen of a good woman, whose religion shows itself in fidelity to all her duties." (Sell.) "One chief purpose of the book seems to be the tracing of the genealogy of David to the Moabitess Ruth, whose name it bears." (Robertson.) "This information gains in significance if we remember that the genealogy of David is at the same time that of Jesus Christ. The story therefore goes to show how Ruth the Moabitess, by birth an alien to Israel, was chosen to become an ancestress of the Savior. Her reception into the communion of Israel also testified to the fact that even in the days before Christ Gentiles might be admitted to the kingdom of God if only they received the promises of the covenant in true faith. - As the genealogy here recorded ends with David's name, it is improbable that the book should have been written before David had become a person of influence and renown among the people of the covenant. We find an additional reason for this assumption in chap. 4, 7, where the author explains a peculiar custom, which had fallen into disuse in his days. - The author remains unknown to us; but it has been suggested that David himself might well have penned this account of a significant episode in his family history," and the record concerning Christ's ancestors was thus completed.

49

Ruth 1

Ruth Accompanies Naomi to Bethlehem.
Elimelech and Naomi in the country of Moab. — V.
1. **Now, it came to pass, in the days when the judges
ruled,** some hundred and fifty years before the reign of David,
that there was a famine in the land, an affliction threatened
by the Lord, Deut. 28, 22-24, and sent from time to time
as a punishment of Israel's iniquity in committing idolatry.
And a certain man of Bethlehem-Judah, the town afterward
famous as the birthplace of our Lord, **went to sojourn,** to live
as an alien, **in the country of Moab,** literally, "in the fields";
for the entire territory was conceived to have been divided
into fields for agricultural purposes, **he, and his wife, and his
two sons.** It may well have been that importations of grain
from Egypt were cut off by the hostility of the Philistines,
and that the inhabitants of Judah, therefore, were almost
obliged to turn to the country east of the Dead Sea, although
the Moabites belonged to the ancient enemies of Israel. V.
2. **And the name of the man was Elimelech, and the name
of his wife Naomi, and the name of his two sons Mahlon**

and Chilion, Ephrathites of Bethlehem-judah, natives of the region, Ephratah being the ancient name of the city and its vicinity. **And they came into the country of Moab, and continued there,** they were there for some time. V. 3. **And Elimelech, Naomi's husband, died; and she was left and her two sons.** The first affliction which befell her was that her husband died in the strange country. V. 4. **And they took them wives of the women of Moab,** an act surely not in conformity with Deut. 23, 3. 4, although the Moabites are not expressly mentioned Deut. 7, 3; **the name of the one was Orpah and the name of the other Ruth. And they dwelled there about ten years;** that was the total length of the sojourn of Naomi. Although the sojourn of this Jewish family in the Moabite country did not prove productive of the blessings which they had anticipated, as the undertaking evidently was not in accordance with the will of God, yet the result was one highly beneficial to at least one of the Moabite women, so that, by God's merciful kindness, it served a great end. V. 5. **And Mahlon and Chilion died also, both of them,** Naomi thus having neither husband, sons, nor property, nor were there grandchildren. **And the woman was left of her two sons and her husband.** Thus God often lays a cross upon His children and chastises them severely, in order to bind them more securely to Himself.

The return of Naomi with Ruth. — V. 6. **Then she arose with her daughters-in-law that she might return from the country of Moab,** for it was understood that the younger women were merely to accompany her for some distance, perhaps to the boundary of the country; **for she had heard in the country of Moab how that the Lord had visited His people,** in mercy, **in giving them bread,** in delivering them from the ravages of the famine. V. 7. **Wherefore she went forth out of the place where she was,** where she had been an alien, where she had not been at home, **and her two daughters-in-law with her; and they went on the way to return unto the land of Judah,** they took the road leading to Canaan. V. 8. **And Naomi said unto her daughters-in-law,** after they had traversed some distance. **Go, return each to her mother's house,** the usual place of refuge for young widows; **the Lord deal kindly with you,** in showing them merciful kindness, **as ye have dealt with the dead and with me.** The relation of these former heathen women, not only toward their husbands, but also toward their mother-in-law had been one of the most tender affection and service, a model, in this respect, to this very day and hour. V. 9. **The Lord grant you that ye may find rest,** quiet and safe happiness, an asylum of honor and freedom, **each of you in the house of her husband,** in a second happy marriage. **Then she kissed them,** as the signal of parting; **and they lifted up their voice and wept,** unwilling to leave Naomi, whom they had learned to love so dearly. V. 10. **And they said unto her, Surely we will return with thee unto thy people.** They found the parting so hard that they preferred to stay with Naomi on her solitary walk through life. V. 11. **And Naomi said, Turn again, my daughters; why will ye go with me?** It was her great love for them which prompted her to deter them, if possible. **Are there yet any more sons in my womb that they may be your husbands?** She was not pregnant with possible sons, who would then be able to perform the duty of levirs toward Ruth and Orpah, Deut. 25, 5; Gen. 38, 8. V. 12. **Turn again, my daughters, go your way;** her love was great enough to bear the sacrifice of their parting with her, since she had only their happiness in mind; **for I am too old to have an husband,** she was past the age when the normal consequence of marriage might be expected. **If I should say, I have hope,** if she should expect the apparently impossible to happen, **if I should have an husband also tonight, and should also bear sons,** v. 13. **would ye tarry for them,** hope to be married to them, **till they were grown? Would ye stay for them from having husbands?** Should they let this very uncertain possibility keep them from becoming happily married in their own country? **Nay, my daughters, for it grieveth me much for your sakes,** that was the bitterest drop in her cup of sorrow, **that the hand of the Lord is gone out against me,** in taking both her husband and her sons. She did not even mention another possibility, namely, that of a marriage in the land of Judah, for her delicacy kept her from mentioning what would probably prove a disappointment, since the sentiment in Israel was strongly against marriages also with Moabites, Deut. 7, 3. 4. V. 14. **And they lifted up their voice and wept again. And Orpah kissed her mother-in-law,** convinced that the way pointed out by her was the best; **but Ruth clave unto her,** clinging to her all the more closely now that Orpah was leaving. V. 15. **And she,** Naomi, said, **Behold, thy sister-in-law is gone back unto her people and unto her gods,** for the one implied the other; **return thou after thy sister-in-law.** Naomi's love for Ruth was so great that she desired her earthly welfare even at the sacrifice of her company. V. 16. **And Ruth said,** as the climax of a scene of wonderful delicacy and unequaled tenderness, in a rivalry of affection which is without a parallel in human annals, **Intreat me not to leave thee or to return from following after thee; for whither thou goest, I will go; and where thou lodgest, I will lodge; thy people shall be my people and thy God my**

God; v. 17. **where thou diest, will I die, and there will I be buried.** She will not be swerved from her intention to cast her lot with that of Naomi. It was not the affection of a daughter to her natural mother nor that of a wife to the husband of her choice, but it was her love toward Naomi which had knit their hearts together. And the highest stage of the devotion which she yielded to Naomi for life was reached in the confession that she had found the God of Israel to be the true God, a fact which implied the highest unity of spirit. **The Lord,** Jehovah, **do so to me, and more also, if aught but death part thee and me.** It was an oath inviting the severest penalty on the part of Jehovah if Ruth should prove fickle in her affection and devotion. V. 18. **When she,** Naomi, **saw that she was steadfastly minded,** that her resolution was unshakable, **to go with her, then she left speaking unto her,** she no longer attempted to dissuade her. V. 19. **So they two went until they came to Bethlehem,** the end of their journey. **And it came to pass, when they were come to Bethlehem, that all the city was moved about them,** there was great excitement on account of their return, **and they,** chiefly the women, **said, Is this Naomi?** It was not a cry of surprise over the fact that she was still alive, but rather an expression of sympathy that she had returned bereft of both husband and sons. V. 20. **And she said unto them, Call me not Naomi** (lovely, gracious), **call me Mara** (bitter); **for the Almighty hath dealt very bitterly with me,** He had inflicted sorrow upon her, as her obvious bereavement showed; the God of fruitfulness and life had withheld His blessings from her. V. 21. **I went out full,** rich, as a wife and mother, **and the Lord hath brought me home again empty,** with neither husband nor sons; **why, then, call ye me Naomi, seeing the Lord hath testified against me,** had declared Himself her opponent by depriving her of her loved ones, **and the Almighty hath afflicted me?** God had made sorrow her portion, to teach her to trust in Him all the more implicitly. V. 22. **So Naomi returned,** such was the nature of her return to the city of her fathers, **and Ruth the Moabitess, her daughter-in-law, with her, which returned out of the country of Moab.** The curiosity of the Bethlehemites was satisfied, and their interest soon died down, since Naomi had sunk into poverty and no longer could take her place with the influential people of the town; but Ruth remained faithful, standing by her mother-in-law in her misery. **And they came to Bethlehem in the beginning of barley-harvest,** about the latter part of March or the beginning of April, fortunate for them, since they were now dependent upon the portion of the poor to get a livelihood, Lev. 19, 9. 10; 23, 22. Thus Ruth, in denying herself the advantages which she might have had in her home country, became a partaker of the blessings of the true God. Whenever we are placed before a decision such as she made, the way which points to the service and worship of the true God must be our choice without hesitation, for in Him we find the eternal blessings of His mercy.

50

Ruth 2

Ruth the Gleaner.

In the field of Boaz. — V. 1. **And Naomi had a kinsman of her husband's,** a relative by marriage, according to Jewish tradition a nephew of Elimelech, **a mighty man of wealth, of the family of Elimelech; and his name was Boaz.** His ability and influence were freely recognized in the community, both in war and peace. V. 2. **And Ruth the Moabitess said unto Naomi, Let me now go to the field and glean ears of corn, of grain, after him in whose sight I shall find grace.** That was a privilege granted to the very poor, to widows and orphans by the precepts of Moses, Lev. 23, 22; Deut. 24, 19, but it must have been a rather bitter experience to one unaccustomed to charity, especially since the permission was not always given in good grace by the harvesters. But Ruth's love for Naomi was sincere and faithful; she was ready to brave the ordeal. **And she,** Naomi, said unto her, **Go, my daughter,** for she was now utterly dependent upon the efforts of her daughter-in-law. V. 3. **And she went, and came, and gleaned in the field after the reapers,** gathering up the ears that fell aside when the harvesters bound up the sheaves; **and her hap was,** it was a providential happening for her, **to light on a part of the field belonging unto Boaz, who was of the kindred of Elimelech.** Unacquainted with the neighborhood as she was, she simply turned her footsteps to the first field she struck, but God guided her in her selection. V. 4. **And, behold, Boaz came from Bethlehem,** to oversee the harvesting, **and said unto the reapers,** in a greeting which might be copied oftener, **The Lord be with you! And they,** as the laudable custom of the country required, answered him, **The Lord bless thee!** If the excellent relationship between employers and employees which this exchange of greetings implied obtained everywhere, there would be no need of arbitration committees between capital and labor. V. 5. **Then said Boaz unto his servant that was set over the reapers,** the foreman of the harvesters, **Whose damsel is this?** Being familiar with all the families in the entire neighborhood, he wanted to know to which of these she belonged. V. 6. **And the servant that was set over the reapers answered and said, It is the Moabitish damsel that came back with Naomi out of the country of Moab;** v. 7. **and she said, I pray you, let me glean and gather after the reapers among the sheaves; so she came and hath continued even from the morning until now, that she tarried a little in the house,** she had not even taken time to rest, so busy had she been. So the overseer praised both the humility and the diligence of Ruth, including the propriety and the reserve of her demeanor. It appears, then, that Boaz freely permitted the poor to glean on his fields, and that his overseer had taken his cue from his master, feeling very kindly disposed toward those in need, especially if they were, as in this case, humble and respectful. V. 8. **Then**

said Boaz unto Ruth, on the strength of the fine testimonial given her by the overseer, **Hearest thou not, my daughter?** He wanted to be sure that she followed his kind directions without hesitation. **Go not to glean in another field, neither go from hence,** for she modestly stayed at a distance from the reapers and binders, **but abide here fast by my maidens,** the women-servants who bound up the cut grain in sheaves; v. 9. **let thine eyes be on the field that they do reap,** right behind the binders, where the gleaning would be most productive, **and go thou after them. Have I not charged the young men that they shall not touch thee?** For they may occasionally have indulged in some rudeness toward the poor gleaners. **And when thou art athirst, go unto the vessels,** placed there for the use of the workmen, **and drink of that which the young men have drawn.** Although Boaz was undoubtedly aware of a certain relationship between himself and this poor woman, he practices no condescension, he assumes no patronizing air, but protects her interests in a manner which would not hurt. V. 10. **Then she fell on her face,** bowing down deeply, so as to touch the ground with her forehead, in recognition of his kindness, **and bowed herself to the ground, and said unto him, Why have I found grace in thine eyes that thou shouldest take knowledge of me,** notice her at all, **seeing I am a stranger?** She felt unworthy of the kind interest which he was showing in her, especially since she was not even a member of the people of Israel. V. 11. **And Boaz answered and said unto her, It hath been fully showed me,** he had been given full information, **all that thou hast done unto thy mother-in-law since the death of thine husband; and how thou hast left thy father and thy mother and the land of thy nativity, and art come unto a people which thou knewest not**

heretofore. She had had a home and parents living as well, all that she needed for earthly happiness; but all this she had left for an unknown country, with people that were strangers to her. It was not only devotion to her mother-in-law, as Boaz very well knew, but faith in the God of Israel which had determined Ruth's course. V. 12. **The Lord,** whom Ruth had chosen as her God, **recompense thy work, and a full reward be given thee of the Lord God of Israel, under whose wings thou art come to trust,** to take refuge. The words of Boaz reveal the truly pious mind of this chief among his brethren. He looks to Jehovah to reward Ruth as richly and abundantly as her love and its expression merited, so that she would miss nothing of that which she had left behind in the line of earthly blessings, but recover them all and more. "In his words there is undeniably the breathing of a pious, national consciousness, such as becomes an Israelitish family-head and hero in the presence of a recent proselyte to his faith and people." V. 13. **Then she said,** with the same modesty which characterized her behavior throughout, **Let me find favor in thy sight, my lord; for that thou hast comforted me, and for that thou hast spoken friendly,** literally, "to the heart," **unto thine handmaid, though,** as she adds in restriction of her apparent boldness in daring to place herself on a level with his servants, **I be not like unto one of thine handmaidens,** not in that relationship of service to him that she might have earned his kind regard. V. 14. **And Boaz,** still more favorably disposed toward her on account of her humility, **said unto her, At meal-time come thou hither, and eat of the bread, and dip thy morsel in the vinegar,** the food which was supplied to the laborers, bread and roasted grain or parched corn, the former being dipped into a refreshing drink, consisting of vinegar and water, perhaps with a little olive oil. **And she sat beside the reapers; and he,** partaking himself of the simple meal, **reached her parched corn,** grain roasted in the ear, **and she did eat, and was sufficed,** she had her fill, **and left,** the uneaten quantity being carefully saved for her mother-in-law. V. 15. **And when she was risen up to glean,** even before the others returned to work, **Boaz commanded his young men, saying, Let her glean even among the sheaves,** not only at a distance in the rear, **and reproach her not,** not in any way interfere with her or heap shame upon her; v. 16. **and let fall also some of the handfuls of purpose for her,** purposely pulling out some stalks from the bound sheaves, **and leave them that she may glean them, and rebuke her not,** by speaking harshly to her. V. 17. **So she gleaned in the field until even, and beat out that she had gleaned,** separating the kernels from the husks; **and it was about an ephah of barley,** over three pecks, a considerable amount for a mere gleaner. God rewards faithfulness in the performance of the duties of life in rich measure, even here in time.

The pleasure of Naomi. — V. 18. **And she took it up and went into the city; and her mother-in-law saw what she had gleaned. And she brought forth,** from a pocket or from a special package, **and gave to her that she had reserved after she was sufficed,** the amount of roasted grain which she had saved from her plentiful meal in the field. V. 19. **And her mother-in-law said unto her, Where hast thou gleaned today, and where wroughtest thou?** This was a question of astonishment at the large quantity brought home by Ruth, for gleaners usually got very little. **Blessed be he that did take knowledge of thee,** showed her a friendly interest. Whosoever treated Ruth thus kindly and loaded her with presents must have intended to show his appreciation of her position and of her virtues. **And she showed her mother-in-law with whom she had wrought,** in whose field she had been busy all day, **and said, The man's name with whom I wrought today is Boaz.** V. 20. **And Naomi said unto her daughter-in-law, Blessed be he of the Lord, who hath not left off His kindness to the living and to the dead.** Through the kindness of Boaz, God was showing mercy not only to the living, Naomi and Ruth, but also to the dead, namely, by providing so richly for the two widows. Naomi recognized God's hand to an extent which made her feel that this would not be the end of the interest which Boaz had taken in Ruth. Cp. Gen. 24, 27. **And Naomi said unto her, The man is near of kin unto us, one of our next kinsmen,** one of those who had the right to redeem the land belonging to Elimelech by marrying the widow of his son. Cp. Lev. 25, 25. V. 21. **And Ruth the Moabitess,** without paying any attention to the hint in Naomi's words, which she probably did not understand at the time, **said, He said unto me also, Thou shall keep fast by my young men until they have ended all my harvest.** This permission to keep with the laborers of Boaz till the end of harvest safeguarded Ruth against rude treatment. V. 22. **And Naomi said unto Ruth, her daughter-in-law, It is good, my daughter, that thou go out with his maidens,** where safety was now assured, **that they meet thee not in any other field,** namely, that she might not be fallen upon and abused in other fields, where she was not protected in this manner. V. 23. **So she kept fast by the maidens of Boaz to glean unto the end of barley-harvest and of wheat-harvest,** well through the first part of summer; **and dwelt with her mother-in-law,** always returning there when she came from gleaning in the evening. Her diligence did not relax, nor did she change her behavior on account of the favors shown her; she was as modest and unassuming as ever, her gentle and virtuous conduct being obvious to all. All such virtues, both those shown by Boaz and those found in Ruth, are fruits of true faith.

51

Ruth 3

Naomi Arranges for Ruth's Marriage.
Ruth lays the matter of redemption before Boaz.
— V. 1. **Then Naomi, her mother-in-law, said unto her. My daughter, shall I not seek rest for thee,** a resting-place in the home of a husband, happily married, **that it may be well with thee?** Naomi's former hopeless sorrow had given way to the joyful hope that Boaz, as a near relative, having taken an obvious interest in Ruth, would be willing to take upon himself the duty of redeeming her property, which she had been obliged to sell and at the same time, as the levir in the case, to enter into marriage with Ruth, Deut. 25, 5. For it was a custom in Israel that, if the dead husband had no brethren to undertake this duty, the nearest male relative would do so, thus keeping the inheritance in the family through the children of such a union. It was the woman's right to ask this duty of the relative concerned, and, far from being considered indelicate, she had a right openly to put him to shame in case of his refusal. These facts must be borne in mind in order to understand the mission of Ruth in this chapter, for

300

otherwise her behavior may seem rather strange to modern ways of thinking. V. 2. **And now,** so Naomi continues, **is not Boaz of our kindred, with whose maidens thou wast?** It was in favor of Naomi's scheme that Boaz had not slighted her on account of her nationality, but placed her on an equality with his Israelitish workpeople. **Behold, he winnoweth barley tonight in the threshing-floor,** this work being done in the evening, after the threshing had been done by the oxen during the day, by stepping out the kernels from the husks, as the stalks of grain were scattered upon the threshing-floor. V. 3. **Wash thyself, therefore, and anoint thee, and put thy raiment upon thee,** paying special attention to the adornment of her person, which she had probably neglected during her widowhood, **and get thee down to the floor; but make not thyself known unto the man until he shall have done eating and drinking,** she was not to let herself be seen until he had partaken of his late supper, which would probably put him into a humor to give more favorable attention to her proposition. V. 4. **And it shall be when he lieth down,** for it was the custom for the master to remain on the threshing-floor all night, **that thou shall mark the place where he shall lie, and thou shall go in, and uncover his feet,** removing the clothes or blankets lying at his feet, **and lay thee down; and he will tell thee what thou shall do.** V. 5. **And she said unto her,** with the same respectful submission which had always characterized her relation toward her mother-in-law, **All that thou sayest unto me I will do.** V. 6. **And she went down unto the floor, and did according to all that her mother-in-law bade her,** especially as to keeping out of sight as long as there were other people near, lest they suspect both Boaz and her of unpermitted relations, of a clandestine meeting with impure purposes. V.

7. **And when Boaz had eaten and drunk, and his heart was merry,** cheerful at the prospect of a rich return for his labor, **he went to lie down at the end of the heap of corn,** of the barley stacked in sheaves at the end of the threshing-floor; **and she came softly,** so quietly, in fact, as not to disturb the deep slumber into which he had immediately fallen, **and uncovered his feet, and laid her down.** V. 8. **And it came to pass at midnight,** when the first phase of deepest slumber was past, **that the man was afraid,** startled out of his sleep, perhaps by having his foot come in contact with the person of Ruth, and turned himself, bending forward in order to see what he was touching; **and, behold, a woman lay at his feet.** V. 9. **And he said, Who art thou? And she answered, I am Ruth, thine handmaid; spread, therefore, thy skirt over thine handmaid,** a proverbial expression by which she reminded him of the duty of marriage, in case he would consider the proposition, Deut. 23, 1; **for thou art a near kinsman,** one of those in the near relationship that had the right to redeem, namely, by repurchasing the field sold by Naomi, which included the marrying of Ruth, the widow of the rightful heir of Elimelech. Ruth did not deviate in the least from the strict path of virtue, and she had faith in Boaz, as a man of nobility and honor, that he would not take advantage of the situation.

Boaz promises favorable action. — V. 10. **And he said, Blessed be thou of the Lord, my daughter; for thou hast showed more kindness in the latter end than at the beginning, inasmuch as thou followedst not young men, whether poor or rich.** She had at first, when she might have stayed in her own country and married among her own people, preferred to accompany her mother-in-law into a strange land, with no other prospect than that of sharing poverty, misery, and humiliation with her. And she had now, instead of setting her cap for some attractive young man, as would have been natural for a woman of her age, shown her obedient disposition toward Naomi in proposing marriage to him, as the levir relative, although he was advanced in life. V. 11. **And now, my daughter, fear not,** she was to lay aside all anxiety and worry, which probably showed itself in the tremulous tones with which she made her request; **I will do to thee all that thou requirest; for all the city of my people,** "literally, the whole gate," standing for all the inhabitants of Bethlehem and the surrounding country, **doth know that thou art a virtuous woman,** she had proved to all that she was a good woman, with no loose morals such as were ascribed to the women of Moab. V. 12. **And now it is true that I am thy near kinsman; howbeit there is a kinsman nearer than I,** this restriction being added by Boaz on account of possible legal complications. V. 13. **Tarry this night,** he would not think of sending her away in the dense darkness, **and it shall be in the morning that, if he will perform unto thee the part of a kinsman, well; let him do the kinsman's part,** in redeeming the land and marrying Ruth; **but if he will not do the part of a kinsman to thee, then will I do the part of a kinsman to thee, as the Lord liveth,** he would cheerfully perform the duty, as he confirmed with a solemn oath. **Lie down until the morning.** There is not an unseemly hint in the entire passage, only naturalness and simplicity and virtue. V. 14. **And she lay at his feet until the morning; and she rose up before one could know another,** before the light made it possible to recognize people clearly. **And he said, Let it not be known that a woman came into the floor.** He wanted to protect, not only his own good name, but that of Ruth as well, particularly since there was still a possibility that the nearer relative might claim her as his wife, and scandalous rumors might have resulted most unpleasantly. V. 15. **Also he said, Bring the veil,** the cloak or shawl which she had about her, **that thou hast upon thee, and hold it. And when she held it, he measured six measures of barley,** a large quantity, **and laid it on her,** as a gift showing his good will. **And she went into the city.** V. 16. **And when she came to her mother-in-law, she said, Who art thou, my daughter?** It was an inquiry concerning the success which she had had, whether her claim had been acknowledged or otherwise. **And she told her all that the man had done to her,** the gift, of course, being a strong hint to Naomi of the result of Ruth's application. V. 17. **And she said, These six measures of barley gave he me; for he said to me, Go not empty unto thy mother-in-law,** visitors usually being dismissed with gifts for their families. V. 18. **Then said she,** Naomi, **Sit still, my daughter,** she was to remain quietly at home, **until thou know how the matter will fall,** what the outcome of the business would be; **for the man,** Boaz, **will not be in rest until he have finished the thing this day.** He was an energetic man, who always went forward toward the goal with open directness. All the virtues which we here find in him and in Ruth, purity, chastity, openness, generosity, a strict regard for the rights of the neighbor, are fruits of faith.

52

Ruth 4

The Marriage of Boaz and Ruth.
The nearer relative declines to act. — V. 1. **Then went Boaz up to the gate and sat him down there,** he went early since he wanted to be sure of finding the man for whom he was looking, and the space just inside the city gate was used for the transaction of judicial business, as well as for the marketplace; **and, behold, the kinsman of whom Boaz spake,** namely, in his talking to Ruth, chap. 3, 12. 13, **came by; unto whom he said, Ho, such a one! turn aside, sit down here,** the legal formula for summoning a person when seeking a judicial decision. **And he turned aside, and sat down.** V. 2. **And he,** Boaz, **took ten men of the elders of the city, and said, Sit ye down here,** this being the customary complement of witnesses. **And they sat down.** V. 3. **And he said unto the kinsman, Naomi, that is come again out of the country of Moab, selleth a parcel of land which was our brother Elimelech's,** she had disposed of this piece of land, the family inheritance. "The name of Elimelech was still on the property; consequently the law demanded its redemption, and

directed this demand to the nearest blood-relative. It is on the basis of this prescription that Boaz begins his negotiation with the unnamed kinsman, in the interest of Naomi." (Lange.) V. 4. **And I thought to advertise thee,** literally, uncover thy ear, to inform him solemnly and officially, **saying, Buy it before the inhabitants and before the elders of my people,** the men sitting by acting as witnesses of the transaction. **If thou wilt redeem it, redeem it; but if thou wilt not redeem it, then tell me, that I may know; for there is none to redeem it beside thee; and I am after thee.** Boaz came only in second place in the right to purchase the field according to law. While reminding the nearer relative of the duty imposed on him by law, he indicates his readiness to render the service demanded, in case the other should prefer to be excused. **And he said, I will redeem it,** believing that it was a mere matter of paying the purchase money. V. 5. **Then said Boaz, What day thou buyest the field of the hand of Naomi, thou must buy it also of Ruth the Moabitess, the wife of the dead, to raise up the name of the dead upon his inheritance,** for such was the law of entailment connected with levirate marriages, the oldest son springing from such a union continuing the inheritance in the family of his mother. V. 6. **And the kinsman said, I cannot redeem it for myself,** he could not fulfill that condition, **lest I mar mine own inheritance,** for he held it possible to decline in the case of a woman of Moab what he would otherwise have considered a plain duty; **redeem thou my right to thyself; for I cannot redeem it;** his mind was definitely made up to step back. V. 7. **Now this was the manner in former time in Israel concerning redeeming and concerning changing,** whenever real estate changed hands, **for to confirm all things,** the author here explaining a custom which had been discontinued, except in the case mentioned Deut. 25, 9; **a man plucked off his shoe and gave it to his neighbor,** thereby surrendering all claims to the right of possession which would have been his had he fulfilled its conditions; **and this was a testimony in Israel.** Similar selfish considerations as those urged by the unnamed kinsman in this case have caused many people to lose even greater inheritances than that of a piece of land. V. 8. **Therefore the kinsman said unto Boaz, Buy it for thee. So he drew off his shoe.** He relinquished all his claims.

The happy marriage of Boaz and Ruth. — V. 9. **And Boaz said unto the elders and unto all the people,** those present at the transaction. **Ye are witnesses this day that I have bought all that was Elimelech's, and all that was Chilion's and Mahlon's, of the hand of Naomi.** He made a formal declaration that he would fulfill the condition, that he acquired the property in question, that he was willing to marry the Moabitess. V. 10. **Moreover, Ruth the Moabitess, the wife of Mahlon, have I purchased to be my wife,** acquired by taking over the obligation connected with the land, **to raise up the name of the dead upon his inheritance, that the name of the dead be not out off from among his brethren and from the gate of his place,** like a withered branch which is cut off a tree; **ye are witnesses this day.** V. 11. **And all the people that were in the gate, and the elders,** responding to this frank appeal and declaration, **said. We are witnesses,** their testimony giving legal standing to the transaction. **The Lord make the woman that is come into thine house,** literally, that is about to come, **like Rachel and like Leah, which two did build the house of Israel,** as the mothers of the twelve tribes; **and do thou worthily in Ephratah,** in raising up sons who would be heroes of strength, **and be famous in Bethlehem,** through the honor brought upon him by the same excellent sons; v. 12. **and let thy house be like the house of Pharez, whom Tamar,** the special ancestress of their own tribe, **bare unto Judah, of the seed which the Lord shall give thee of this young woman.** It speaks well of the love and respect in which Ruth was held that the people were so unanimous in bestowing this blessing, with its prayer for such great and wonderful earthly advantages. V. 13. **So Boaz took Ruth, and she was his wife,** the marriage took place without delay; **and when he went in unto her, the Lord gave her conception,** for children are Jehovah's gift, Ps. 127, 3, **and she bare a son.** V. 14. **And the women said unto Naomi,** for she no longer was lonely and wanting in women interested in her as at first, when she returned from the land of Moab, poor and bereaved. **Blessed be the Lord, which hath not left thee this day without a kinsman,** to redeem her from the disgrace of childlessness, of having her family cut off in Israel, **that his name may be famous in Israel,** being on the lips of many people with words of praise. V. 15. **And he shall be unto thee a restorer of thy life,** to refresh and cheer up her soul, **and a nourisher of thine old age,** by taking care of her in her declining years; **for thy daughter-in-law, which loveth thee, which is better to thee than seven sons, hath born him,** surely a very high praise for Ruth, showing the regard in which she was held by all the women of the city and neighborhood. V. 16. **And Naomi took the child, and laid it in her bosom,** like an actual grandmother, **and became nurse unto it,** a foster-mother instructing the boy in Israelitish life and customs, an instructress in the Law of God. V. 17. **And the women, her neighbors, gave it a name, saying, There is a son born to Naomi; and they called his name Obed** (servant), with reference to the fact that the boy would take care of her, as they had pictured it in their effusive congratulations; **he is the father of Jesse, the father of David,** and thus one of the ancestors of Christ, Matt. 1, 5. 6. V. 18. **Now, these are the generations of Pharez,** the list being appended to the book for quick reference; **Pharez begat Hezron,** 1 Chron. 2, 4, v. 19. **and Hezron begat Barn, and Barn begat Amminadab,** v. 20. **and Amminadab begat Nahshon,** Num. 1, 7, **and Nahshon begat Salmon** (or, Salmah), v. 21. **and Salmon begat Boaz, and Boaz begat Obed,** v. 22. **and Obed begat Jesse, and Jesse begat David.** Note: To this day the Lord measures out joy as well as sorrow to His children. He may send affliction and tribulation for many years, but He will often grant a peaceful old age. Our trust in Him must never waver, for His compassion fails not, and His merciful promises will not fall to the ground.

Made in the USA
Monee, IL
07 July 2026

56544291R00184